YOUR
DOCTOR IS NOT IN

YOUR DOCTOR IS NOT IN

HEALTHY SKEPTICISM ABOUT NATIONAL HEALTH CARE

JANE M. ORIENT, M.D.

CROWN PUBLISHERS, INC.

New York

Grateful acknowledgment is made to the following for permission to reprint previously published material:

Alpha Omega Alpha Honor Medical Society: Paragraph from "Medicine and the Social Contract" by David E. Rogers. Copyright © 1991 by Alpha Omega Alpha Honor Medical Society. Reprinted by permission from *The Pharos*, Summer 1991. *Journal of the American Medical Association*: "The Physician's Oath and the Prevention of Nuclear War" by Christine K. Cassel, Andrew L. Jameton, Victor W. Sidel, and Patrick Storey, *Journal of the American Medical Association*, 254: 652–654, August 2, 1985; oath taken by Soviet physicians from *Journal of the American Medical Association*, 1985, 254:562–654. Copyright © 1985, 1991 by the *American Medical Association*. *Medical Ethics*: Excerpt from "Striking the Balance between Fidelity and Justice" by Nancy S. Jecker, Ph.D., *Medical Ethics*, February 1992, Vol. 7, No. 1. The KSF Group, 630 9th Avenue, Suite 901, New York, New York 10036. Excerpt from "Euthanasia Debate," *The New England Journal of Medicine*, Vol. 323, pp. 1770, 1771. *Psychiatric Times*: Excerpt from "In the Interest of Justice: Abuses in Medifraud Investigations" by Donald Zerendow, J.D. and Howard Fishman, M.Ed., M.S.W. Copyright © 1990. All rights reserved. Reprinted with permission of *Psychiatric Times*.

Published by Crown Publishers, Inc., 201 East 50th Street, New York, New York 10022. Member of the Crown Publishing Group.

Random House, Inc. New York, Toronto, London, Sydney, Auckland

CROWN is a trademark of Crown Publishers, Inc.

Manufactured in the United States of America

Library of Congress Cataloging-in-Publication Data

Orient, Jane M.
     Your doctor is not in : healthy skepticism about national health care / Jane M. Orient.—1st ed.
     Includes index.
     1. Medical care—United States.   2. Health care reform—United States.   I. Title.
     RA395.A3074   1994
     362.1'0973—dc20   93-38180
                                                                CIP

ISBN 0-517-59011-5

10   9   8   7   6   5   4   3   2   1

First Edition

This book is dedicated to
Ellen Brown Hanley ("Nellie") (1854–1943),
my great-great-grandmother,
who was a midwife in Missouri

CONTENTS

Doctors are human, just like you—see how you would feel about it if it were happening to you (remember that your doctor's feelings about you are likely to affect your treatment).

18. **GETTING IT RIGHT**
If our goal is to make the sick and the injured well and whole, then the patients, not the managers, have to hold the power.

APPENDIX: PHYSICIAN OATHS

REFERENCES

INDEX

GLOSSARY

assignment: payment by an insurer directly to a "provider" of medical services, instead of to the patient or beneficiary. A provider who "accepts assignment" from Medicare agrees that the amount approved by Medicare will be accepted as payment in full. (Part of that amount, however, will actually be paid by the patient; see "copayment.") Although some promote assignment as a method of moderating fees, an assigned fee may actually be substantially higher than the fee a physician would have charged a patient who was paying out of pocket. The key feature of assignment is that it effectively makes the third party, rather than the patient, the physician's employer.

attestation statement: a statement that must be signed by physicians every year if they wish to retain their hospital privileges. It certifies that the physician knows that providing false information in the chart is a federal crime.

balance billing: billing a patient for the difference between what the doctor charges (his fee) and what the insurance policy covers (the "approved" charge); often believed to be synonymous with "overcharging" even if the approved charge is the same as it was ten years ago.

capitation (*Kopfausschale*): payment by the head. In some socialized systems (such as Britain's) and in some managed care plans, a physician is paid a set amount for each patient on his "list" or "panel," regardless of how much service the physician does (or does not) provide. The idea is a little different from paying farmers not to grow corn. In agriculture, the same thing would be achieved by paying a farmer by the acre no matter how much corn he grew.

1

concurrent care: rationale used by Medicare to deny payment for a service when the patient received a similar service on the same day (usually a visit to another physician for the same diagnosis).

copayment: the percentage of the approved charge that the patient is supposed to pay.

CT scan: x-ray that uses computer analysis (computed tomography) to combine views taken from many different angles; a technique that shows much more detail than a standard x-ray.

deterrent: (1) a penalty that is not considered a "punishment" and therefore may be imposed without giving the accused the benefit of due process of law; (2) a user's fee paid at the time of service, applied in some socialized medical systems to discourage over-utilization.

Diagnosis Related Groups (DRGs): A set of some 400 to 500 codes for patient diagnoses, used as the basis for "prospective" payment to hospitals for Medicare patients. The hospital is paid on the basis of what Medicare thinks it should spend for the average patient with a particular diagnosis, rather than on what the patient's care actually costs (in retrospect).

document: to write something down on a piece of paper that thereby becomes a legal document. (It sounds legalistic because it is.)

fraud and abuse (current, technical meaning used by HCFA): means used to collect money from an insurer, most commonly Medicare or Medicaid, in a way that the government does not approve. Examples: routinely failing to bill patients for the copayment; using the wrong code for a service; or billing for services that were not actually provided or are supposed to be a part of—"bundled" with—a service that was provided.

gatekeeper: a person holding the degree of M.D. or D.O. whose function is to prevent access to medical care and accept the liability for such activity.

global budget: a budget that is supposed to cover everything. The payor sets an amount, and the providers divide it up. For example, a hospital is given a certain amount and decides what to allocate to personnel, maintenance, capital expenditures, etc.

global fee: similar to a global budget or a DRG, applied to a physician's service. It replaces an itemized bill. For example, a surgeon is paid a certain amount for a hip replacement, and the amount is supposed to cover the surgery, the postoperative care, and possibly any equipment that is needed.

health care system: current jargon for American medicine with all its institutions, appurtenances, appendages, and governmental infrastructure somehow related to or derived from the original purpose of caring for the sick and the injured. The purpose is now being generalized to encompass anything that is somehow related to health in the broad sense of well-being.

H₂S or HHS: the U.S. Department of Health and Human Services.

HCFA: Health Care Financing Administration, an agency under the U.S. Department of Health and Human Services, which administers Medicare.

HCFA 1500: the form that HCFA requires physicians to submit for every covered service that is rendered to a Medicare beneficiary.

HMO or Health Maintenance Organization: a type of prepaid managed care plan.

indemnity: insurance payment to compensate a person for a loss; a payment of a specified amount for a particular medical procedure or condition.

insurance: a voluntary method of sharing risk of catastrophic loss. The term is often used incorrectly to refer to a method of prepayment for the consumption of (usually medical) goods and services. The "business of insurance" is the pricing of risk, not the provision of goods and services.

LMD: local medical doctor, a term of derision used by significant persons such as full professors to refer to doctors in the world outside the academy. The term connotes a bumbler or hick who somehow got an M.D. degree.

lock-in provider: a physician assigned to a patient considered to be an overutilizer of services covered by Medicaid. The lock-in provider is supposed to lock the patient *out* of other medical services that are considered unnecessary.

managed care: prepayment plan for medical services, provided under the supervision of persons primarily concerned with the plan's financial solvency.

managed competition: originally, a proposal developed by the Jackson Hole Group, a group composed primarily of academics. It has been applied to so many ideas that conflict with the principles of the original that it no longer has a precise meaning. Generally, however, such proposals emphasize managed care and would forbid or discourage true free-market (unmanaged) competition.

Medicaid: federal-state program to finance medical care for the poor.

Medicare: U.S. government program established to help pay medical bills for the elderly (over the age of 65) and the disabled, financed through payroll taxes and (in the case of Part B) partly through a beneficiary premium.

Medicare carrier: the insurance company that has the contract to administer Medicare payments within a certain geographic area. It is privately owned, but government controlled, at least for purposes of Medicare.

Part A: The Medicare plan that covers hospital benefits.

Part B: The Medicare plan that covers physician and outpatient services.

participation agreement: a contract with an insurer, for example, Medicare. A physician who participates in Medicare agrees to accept assignment in all cases.

PCP: (1) phencyclidine, a drug of abuse. (2) an acronym for "primary care provider" (qv).

PPO (Preferred Provider Organization): a type of managed care plan, in which patients are strongly encouraged or required to receive services only from "preferred providers" (qv) who have signed a contract with the organization.

practice guidelines: instructions on how to manage certain medical problems in ways approved by the government or some other authoritative body; the AMA's solution to high costs and variable quality. Not to be confused with "cookbooks." A cookbook is a precise, comprehensible guide to an appetizing product, not a stew of half-baked, untested ingredients designed for force-feeding.

precertification: the procedure for getting the insurance company's permission to offer a certain test or treatment, to ensure that the patient's claim is not denied.

preferred provider: someone who has signed a contract with an insurance company, generally to provide services at a discounted fee according to the rules of the plan.

primary care provider ("primary" or "PCP" for short): a physician or other clinician who is responsible for the overall management of a patient; operationally, a gatekeeper. PCPs do provide some medical care, but the reason for calling them PCPs instead of doctors is their role in keeping patients from seeing specialists whenever they like. While specialists are usually paid only for services they actually provide, PCPs are rewarded for services that patients do *not* receive, through receiving a share of the prepayment that is withheld until the plan's financial status is reviewed.

provider: a person or entity that provides a medical good or service; examples: physicians, physical therapists, hospitals, pharmacies, suppliers of wheelchairs or other equipment, nursing homes, and home health agencies.

single-payor system: a system in which all medical bills are paid by a single entity, a governmental agency.

standard of care: what doctors say is the accepted way to treat a condition, at least when they are testifying in court. Practice guidelines are an attempt to define the standard in advance, instead of after the fact.

third party: an entity other than the doctor and the patient that is involved in a medical transaction, usually because of paying part of the bill. Examples: Medicare, Blue Cross, Aetna.

utilization review: a mechanism whereby an agent of a third party or a hospital reviews a patient's record to determine whether the physician's care is appropriate or constitutes overutilization, i.e., whether the third party will pay for it.

1

WHAT TO EXPECT FROM THIS BOOK

This book explains where we are, how we got there, and where we ought to go; it is a road map, not a panacea.

THERE ARE many books on the market today deploring the ills of our health care system and prescribing a "comprehensive" cure. This is not one of them, although I do believe that medicine is being destroyed and that something must be done about it.

Nevertheless, I cannot and will not prescribe a detailed "plan."

That statement is perhaps the main point of this book. We can define principles (as I shall try to do), but we cannot tell people exactly what to do, not without becoming little tyrants. That's how the free market that I advocate is so different from other proposals. It just sets up some basic ground rules and lets the players determine their own strategies for the game.

For example, I will advise people to buy true (catastrophic) insurance (I'll explain later what I mean by that), but I will not try to define a "basic package." And I will not advocate forcing people to buy the package that *I* like. The insurance company and subscribers should choose the plan and not leave that up to some government agency.

Likewise, I will not advocate that Congress force ("incentivize") medical training programs to produce a specified proportion of "primary care" physicians. (Today, the "50 percent solution" is proposed.) I don't know how many of each specialist we need, but neither does anybody else. For all we know, the current structure of medical specialists is absurd and should be reorganized. That will never happen if we set up quotas in stone.

This book is written by an internist, a doctor who used to be called a diagnostician. Sometimes patients ask internists for a prescription after the first mention of their complaint. However impatient they may be, a competent physician cannot accede to this demand. Before the prescription comes the diagnosis. And before the diagnosis, the history and physical examination. If the prescription is written too soon, the diagnosis will be missed, and the wrong treatment will be started. (Sometimes the wrong treatment is started even when the diagnosis is correct.) I believe most of the books on America's medical care, not to mention most of the bills passed by the legislature, offer dangerous treatment based on faulty diagnosis. They are getting it wrong, as I will show in the next chapter.

Internists often see patients with a long history of complex medical problems and many seemingly unrelated symptoms. In such instances, the most useful part of the examination might not be to listen to the patient's chest but to examine the shopping bag filled with the patient's medicines. The first one might have been prescribed for the wrong diagnosis, the second for the side effects of the first, the third to counteract the interaction of the first two, and so on. And there might be some medicines that are causing idiosyncratic side effects.

Sometimes, one can become a real medical hero very simply: Just *stop all the medicines.*

Note that this is not the same thing as stopping all treatment and abandoning the patient. It is a diagnostic maneuver and *possibly* a therapeutic one as well. It is accompanied by careful observation to determine whether in this case the treatment is worse than the disease, or even *is* the disease. One of the first things we learned in pharmacology class—or was it during internship?—is that "every drug is a new disease."

One example is certain drugs used to treat premature heartbeats. These can trigger ventricular fibrillation, a condition in which the heart writhes like a bag of worms without pumping out any blood. For years, it was common to prescribe drugs to suppress premature beats. We could show that the number of abnormal beats decreased. We thought we were doing a good thing, reducing the patient's risk of a fatal rhythm disturbance by "regulating" the heartbeat.

Then careful studies showed that more of the treated patients suddenly dropped dead. In many cases, it is much better just to leave the abnormal heartbeats alone.

I think that American medicine is like a patient who suffers from polypharmacy (too many drugs), and the effects of some highly toxic drugs, some of them prescribed to "regulate" conditions that were best left alone.

The twentieth-century solution to any social problem is to pass a law.

But what if it was a law that caused the problem in the first place? Why not *repeal the law?*

Do we have 37 million uninsured? We might pass a law that will require them to get insurance, through a government program if necessary.

The "35 to 37 million uninsured" has become a mantra. That's the number who are uninsured for some period of time during a year, most often because of changing jobs. The number uninsured for prolonged periods is about 9 to 11 million, according to U.S. Census Bureau figures.[1]

But what if the basic problem (the outrageously high cost of medical care and hence of insurance premiums) is *caused* by laws that we already have? We'll consider that hypothesis.

Can we find some medical horror stories? Undoubtedly, we can. Does this mean we should put all doctors, hospitals, laboratories, drug companies, and others under strict government regulation of every move they make? That is the direction in which we are heading.

Would-be reformers are attacking every glitch in the system, trying to suppress every premature heartbeat. You would definitely not like to have a doctor who treated your body that way. The supposedly well-intentioned ministrations of the reformers are about to stop the patient's heart.

The heart of medicine is the relationship of one doctor to one patient. In medicine, as opposed to a "health care delivery system," the training and experience of the physician are placed at the service of a sick person, under conditions agreeable to both. In medicine, the patient is at the center of the universe. The hospital, the CT scanner, the pharmaceutical industry, all the appurtenances of modern diagnosis and therapy, should revolve around the patient, not around the heads of the "system."

So there you have it, right up front: an admission that this book is really radical. Now "radical" does not mean one of the perennial variants of the plan to replace the present system with one that has more central planning and more government financing. Advocates of such plans may *think* that they are radicals, but they are really just asking for more of the same, only worse.

The really radical question to ask is: Why do we need a *national* system or a *national* program at all? We will always have institutions, each one being its own little system. But why do they have to be subordinate to and ruled by a giant national monolith? Maybe decentralization (the would-be reformers call it "fragmentation") is our *strength*, not our weakness. As the physiologists are discovering, a certain fundamental chaos is necessary to produce an orderly heartbeat, paradoxical as that may seem. (Chaos, indeed, underlies much of the order of the universe and is becoming a field of study in its own right.)

My purpose is to make the case for freedom of *enterprise* as well as freedom of *inquiry* in medicine. That's the radical remedy people are now stumbling toward in Eastern Europe, their centrally planned paradise having fallen apart. Having exported the concept of a free market to Poland (and Argentina, Singapore, Mexico, and even Britain and Sweden), we in the United States might try it out ourselves instead of turning the clock backward to mercantilism or socialism or other failed experiments of the past.

Yes, I know, people use the phrase "turning back the clock" to refer disparagingly to free enterprise as in our early tradition. They could, with equal aptness, apply the expression to other rediscoveries, say that of gunpowder, which was used in ancient times by the Chinese. (It worked then for firing projectiles like toy rockets, and it works now for propelling projectiles like bullets.) Free enterprise propelled the U.S. economy in the nineteenth century and is building the economies of the Pacific Rim today. Its startling success in improving the lives of ordinary people—wherever and whenever it has been tried—demonstrates that it does not depend on the century, the size of the country, the number of natural resources, or the population density (consider Hong Kong).

I will not pretend to show that a free market in medicine would be utopia or would solve all our problems once and for all. *There is no utopia.* I will only maintain that a free market is the best of the available alternatives and the one that does the least harm. Free enterprise does not create a system that is at equilibrium and is free of errors and problems. There are systems like that. They are all dead.

Because so many people assume otherwise, I must specifically state that free enterprise does *not* mean anarchy or lawlessness. Quite the contrary. There is no such thing as "unrestrained capitalism" (unless the term *capitalism* is taken to include state capitalism or fascism, under which the state, not the economy, is unfettered).

In the first place, free enterprise is governed by the laws of economics. Like the law of gravity, and unlike acts of Congress, the law of supply and demand cannot be repealed. Even Stalin, Mao Tse-tung, and the Khmer Rouge couldn't do it, despite the impressive forces of repression at their command. Of course, one can ignore the laws, say because one does not believe in them. But faith is not required. A person may firmly believe that the law of gravity does not apply to him under a particular circumstance. But if he tests his belief by jumping out of a twenty-first-story window, there is no doubt about what will happen.

One economic principle is that "honesty is the best policy." More broadly stated, *in the long run* cooperation wins and cheaters lose in a free economy. (In the short run, of course, cheaters can gain a temporary advantage. Beware of fly-by-night operators!)

This principle has been demonstrated in computer game theory. Robert Axelrod describes the winning program named "Tit for Tat" in a brilliant little book called *The Evolution of Cooperation.*[2] The game was a variant of "Prisoner's Dilemma," played repeatedly. Competitors devised more or less complicated strategies, some designed to take advantage of their opponent. The simple strategy of always cooperating, except for retaliating exactly once against every episode of cheating, won hands down—*if and only if* the game was played repeatedly. (In societal terms, this means that cooperation comes about naturally *if and only if* people have to bear responsibility for the long-term consequences of their own actions.)

Free enterprise cannot exist in the absence of the rule of law—a government that enforces contracts, protects property rights, and restrains those who would use violence against their neighbors. Such a rule of law establishes basic fairness, requiring that everybody has to play by the same rules. Note that this is *not* the politically correct definition of fairness; the latter definition judges by the win-loss record, not by the ground rules.

The record of free enterprise is of course imperfect. But then if there were no lawbreakers, there would be no need for a law.

Lawlessness threatens everyone, from entrepreneurs to the neediest of the poor. Lawlessness is rightly to be feared and today is everywhere to be found. Not just on the streets of Los Angeles, but in the halls of government itself. As we will see, the government is rapidly moving forward in its campaign to control the practice of medicine. "Physicians must be fettered," states William Roper, former head of the Health Care Financing Administration, which administers Medicare. "We need to control the health care system—the whole thing," proclaims Judith Feder, director of health policy on President Clinton's transition team. In order to establish control, the government is removing the fetters of constitutional law from itself, gradually, slowly. Each step of increased control over citizens (and decreased restraints on Leviathan) is proposed as a cure for a problem, seemingly with the best of intentions.

At this point, the reader may think this book is the work of an ideologue. If so, let him raise the same concern about the proposals written by Congress or by the scholars at the *Journal of the American Medical Association* (JAMA). Consider the question of how to identify an ideology:

Gorbachev was driving in a limousine through the countryside and saw a Russian plowman walking behind a horse-drawn plow, so he asked his driver to stop, walked up to the plowman, and said, "Comrade, tell me, is socialism an ideology, or is it a science?"

So the plowman scratches his head and his beard, and meditates, and finally replies: "Your Excellency, it is an ideology."

"You're right!" Gorbachev said. "And how did you reach this conclusion?"

"Well, Excellency, I figured that if it was a science, they would have tried it on the dogs first."

Theory underlies science, but the mark of science is observation of actual results. A prescription must be judged not by the doctor's intentions but by the patient's outcome. Are national health programs supposed to help the poor? All the proponents say they are. Do they actually bring better medical care to the poor? They do not, as I propose to show. Are Medicare rules and regulations supposed to benefit the elderly? All the congressmen who voted for them say that they are. From a short-term perspective they do benefit some elderly persons. All government programs have beneficiaries, who get a privilege at the expense of others, in this case, members of the next generations. But the beneficiaries pay for it in the long run. The bills are now coming due, and the result will be *restricted* medical care to the elderly, including those who didn't need the benefits in the first place. In addition, the elderly will face increasing resentment from younger persons, including their doctors. And they will be treated by doctors who are generally rewarded for lying and cheating and punished for being conscientious.

Despite the increasingly heavy dose of medications being forced upon the medical economy, the system is getting sicker. The doctors are feeling the symptoms first.

As I describe doctors' dilemmas, the reader may think that I am appealing for sympathy for the doctor. That is not my purpose at all.

Appeals for sympathy do not work. As my grandfather once said, "If you want to find sympathy, look in the dictionary." He said this not because he was a hard and unfeeling man. On the contrary, he was the kindest man in the world. Everybody who knew him thought so. He was simply stating a fact of life—a fact that is becoming the more true, the more we hear talk of "compassion." (Remember the song from *Hair:* " 'Specially people who care about strangers, Who care about evil and social injustice. Do they only care about the bleeding crowd? How about a needing friend?")

Physicians are becoming scapegoats now, as I will illustrate later on. But others have been scapegoats before and treated far more viciously than today's physicians. One example was the Jews of Shakespeare's time (as well as other times). In *The Merchant of Venice*, Shylock makes an eloquent appeal for understanding:

"Hath not a Jew hands, organs, dimensions, senses, affections, passions? . . . If you prick us, do we not bleed? . . . If you poison us, do we not die?" (act 3, scene 1). He made the point that Jews, too, were human.

What could the eloquence of a Shakespeare accomplish for English Jews? Probably very little. What could he do against the overwhelming anti-Semitism of society? So what can my words accomplish for the public perception of doctors? On the other side are Ralph Nader, the FBI, the media, trial lawyers, and a lot of prestigious physicians.

There are other reasons why doctors should not ask for sympathy. Many of them don't deserve it because they played their part in creating, or at least tolerating, the situation as it now is. And most of them don't need it. Doctors don't get through medical school, much less internship, by being stupid or weak. If they survive, they are tough. They will adapt to the situation, turn it to their own advantage, or escape from it.

Readers should care about the plight of doctors for one and only one reason: Someday they might need one.

Doctors are human. If you kick them, they resent it. If you reward them for behaving like petty bureaucrats, they'll start to act like petty bureaucrats. If you punish them for putting their patients first, they'll think twice before going to war for the patient. In fact, if you punish them for being doctors, there will eventually be no doctors. No *real* doctors, that is. There will be people with academic degrees performing the official functions assigned to them.

Patients want a doctor who will be skillful, competent, and intelligent. They also want a doctor who will have sympathy for *them.* They do not want to be treated the way some patients were treated in *The House of God.*

The House of God is a novel about internship in one of our most prestigious (and purportedly best) teaching hospitals. The novel has been deplored in the *New England Journal of Medicine* and other hallowed medical publications for its irreverent attitude and biting cynicism. (How could the author "Samuel Shem" *dare* tell this story to the reading public!) But the interns and residents all love it. They know that Shem speaks the truth—the ugly truth. They know just how the characters in the story feel. *You* need to know that, too, so read the book and wonder: Does your doctor think of you as a "gomer"? (Law II of *The House of God* is that "Gomers go to ground." According to Shem, GOMER is an acronym that means "Get Out of My Emergency Room.")

This is a relatively recent phenomenon. Interns have always had a tough life. They are always tired and frequently irritable. When I was an intern at Parkland, one of my residents, a thoroughly humane and civilized man, confided in me that one time he could barely restrain himself from hitting a belligerent patient with an IV pole. Later, I understood exactly how he felt. But the deep-seated, chronic, bitter cynicism is something new, I think. And it affects not only interns, but the entire profession, including those physicians who always before loved their patients, loved their profession, and hoped to practice until the day they died.

One grandfatherly physician told me about his vain efforts to get patients to understand his troubles and the reasons he plans to retire early.

"After I finished, the patient asked, 'Well, when you quit, will you find me someone who will take care of me?'

"I said, 'No, I won't. I hope you get sick and die. It would serve you right.' "

And this was from a kindly man, the type of physician you would choose for yourself or your mother, partly because of his excellent judgment and technical skill and partly because of his personality. I don't know whether he really said that to a patient. Probably not. But I do know that he felt it, at least for a moment. He is human. One of the best human beings you will find, but still human.

A survey done in 1991 showed that nearly 75 percent of physicians thought they might retire earlier than they would have thought possible five years ago. Some physicians who actually changed their occupations were shown on a *60 Minutes* program: One became a carpenter and one opened a pet store.

Good riddance, you may say. But first, think about it. If you are not 100 percent sure that you are right, please read on.

To summarize what this book is not: It is not a sixteen-point promise to bring universal access to the highest quality care for all Americans at a contained cost. (You'll have to find some AMA propaganda if you want that.) It is not a blueprint for a "new" national system, some variation on the Swedish or the Canadian or the German or the British or some other plan. Try looking through almost any standard medical journal if you want that, although I will touch on these experiments. It is not a cookbook or a prescription at all. And it is *not* an appeal for sympathy for physicians. Save your sympathy for the patients. They are going to need it.

In other words, I will *not* suggest a blue-ribbon commission, a national academy, a task force, a quality assurance committee, a nationwide educational program, a cabinet-level post, a multidisciplinary approach, a congressional inquiry, or a national Doctors Appreciation Day.

What this book does strive to be is a description of how things *are* and how they got that way (the symptoms and signs, the diagnosis, the etiology, and the pathophysiology); an attempt to plot the future course of the disease (the prognosis); and an outline of what medicine ought to be like and how we can make the situation better (a treatment strategy).

Here is a preliminary warning: Some readers may find this material offensive. I will promote the most unpopular idea on earth: individual responsibility. That is the alternate to the usual remedies, all of which boil down to "Have George do it." Inevitably, George will be, at best, a replay of George III, the one in charge before the radicals had that tea party back in 1773. The new George, like the old one, won't really be capable of doing anything except *forcing* others to act or refrain from acting.

Here is a list of people who may want to save themselves time and vexation by putting this book down immediately:

• Those who are 100 percent certain that private doctors are all robber barons or buccaneers (a word I borrowed from the editor of *Arizona Medicine*) or should be treated as if they were.

• Those who are 100 percent certain that patients are not capable of making wise decisions about their medical care, of which the first is the choice of physicians and others to advise them (the dean of our medical school seems to think that).

• Those who would *never* take the word of *any* mere physician (LMD) over that of one of the following: an author of an article in the *New England Journal of Medicine*, a person with a Ph.D. degree from Harvard, the head of the department of medicine at an accredited medical school, a credentialed ethicist or sociologist, or the head of an important government regulatory agency.

• Those who are adamant in insisting that health care is a "right" or *should* be declared a right by the government (as I see it, the government can either respect or trample on rights but cannot create them). Medical care is *not* a right, and if we treat it as a right we will receive worse medical care.

• Those who think there is nothing to be learned from a physician who lived around 400 B.C. or from events that occurred between A.D. 1917 and 1989, human social evolution having outpaced Darwinian evolution in which epochs lasted for millions of years.

• Those who believe there are no absolutes (except perhaps the right to health care) and consider any belief in an absolute to be arcane, eccentric, discredited, or even sinister.

• Those who are grievously offended by the words of nineteenth-century French economist Frederic Bastiat, who came to the following conclusions about French experiments in socialism following the Revolution:

> Away with the whims of governmental administrators, their socialized projects, their centralization, . . . their regulations, their restrictions, their equalization by taxation, and their pious moralizations!
>
> And now that the legislators and do-gooders have so futilely inflicted so many systems upon society, may they finally end where they should have begun: May they reject all systems, and try liberty. . . . [3]

2

. . . .

GETTING IT WRONG

. . . .

Most proposed remedies for the "health care crisis" are snake oil, and you shouldn't swallow them.

THERE, I have already made an absolute statement in the very title of this chapter. (People offended by a belief in an absolute have been warned.)

In mathematics and the hard sciences, problems have a right answer. That's one thing I like about them.

There are also an infinite number of *wrong* answers.

The difference between right and wrong is not simply a matter of opinion or taste. The right answer agrees with observation (with reality). The wrong answers don't.

You may consider what follows to be a digression. You may skip it if you want, but you shouldn't. At least if you think doctors need to know more about sociology and humanities, you should be open to the idea that everybody needs to know more about science and mathematics. And for your sociologic interest, here is how a former teacher of physics and geometry thinks about things.

The right answer is not necessarily the one that is in the book. "True" is not a synonym for "accepted." In physics, wrong theories can be propounded for centuries. But when the theory is shown to conflict with the experimental evidence, it has to be discarded.

The fact that we haven't *found* the right answer doesn't mean that it doesn't exist. However, there are some questions that don't have a right answer. Even in mathematics there are some propositions that

19

cannot be decided one way or another. (This is Goedel's famous theorem.)[1]

Outside of the hard sciences, there are more unanswerable questions and many matters of opinion or taste. But some propositions are still right, and an infinite number are still wrong. And the right answers stay right, whether anyone accepts them or not. What was *true* (as opposed to what was believed) in the fourteenth century is also true in the twentieth century, and vice versa. For example: Water doesn't run uphill; leprosy is caused by *Mycobacterium leprae*, not by a devil's curse; and human beings who are allowed to keep the fruits of their labor work harder than those who aren't. (Another scientific digression: I am speaking of principles and constants. Variables are, well, variable, and have different values at different times: for example, the age of puberty, the average height of a human being, and the percentage of the population engaged in agriculture.)

Because human beings are fallible, we must constantly keep the possibility of error in mind and exercise great caution about forcing our answers on others. We don't want another Spanish Inquisition. Any "solution" that requires the use of coercion should be viewed with great suspicion. Something that is right and true remains so no matter how many people the inquisitor burns at the stake. As Galileo said, the earth still moves.

Those who speak with the greatest confidence and authority today want to *impose* their theory on American medicine, not to wait for people to accept it. But they have got it all *wrong*.

It's perfectly fair for you to say that I'm the one who has it all wrong. So let's have an experiment—a controlled experiment—instead of an argument in which assertions by various authorities are exchanged.

At the end of the book, I will outline the ideas that I think we should try in medical reforms. This is not a murder mystery—go ahead and read the last chapter first if you like. A lot of people read books that way. To me, it seems more logical to look first at observations that we already have made. We have done a lot of experiments although not with rigorous controls in the scientific sense. (Scientific controls are carefully matched groups treated in different ways, not punishments for dissenters.)

PLANS FOR THE NEW ORDER

Every aspirant to political office and every branch of organized medicine has a plan. They all sound alike to me: more subsidies, more "management," more "documentation," more "guidelines," more government inspectors, more committees, and, inevitably, rationing (either explicitly as in the Oregon plan, about which more later, or by means of the global budget, which puts a lid on how much could be spent for medical care). This means less freedom and less privacy for both doctors and patients, less innovation, and less private profit (at least to physicians and others who actually do the medical care). And what will you get as a result? Let me tell you: a freeway to clinics that dispense aspirin, oat bran, and well-baby checks, with access impeded mainly by traffic jams; roadblocks on the way to the hospital that offers lifesaving technology to the sick and the injured; and higher, more expensive hurdles for new technology that might enable the deaf to hear or the paralyzed to walk.

Of course, proponents of the plan don't put it that way. Their wording is like that of the New Jersey ballot initiative, which won overwhelming voter approval:

> Shall the State urge the United States Congress and the President of the United States to enact a national health care program which provides high quality comprehensive personal health care including preventive, curative, and occupational health services, is universal in coverage, community controlled, rationally organized, equitably financed, with minimal out-of-pocket expense to taxpayers; is sensitive to the particular health care needs of all persons; and aims at reducing the overall costs of health care.

Notice the semantics of this proposal. "Community control" means *public* control, not *private*. Operationally, *they*, the managers, control the system; *you* don't (whether you are a provider or a recipient of the actual medical service). "Minimal out-of-pocket expense to taxpayers" means minimal at the time of service (if any), not at the time of tax collection or on the day of reckoning for the national debt. And the service might be "sensitive," but not necessarily responsive, especially to those whose particular needs are low on the societal priority list.

Such a system promises to turn the medical profession into a New Order, rather like a religious order. Instead of carrying out the will of God as conveyed through the voice of Mother Superior, the health care provider will carry out the will of society as conveyed through the voice of managers who interpret the Revised Standard Version of the HCFA-AMA Practice Guidelines (you might not have heard about these yet, but they will affect your life—more about them later, alas).

The New Order will open the way to paradise. A paradise has been promised for decades. Congressman Pete Stark (D-CA) defined it in words that mean "from each according to his ability and to each according to his needs."[2] That's not his original idea, of course, even though he cites it without crediting Karl Marx.

Not everyone finds the New Order appealing. But everyone *is* looking for a way out of the current crisis.

IS THERE A WAY OUT?

In Britain and Germany, there is a way out: private doctors. In Canada, there is a way out: an open border to the south. In the United States, there is a way out of government medical care: the private sector.

Many reformers think that the way out is part of the problem, and they propose to plug up the escape hatches. Instead of letting "greedy" and "selfish" people spend their own money for their own medical care, the reformers would make them put it in the community pot and then get their own care from that same pot. If only *everybody* (except the reformers) had to go to the Medicaid clinic, there would be political pressure to make that clinic better for all, or so they say.

And how is the clinic to be made better?

There are two possibilities: patchwork reform or a complete overhaul.

Patchwork reform is a Marxist term for a process that is deplored because it accepts the existence of a capitalist system. But most people who use the term probably mean symptomatic treatment that won't cure the problem.

One example is the approach to the rampant problem of thievery. Congress responds as Parliament did after the inception of the National Health Service. Dr. Donal Sheehan, a British physician, stated that funds were grossly mismanaged, and that "having made the assumption that all doctors must be thieves, the state has had to pay for hosts of other thieves to watch 'em."[3] We'll talk about the war on fraud and abuse later on.

To many, patchwork reform seems to be the only politically feasible course. That's because we are trapped by what Milton Friedman calls the "tyranny of the status quo." Once a controversial bill passes Congress, the only debate concerns whether the budget should be increased by 5 or 15 percent. The new program is protected by the iron triangle of direct beneficiaries, the congressional oversight committee, and the federal agency that administers it. (Still, there might be hope: the "catastrophic" extension of Medicare was repealed.)

According to some reformers, the way out of patchwork reform is to seal off the exits, then blow up the building (destroy the free enterprise system). Then you can start over, building a new system (and remaking human nature).

The way of most physicians (and politicians) is to try to delay the day of reckoning. For years, physicians have been going along to get along. They support AMA proposals to tinker with the system to make it slightly more tolerable, or to slow the rate of its decline.

The reckoning cannot be postponed indefinitely. Even the most cooperative are now learning that Law VIII of *The House of God* ("They can always hurt you more") does not just apply to medical interns.

Evasive action is not the answer. Physicians might escape from Medicare—for a few years or even a few decades (as I have done—see chapter 6). They might try digging a tunnel after the last doorway is barred. But none of us can escape from the human condition. The fact is that we might someday become patients—if we live long enough, Medicare patients. At that point, we will probably get the medical care that we deserve—the kind we asked for, or the kind we didn't bother to fight.

REMEMBER THE OBJECTIVE

If we're trying to decide whether our reforms are taking us in the right direction or the wrong one, we have to first figure out where we want to go.

In medicine, the objective is not to enforce an abstract concept like the "right to [equal] medical care" or to be able to say that everyone is "insured." *The objective is to do right by our patients.* As doctors, our job is to take care of patients to the best of our ability: to extend and improve life, to relieve pain, and to diminish disability, always following the moral law. The moral *law*, which is not necessarily the same as the bureaucratic *rules*. The moral *law*, not the moral *theory*. The law is summarized pretty well in the Oath of Hippocrates—see page 255, arcane as many academics believe that to be.

Our goal is to have as many people benefit as much as possible from our medical knowledge. And we want that knowledge to advance, not to stagnate and regress.

Physicians take care of patients one at a time. (People who are offended thereby might call this approach a patchwork style of practice.) As physicians (as opposed to social engineers), we are interested in any method that will help one patient with one problem. We'd like to help as much as we can in restoring health and optimal function to each of our patients. Fulfilling a norm or complying with a "guideline" or directive is a goal for bureaucrats or assembly-line workers, not for physicians.

It is said that "society can be encouraged to accept and demand reasonable limits to health services."[4] But physicians want to accomplish more, not to learn to make do with less. (I said *accomplish* more, not spend more money. The two are not necessarily related.) And what patient would not feel the same way?

All proposals should be evaluated on the basis of whether they move us toward that objective or away from it: It's the *results*, not the *intentions* that count. If we're moving away from the destination, then we'd better take a look at the way the guideposts (the assumptions underlying the reform) are pointing.

These are basic assumptions underlying both the health care patchwork reform plans and the ultimate radical New Order:

- There is a right to health care.

- The government is the definer, guardian, and enforcer of entitlement rights, such as the right to health care. (Entitlement rights are to be distinguished from freedom rights, such as the protection of life, liberty, and property.)

• There are no moral absolutes (such as the ones in the Oath of Hippocrates), at least none that override the "rights" of "society."

In this book, I intend to show that these assumptions are wrong a priori and that as currently implemented they have disastrous results in the daily practice of medicine. Then I will examine the question: Where do we go from here?

You may be outraged by the very suggestion that you don't have a natural right to health care. At this point, let me just say that if you demand that the government try to *create* this right, you are going to have to trade in your fundamental rights to life, liberty, and the pursuit of happiness (and the right to property, which is fundamental to all three). This is *not a good bargain* for patients or physicians. (For doctors, I think it is a Faustian bargain.) Read on to see how I came to this conclusion.

3

PERSONAL DATA, INCLUDING THINGS IT DIDN'T
SAY ON MY MEDICAL SCHOOL APPLICATION
(WITH SPECULATIONS ON WHETHER THE
ADMISSIONS COMMITTEE MADE A MISTAKE)

*Medical school admissions committees are trying to undo their
past mistakes—admitting people like me—but you the reader
ought to find out more about us.*

EVERYBODY who applies to medical school is asked the obvious question: Why do you want to be a doctor? I ask it of the candidates I interview. And of course somebody once asked it of me. I'm not sure why we ask, because the answer is usually the same. The person claims to like working with people, to be interested in science, and to want to serve humanity. The claim is probably a sincere belief, based on little knowledge. Medical school applicants are too young to have had much experience in the realities of serving humanity.

I don't remember what I said at the time, but it probably wasn't the whole truth. I didn't know what the whole truth was. And if I had, I wouldn't have expected the interviewer to be impressed.

Whatever the original motive to become a doctor—I had wanted to do it as long as I can remember—the catalyst was a very mundane object. A spitwad. I was a schoolteacher at the time. That job just came naturally; I started my teaching career as soon as my little sisters were able to sit up in front of a blackboard. And for two years, I taught professionally.

One day, one of my reluctant math students aimed a very wet spitwad in my direction, and it splattered on the blackboard, narrowly missing my face. I am not sure whether his aim was a little off or extraordinarily good. But he expressed rather eloquently the general attitude that most of my public school students had about learning—as well as the opinion that the administration secretly cherished about upstart teachers who thought it was really dumb to insist that seventh graders try to prove theorems about the Babylonian number system. They can't do it. Nobody can teach them to do it. But I was sure that I could teach the students to multiply fractions, even though their previous teachers hadn't. And from a psychological standpoint, I thought that overcoming mathematical ignorance does wonders for math anxiety—one of my many reactionary attitudes.

I have always been grateful to that kid. (I never found out who it was, although I'm sure it was a boy. Girls never throw spitwads. At least they didn't back in 1969; perhaps we have evolved since then.) Partly because of him, I reactivated my applications to medical school. I thought I might be able to overcome my tendency to faint at the sight of blood or the mere description of an operation. And I thought I could probably accomplish more in medicine than in the benighted public school system, even if teaching was the more valuable service to humanity.

At the time, I never suspected that I would see worse things than spitwads routinely thrown at doctors. Not just lawsuits. Abuse by patients and administrators; fines; threatening letters from Medicare or Medicaid; criminal charges; asset forfeiture; and the book—the book from which they read the rights to rapists and murderers, which has no such rights listed for physicians. More about these things later.

At home, we were always taught that everybody (including girls) needed to learn to be useful as well as ornamental. Had I been a boy, I would probably have learned to lay brick and do carpentry, like my father. I had neither the strength nor the inclination for such endeavors. But medicine always impressed me as women's work (which is not to say that men can't also be very good at it). Women have always taken care of most of the sickness in the world. A few of these women were physicians, some were nurses, and some were mothers and grandmothers without additional medical qualifications. My mother, whose total medical training was a short period of working with an ENT (ear, nose, and throat) surgeon, was the medical consultant of first choice for most of the other mothers of her acquaintance. I still rely on her remarkable clinical judgment.

It could be that an interest in medicine is partly hereditary, like a propensity for troublemaking. My mother's great-grandmother, Nellie

Hanley, was a midwife as well as a farmer and the mother of eight. But unlike many of my classmates, I had no living relatives with professional training in medicine. (My earliest contact with medicine was playing with the surgical instruments that my grandfather found; he drove the laundry truck that collected the dirty linen from the county hospital.) Thus, I had no way of knowing what I was getting into. And perhaps neither did my classmates. Very few people foresaw what would befall the medical profession. (Back in those days, physician parents generally encouraged their children to follow in their footsteps instead of threatening to disinherit them for doing so.) In many ways, medicine has recapitulated the history of the teaching profession, lagging a couple of decades behind. One can observe that the onset of the professional decline just happens to coincide with the infusions of government funding and the beginning of a steep rise in costs. Sometimes I think that I was born about twenty years too late to be a doctor, as well as forty years too late to be a teacher.

On the other hand, in an attempt to be fair, let me present another side of the story. It could be that the admissions committee to my medical school made a mistake. Maybe the dean was a little reactionary that year, having tired of sit-ins in his office.

Except for being out of school for three years, I was the epitome of the desirable medical school applicant of the day. I was a science major; actually, I had a double major in chemistry and math. I had straight A's in all my academic subjects, my average being spoiled only by PE (physical education), which I cordially hated even before I got a C in it.

I had an extracurricular activity, since that was considered important. I was on the debate team. I worked my differential equations problems in the backseat of the car on the way to tournaments in places like Lubbock, Texas. I was not a particularly contentious person—not then. I didn't write polemics as I do now; I just prepared both sides of the case as debaters (most of them prelaw students) are required to do. I suppose my political opinions would have been called conservative, but I wasn't a very political person. I didn't even win very many debates.

I did not, however, have some of the qualifications considered indispensable to medical school candidates today. I had not done volunteer work, and the medical school interviewers never even asked about it. (Now applicants tell the interviewer about it even if not asked.) I had not demonstrated social concern. I was too busy studying, and in college I also had to work in the chemistry lab for rather less than the minimum wage. (I needed the money because my daddy wasn't rich. I did not complain, and I did not feel the least bit abused, because I was learning a lot about chemistry.)

I was like a lot of my classmates in medical school, the shy, studious, scientific type. Not very colorful, and possibly not even well rounded. (Straight or square would be more like it.)

My classmates and I (and our older colleagues who are like us only more so) are now either explicitly or implicitly under attack for the way that we are. And we of course are increasingly frustrated by developments in the medical system.

One answer is to say that we are not fit to be physicians, and that society needs a New Physician. And that we need less emphasis on grades, and more on caring.

It is true that physicians graduated in the bad old days were far from perfect. The stereotype of the premed, a drudge who cared about nothing except getting the right answers on tests so that he could get into medical school, probably has a lot of truth to it. To be sure, I never met very many premeds on the road to Lubbock or in the library or chemistry lab. But my medical school class had its share of social climbers, money grubbers, and psychotics. The question is whether the treatment—changes in admission policy and curriculum—could be worse than the disease, and whether the treatment even helps the disease. There is no evidence that ethics lectures, novel-reading assignments, or volunteer work can turn a jerk into a Marcus Welby.

We are, in fact, getting less emphasis on grades. Admission to medical school is much less competitive than it used to be. There are now fewer than two applicants for every position, and different types of people are applying. Not just more women and more minorities, but people with different aspirations, different personalities, and different abilities.

The selection process works both ways: in the self-selection of applicants, and in the selection of successful candidates by the admissions committee.

By one means or another, the system is trying to drive out people who bother it or will be bothered by it. But no one has figured out how to tell who *should* become a physician. Deemphasizing grades is easy. But how do you select people who care? (If you know what questions I should ask medical school applicants, please tell me.)

One problem is defining what they should care *about*. My generation does care about a lot of things. We care about our autonomy. We care about doing a good job. Surgeons take pride in speed, technical finesse, beautifully healed wounds, and excellent functional results. Internists take pride in accurate diagnoses and effective treatments. We all care about having the respect of our colleagues and patients. We have at least as much capacity for human kindness as other people do and probably quite a bit more. And, yes, we do care about financial security, too (don't you?). Not all of us are paragons. Some of us are even downright mercenary and are just as bad as some businesspeople, lawyers, and politicians. Some are arrogant snobs who crave adulation. (But some people like that are also technical geniuses.) We have all the failings of human beings.

Reformers tell us that physicians need to care more about money, in the sense of saving money for the government and the insurance company. In most of these proposals, the patients don't get to share in the savings. However, physicians should not care at all about making money for themselves. (Today's incentives, as we shall see, are going to take care of that automatically. People won't be attracted to a field for the money if there isn't any money in it.) How to tell whether they *do* care too much about money in the wrong sort of way is another question. No medical school applicant has ever, ever told me that he wants to become a doctor in order to get rich. Should we give them a lie detector test? Even if polygraphs were reliable (and they are not), I don't think this would help. Entrants to medical school tend to be idealistic. Their mercenary nature comes out later, perhaps at the same time as the bills for their education.

Of course, everybody thinks that physicians should be humane. So how can you tell? There is a tendency to assume that people who study science are less humane than people who study humanities, but I know of no evidence that this is so. Among my personal acquaintances, I know hard-core, brilliant engineers and scientists who are such bleeding hearts that they bleed their own blood (they take in stray cats and would do almost anything for a friend in need). And I know liberal arts majors who speak the finest sentiments while they stab their friends or their mother in the heart. Can you tell them apart by looking at their college transcripts?

The new ideal physician tends to care more about other things, too, the things that are thought to make one well rounded. Social life. Athletics. Travel. Politically correct causes. And, of course, leisure time. Here I will reveal one of the worst of my reactionary attitudes. I don't care in the least about any of these in my physician or the physicians to whom I refer my patients. My question is simply this: Will the physician show up when there is work to be done? And will he be really good at doing the job?*

Give me the old-fashioned, workaholic, technically overtrained, and socially inept surgeon who actually *likes* blood and guts. Even if he does like to make a lot of money. When there is surgery to be done, he will be there. He will not be out training for his next marathon or making a speech at a political rally. And who can say a person does not care enough when he is readily available to *take* care of a problem? That is my opinion as a patient. Maybe you as a patient feel differently.

Of course, I am speaking of conservative surgeons, those who are not knife happy. Conservative surgeons respect their art and know that it can kill people. If I see one patient who has a surgical scar for no good reason, I never again refer a patient to that surgeon if I can possibly help it.

I realize that surgical technique is not the only ingredient in healing, even in surgical diseases. The patient's relationship to the physician is also extremely important. Some physicians seem to have a healing touch. I can't connect this ability to any readily apparent aspect of their personality. I know of no reliable measuring instrument to identify healing skill in aspirants to medical school. My intuition as interviewer is the only tool that I have. (It would be nice to have a way of checking this out ten years later!)

The old way of choosing people for medical school was all right,

---

*A note on personal pronouns: For the record, yes, I do know that women are physicians and surgeons, too. The default option for the third-person singular English personal pronoun is "he," and this may refer to a person of either gender. Call it a contraction for "she," if you will. Wherever you see "he," it means "he or she" or "she or he" unless the antecedent is clearly a male person. Likewise, "him" may mean "him or her" (or "her or him") and "his" may mean "his or hers" (or "hers or his").

even if not perfect, in my opinion. It emphasized what was measurable. And academic achievement did at least correlate strongly with the ability to comprehend the difficult curriculum of medical school, a necessary if not sufficient condition for becoming a good physician.

I even like the idea of one aptitude test that is given to some applicants for a residency in orthopedic surgery. The candidate is given a two-by-four and some hand tools and told to build a "T." The ability to do so tells you nothing about the candidate's humaneness (except in the sense that a person should not want to enter a field for which he has no talent, because he might hurt somebody). But if the surgeon botches the job on your hip because of not being good with his hands, you might not care too much about what a compassionate personality he has.

What are the results of our present efforts to do a better job of selecting the new ideal physician? In 1990, a record 16 percent of medical graduates flunked the national boards, compared with 9 percent in 1984.

There is another effect of deemphasizing technical competence in the selections process: People whose ability exceeds the minimum needed for the task tend to have more self-confidence and to demand more autonomy. People whose ability is marginal are easier to manage.

The old selection process produced some troublemakers, including this one. The new one might expedite the elimination of the independent physician, as described in the next chapter.

4

....

JUST ANOTHER ENDANGERED SPECIES?

....

The private doctor is an endangered species, and you should care about it even if you don't care much about the various other threatened insects and worms.

WILL PRIVATE MEDICINE BECOME EXTINCT?

IT SEEMS to me that the private doctor, the independent solo practitioner, has been under sustained attack for at least ten years. But how, and why, could this be?

Everyone says that the horse-and-buggy doctor is one we all admire and need the most. People read a eulogy for each beloved physician and deplore the loss of a noble tradition. Then they clamor for more programs that hasten the demise of the independent physician and the ascendancy of the depersonalized corporate medical machine that they profess to abhor.

Most people don't know what is going on. Could it be that *nobody* knows what is going on? Or simply that nobody cares?

It is possible that history is an accident, a phenomenon of pure, blind chance. Or that some mysterious force of nature is at work, bringing about the survival of the fittest and the extinction of the unfit, even if it looks as if the exact opposite is actually occurring.

Some people say that private doctors are dinosaurs, but I say they have it backward. Private doctors are small mammals, and bureaucratic medicine is the dinosaur. Consider: The dinosaur was a huge lumbering beast. Some species had two brains. The bigger one was at the wrong end of the spinal cord, but all the orders still came from the one on top. What could be a better analogy for the VA? (I used this analogy in a panel discussion before a class of medical students. The students found it amusing, but the professor never asked me back.)

I used to take comfort in this analogy. But the current theory holds that dinosaurs ruled the earth until it collided with a ten-kilometer asteroid.

It certainly seems to me that the ruling dinosaurs aren't waiting for natural selection (or a catastrophic impact with an extraterrestrial body) to weed out the supposedly maladapted private doctors. Instead, private medicine is under sustained attack. Why?

Private doctors often charge lower fees. They are more available. They offer freedom of choice. They contribute to diversity and pluralism, which are supposed to be good things, aren't they? Why not just leave them alone?

A hypothesis occurred to me while I was visiting some friends who live on a farm.

Early one morning, this city girl made a remarkable discovery: *You can't herd just one sheep.* At least, this fact seemed remarkable to her. To the children, it was obvious.

I was up earlier than the rest and happened to notice that there was a sheep in the backyard. The children had apparently missed that one when they chased the rest out the night before. Something had to be done. Sheep can die from eating too much grain, and there was a lot of loose wheat and corn on the trailer parked in the yard. The sheep was busy munching on it.

No problem, I thought. The gate was not far away. I had seen the children herd large numbers of sheep just by getting behind them. You need to get one sheep to start heading in the right direction; the rest of the flock follows. You have to see this phenomenon to comprehend the meaning of the expression "like a herd of sheep."

So what is easily done with thirty sheep, must be a cinch with just one, right?

Wrong.

My opinion of sheep's intelligence underwent a major revision. I could swear the animal was playing games with me, evading me by ducking around objects, playing hide-and-seek as cleverly as a child.

When I stopped, it stopped. It stared at me brazenly, as if to say "Nya, nya, nya."

Finally I gave up. The sheep was too large for me to pick up, and the sheepdog had recently died. I didn't have a shepherd's crook (now I can guess what they're for). The animal won. The best I could do was chase it away from the trailer when it got too close. No way would that animal go through the gate to be with the other sheep in the field.

"Right," the farmer told me, when I explained what I thought was a brilliant original observation. "You need at least two sheep, and some people say three."

In many ways, human beings are like sheep. They behave very differently in a crowd or a group. Without speculating about the perpetrators' motives, let us consider the results of policies that keep human beings in the herd at all times. What if we always make schoolchildren work in groups rather than alone? What if solo practitioners are driven out of business and physicians practice in large institutions or not at all?

In the herd, sheep are much easier to control. They don't play games with the sheepherder. They are content in the pasture where they are placed and don't usually wander off to find something better for themselves. They behave—like sheep.

In a group, human beings are much more malleable, too. What is normal inquisitiveness in any human child left alone occurs only under the most unusual circumstances within the "group" culture. There might still be some deviants, some aberrations. But many fewer.

At present, it is said that if you ask five doctors their opinion about your treatment, you might well get five different opinions. And what's wrong with that? Usually, if there are wide variations, it means that none of the treatments is clearly better than the rest. Take back pain, for example: There are remedies from A to Z for that. And doctors keep inventing things so fast that the regulators can't keep up with them. There is no herd immunity to innovation.

But times are changing fast. Soon we will have practice guidelines, determined by a government-sponsored committee. The sheep will be fenced in. If they can still run faster than the sheepherder, it won't matter, especially since we're breeding an abundance of sheepdogs to chase down the occasional stray.

We'll have a herd, a nice, placid, socialized, tamed, cud-chewing herd. It will keep the rulers' grass manicured and fertilized. In return for the privilege of grazing on the rulers' grass (the only grass that fenced-in sheep are permitted to have), the sheep will periodically be shorn. And when people become discontented with the system, a supply of sacrificial lambs will be available. (If you think I am being paranoid about doctors being blamed and punished for the failings of our medical system, please read on.)

So What?

As American politicians and social engineers rush to the rescue of the health care system, code 3 (with sirens blaring), Americans might be inclined to ignore them. They are used to sirens.

But most Americans are aware of at least one symptom of the critical illness: the pain they have in their pocketbooks whenever they pay an insurance premium or a medical bill.

For many, that's the only concern. They are ready to believe that private physicians are responsible for their pain, since that is what they are repeatedly told. Why should the average citizen worry about the plight of independent doctors, even if they are an endangered species? Aren't such doctors all greedy and rich?

The first reason you should care is that you might someday need a physician—a private physician.

Ask yourself this question: Is there now, or might there ever be, something in your medical record that you don't want the world to know about? Or that you don't even want a particular clerk to know about? An episode of venereal disease? A panic attack? A spell of depression? A hangover? A marital problem? An altercation with your boss? An exposure to AIDS? In submitting an insurance claim, you have to give permission to have that information released. It's confidential, of course, but no one is sure what that word means, especially in the computer age. Do you want photocopies—or electronic copies— of a record you probably haven't seen yourself proliferating from one provider, plan, or government agency to the next?

Or is it possible that you might someday want to have an "unnecessary" or "unapproved" type of diagnostic test or treatment? Even one that has not been "proved effective" to the satisfaction of the National

Health Board? (People are willing to try almost anything when medicine has no proven cure for their particular ailment.)

Do you have the right to privacy or to unorthodox or "excessive" treatment? Would such rights for individuals like you infringe on the rights of society?

Maybe you are confident that you will always have a right to *seek* these things. But what if a physician does not have the right to *offer* them? Or what if the doctor just isn't in the next time you call, or ever again?

There is another reason you should care about what is happening to doctors. If physicians can ever be treated as I will describe, can others be treated in that way also? And even if special treatment is intended only for doctors, what about the doctors' patients?

During raids on physicians' offices, the officers of the law often seize records of patients, without their knowledge or consent. And after visiting the doctors, the officers have knocked on the patients' door also.

Such events may make you think of the word *Gestapo,* which I have heard with increasing frequency, sometimes with a distinct Hispanic accent. (It happens that American-born minorities and foreign-born physicians have been overrepresented in fraud investigations. This does not necessarily mean that more of them are guilty of fraud. It could mean that they are becoming the politically correct scapegoats.)

To voice a fear that socialized medicine could be the entrée to a repressive tyranny over physicians (and eventually patients, too) carries a heavy risk: One's entire work may be dismissed as the ravings of an eccentric crank.

Maybe it can't happen here. We live at "the end of history," with liberal democracy permanently triumphant over all the earth, according to Professor Francis Fukayama.[1]

It is history that the precursor of socialized medical systems was advocated by Bismarck, known for *Blut und Eisen* (blood and iron) rather than for compassion. In calling for the adoption of his accident insurance law by the Reichstag, Bismarck explained:

> To find the correct ways and means for providing this care is one of the greatest challenges to every community. . . . The . . . concept . . . of a corporate association under state protection and guid-

ance . . . will also make possible the solution of the problems which prevent the Sovereign Power from flourishing to the full on its own. [Translation into English: The Kaiser needs this program to secure and increase in power.]

The social insurance structure established under Bismarck—especially the sickness division—was used by Hitler in facilitating the rise of the National Socialist (Nazi) party, even though this was *not* the original intention of the program. The medical records held by the program contained volumes of information useful in controlling the population. The Canadian Parliament's committee on health insurance stated in March 1943:

> During the early years of Hitler's regime, the government's medical programme was looked upon by many observers as one of the greatest props of the totalitarian state.

That is history, and perhaps the result of unique circumstances that cannot occur again. On the other hand, no one would think the rise of a Hitler a reasonable price to pay for a universal medical system.

The fact that Hitler abused government-controlled medical records is not a reason to do without medical records. However, if the government wants your medical records, you should ask why it really needs them (insurers might like to have access to a centralized system to find more reasons to deny insurance coverage). Despite what promoters may tell you, your chances of recovery if you land unconscious in a remote emergency room will not be materially improved by having your past history in a central computer or on a SmartCard. Wear a Medic-Alert bracelet if you have allergies, diabetes, or another condition that will affect emergency treatment.

To give another example, Lenin thought the Soviet system of medical care was essential in building Communism. Of course, the medical system was not sufficient to ensure Lenin's power. That regime, after lasting only some seventy years, is history.

The principles underlying reform of the Soviet system at the "end of history" were outlined by Fukayama. I do not know how well they are being implemented in Russia (not very well, according to Fukayama). What concerns me is the erosion of the same principles here in the United States of America. They are the basics we learned in seventh grade civics class in the late 1950s: individual responsibility, the protection of property rights, the supremacy of the rule of law (as opposed to arbitrary police actions), and the accountability of the government. Will they, too, become history? Will the land of the free eventually become still another laboratory to repeat the failed experiments of the past? Can we experiment with suppressing freedom in medicine, in the name of noble-sounding buzzwords like *access* and *equity*, without worrying about the erosion of freedom in other institutions?

It could be that doctors have an exaggerated sense of their own importance in thinking that the fate of their own little profession portends disaster for the whole civilization.

I hope that we do not really stand at the end of Western history, and that the Republic will survive even if medicine as we know it is ruined.

I think that all citizens have the responsibility to reflect on the worst possible long-term consequences of political changes that they advocate. After all, doctors have to worry that the wonderful headache remedy they prescribe today could cause cancer thirty years from now. Still, it could be that a mere physician, not being a credentialed historian or political scientist, should not even presume to speculate on general issues related to the governance of our society.

Therefore, I will go on to parochial specifics. I will present the case that my profession is being destroyed, to the detriment of patients.

The next chapter will give some vignettes based on true experiences, my own or a colleague's. My mother always told me that the only way to learn was through experience—and it had better be someone else's experience. Besides being in solo practice, I sit on a lot of hospital committees and answer the telephone for an association of private physicians. I hear about a lot of gruesome experiences, in addition to the ones I have endured myself.

You are invited to participate in a role-playing experiment in the form of a quiz. You will be asked to imagine yourself in a number of different situations, mostly related to Medicare or Medicaid. If you are not involved in either of these programs, at least not yet, don't think that the examples don't apply to you. Proposals before Congress would extend Medicare-like rules to everyone.

5

TRYING ON YOUR DOCTOR'S MOCCASINS

Doctors are human, just like you—see how you would feel about it if it were happening to you (remember that your doctor's feelings about you are likely to affect your treatment).

ONE CAUSE of the supposed health care crisis is said to be the behavior of doctors. There are bad doctors, and there are others who are not as efficient, cost-conscious, or cooperative (compliant) as they should be. The idea is to force them to be better. Yes, the actual word *force* is used, although sometimes it is called "education" or "incentives."

Two of the "bad" character traits that need fixing are: a tendency toward deviance (wanting to do things their own way) and greed (wanting to be paid for their work).

This chapter will describe some of the reform-school methods that doctors are now experiencing. To understand their likely response, you be the doctor in this series of thought experiments. Remember that doctors are human beings, like you. Their reactions are probably not much different from yours.

In this multiple-choice test, you should mark all the answers that apply, if any.

You are a surgeon and have practiced in your community for twenty years. You have the respect of your colleagues. Other doctors refer their mothers to you. You are very busy, and do not need to add cases to your operative schedule. In fact, if you add this case, it will mean working late at night.

You are calling the patient's insurance company for precertification.

If you do not get a precertification number from the clerk, the insurance company will later deny the patient's claim, no matter how urgent the operation was. Well, they're not supposed to deny emergencies, but if you can schedule a procedure, it is not exactly an emergency. You have been on hold for ten minutes. You know that if you hang up, you or your secretary will spend fifteen minutes pushing the automatic redial button.
You should:

a. Practice a biofeedback exercise to raise the temperature of the tip of your left fourth finger—it's supposed to reduce stress.

b. Make good use of your time reading the latest $50 revision of the Medicare ICD-9 code book to familiarize yourself with changes in the fourth and fifth digits of the diagnostic codes—if your secretary puts down the wrong code, you won't get paid, or conceivably you could be fined $2,000.

c. Decide—again—that patients should make the calls to *their* insurance company, even though the insurer refused to talk to the last patient who called.

Finally the clerk answers. She sounds very young. She is probably a high school graduate. She wants to know how big the hernia is. Apparently, if it isn't big enough, the insurer will not pay for having it fixed.

You should:

a. Explain to her (patiently, now!) that (1) the size of hernias is variable, depending on whether the patient is lying down, standing up, or straining; (2) little hernias are more likely to strangulate than big ones; (3) anyway, this patient has a hiatal hernia, not an inguinal hernia—it is possible that the clerk *might* be able to understand the difference between the stomach bulging up into the chest and a lump in the groin.

b. Demand to speak to the guy who thought up that stupid question.

c. Make something up and hope you guess right about the criteria for a hernia they think should be fixed. The criteria, of course, are a secret.

d. Call your country club to schedule a tee time, instead of the operating room to schedule an operation. Refer the patient to the university hospital or some other large institution, where they have an army of clerks or resident physicians to take care of precertification and other such details. Or to the VA, which being a government agency is probably exempt from such requirements.

You are a successful urologist. You are speaking to a representative of EquaCare, a managed care plan, which has just bought out another managed care plan that went through bankruptcy. They want to add you to their list of preferred providers. All you have to do is to pay $1,000 and sign a contract to hold them harmless in case of bankruptcy or malpractice suits. They promise to refer you to a lot of patients, and you will fix their prostates at a substantial discount. Or you will try to manage them medically if the prostate isn't big enough to require fixing (by their definition). For example, you can advise them to stay close to a bathroom and within reasonable distance of an emergency room that can catheterize them if they get an acute obstruction. The plan probably does *not* cover new drugs such as Proscar because they are so expensive. It probably designates them as experimental.

You should:

a. Sign on the dotted line. The payment barely covers overhead, but you can make it up on volume and by raising prices to patients who aren't on the plan.

b. Find out whether your number-one competitor is signing up. You don't want to lose all your referrals to him.

c. Call your lawyer to find out about the antitrust implications of not signing up. This is especially important if your number-one competitor is not signing up. If you have spoken to him recently, the two of you might be accused of a conspiracy to boycott the plan.

d. Throw the salesman out of your office and the proposal in the trash.

e. Buy stock in the corporation. The discounts for surgeons are so deep that you think the company might make a profit. You can make more money as a shareholder than as a surgeon, and capital gains are not subject to Social Security tax. You'll just have to remember to sell the stock before too many liabilities accumulate.

You are a family doctor. Many of your patients, under pressure from their employer, have joined a managed care plan. Not wishing to lose them as your patients, you join, too. It is now 3:00 A.M., and you have been awakened from a sound sleep. It is the clerk in the Samaritan Hospital emergency room. A patient who has chosen you as his doctor (or who has been assigned to you), whom you have never seen, has come to the emergency room with what sounds like the flu. The clerk wants to know whether they can see the patient.

You should:

a. Tell them to send the patient home with instructions to call you when the office opens in the morning. He probably isn't very sick. If the ER sees him, it will cost the plan a lot of money, which will be deducted from the primary doctor's pay at the end of the year.

b. Tell them you'll be right there. Though unlikely, the patient might really be sick. You won't be paid anything extra (above the six dollars per month you get for having the patient on your list), but it will save the plan the cost of the ER doctor's fee.

c. Say "Okay, go ahead and see him." You know that's what most of your colleagues will do. They're afraid of getting sued. All the ER charges are deducted from the pool of withheld fees, and you figure you'll never see any of it anyway.

d. Be thankful for the interruption. The middle of the night, when you can't sleep anyway, is a great time for getting caught up on all the extra paperwork. Or on reading your new $39.95 copy of A Guide to Filling Out Health Insurance Forms. Or your $295 copy of Clinical Laboratory Regulations. Or the $319 copy of a guide to coding procedures and office visits so that Medicare won't accuse you of fraud.

You have been in practice for twenty years and find that you are working harder and making less money. Your patients get notices from Medicare saying that you are overcharging them, even though the Medicare-approved "reasonable" fee dates from the 1970s, when your expenses were much lower. The patients believe Medicare. You frequently have to stay late at the office to respond to threatening letters from the Medicare carrier.

You should:

a. Take a night course in real estate.

b. Play a tape recording of a speech given at the last meeting of the American College of Physicians—the one that tells how privileged you are to be a physician and how you need to maintain a positive attitude about life and the practice of medicine.

c. Threaten to withdraw all financial support from any of your children who apply to medical school.

d. Sign up for a $600 course in how to code things properly in order to "optimize reimbursement." For example, you have heard that there is a code that will allow you to charge $60 over and above the fee for an office visit if you take the blood pressure in all four extremities.

e. Sign a participation agreement with Medicare. That way, payment will be between you and the government, and the patient will be left out of the loop. You might not get paid, but at least the patients won't get disparaging letters about you.

f. Sock your money away for early retirement.

g. Apply for a residency in a subspecialty that does not involve primary patient care.

h. Close your private practice and go to work for a big clinic. Punch the time clock, do what you're told, and let the administrators deal with the third parties.

You are asked to be a "lock-in provider" for Medicaid, that is, to take charge of certain patients who tend to "overutilize." Some of these patients have complex medical problems, and some are hypochondriacs. The idea is to keep them away from specialists, emergency rooms, and expensive tests, in order to save the program money.

You should:

a. Rent a bigger office and hire more help so you can turn over sufficient volume to make money on the six dollars per month per head that the program offers. Buy a word processing program that can spew out a beautiful note for the chart if you push a few buttons. Properly managed, each patient should only require about thirty seconds, and the documentation for the benefit of the utilization reviewers, quality assurers, and malpractice attorneys will be above reproach. Hire a consultant to be sure that you are in compliance with every line of the most current Medicaid regulations.

b. Tell Medicaid to get lost. You'd rather see the patients without any expectation of payment.

c. Move to the suburbs.

You have a patient that, in your opinion, should have a CT head scan (a computer-enhanced x-ray). The Utilization Review Committee of his HMO denies permission. You have already been through the appeals process three times this month and have received a telephone call from the medical director, expressing his concern that you are not a good team player. An HMO quality reviewer has criticized you for having some drug samples stored on the floor. You are afraid that they are trying to find a reason to boot you out of the HMO, which will mean an immediate loss of 20 percent of your gross income. You are only moderately concerned about this patient.

You should:

a. Advise the patient that you think he should have the scan, but that the plan will not pay for it. Offer to arrange it for him on a private-pay basis (for about $550).

b. Tell the patient that he doesn't really need a CT scan. You realize that if you tell him the whole truth, you will be violating a clause in your contract that forbids you to criticize the plan.

c. Advise the patient to take a mild painkiller and come back in two weeks. Make sure his appointment is at a time when you will not be there so that somebody else will become responsible.

d. Look into the procedure for withdrawing from the plan, even though it will cost you. It is better to resign before they throw you out.

e. Apprentice yourself to a plumber.

f. Go through the appeals process again. It's your job to be the patient's advocate.

Had enough? So have a lot of doctors. Some of them are even asking for the previously unthinkable, such as national health insurance. *Anything*, they think, would be better than the current situation.

On the other hand, maybe things could be still worse. . . .

....

6

WHY I AM NOT MAD AT THE WORLD

....

Don't feel sorry for me, because I am very fortunate—it's the patients you should worry about.

SOMETIMES when I speak of matters like those in the last chapter, people think I must be an angry, bitter person.

They are wrong. On the whole, I have more fun than people should be allowed to have. That might be because of my unusually fortunate personal circumstances, which I will recount in this chapter. Many of my colleagues, however, are, in fact, very bitter and cynical—so bitter that people might fear to consult such a physician if they only knew how he really felt. Or if the physician is not inclined to direct his hostility toward others, he may take it all upon himself, becoming depressed.

About 1983, I attended a meeting of the American College of Physicians. They had a graduation-type ritual, complete with gowns and mortarboards, solemn trumpet music, and speeches. The occasion was to advance hundreds of physicians to fellowship in the college and a chosen few to still more prestigious heights. (Now I get to write F.A.C.P. after my name, unless they make me stop doing it because of failure to pay my dues.)

One of the speeches reminded us of what an enormous privilege it was to be a member of our esteemed profession and still more exalted specialty of internal medicine. (I will say more later about the implications of this "privilege.") In case any of us ever felt depressed about the reality of our situation, we needed to see a psychiatrist or other mental health professional. From counseling, we would learn to change our frame of mind. We would stop feeling persecuted. We would become accepting of (or adjusted to) our circumstances. In other words, if we weren't happy, it was because we needed and would respond to therapy.

I think that internists have always tended to be depressed. It is partly the nature of the field and partly the type of person that the specialty attracts. Internists see themselves as an intellectual elite. Perhaps they are smarter than the average surgeon, but certainly they intellectualize a lot more. They tend to ruminate. They are especially susceptible to guilt. And they see a lot of grief, a lot of sickness that modern medicine cannot cure, and a lot of the ravages of aging.

While in medical school, I seldom enjoyed the company of internists. I liked the surgeons much better. You could enjoy a steak sandwich with them at midnight and never hear a lecture about cholesterol. Surgeons might be up all night, up to their elbows in blood, but still be cheerful. Few internists were *ever* cheerful. I thought of becoming a surgeon, just because I liked being around surgeons and could appreciate their attitude that a "chance to cut was a chance to cure." But I lacked the necessary stamina, self-confidence, and talent.

It could be that my early education was deficient. When I was helping my father build some steps in my house, he asked me: "Don't you even know how to hold a saw?"

"No, Papa, I don't. You never taught me."

Probably nobody ever taught him either. He just *knew*.

Natural-born surgeons seem to just know how to do certain things (such as visualizing three-dimensional structures) that I can learn only with great difficulty. Whatever the reason, there is no point in complaining. I am also unable to swing a hammer competently and certainly not while being dangled out an upper-story window by my ankles. In his youth, my father could do that, and I have never envied him for a moment, although my admiration is boundless.

Clearly, I was better suited for internal medicine than either carpentry or surgery. I liked figuring out the diagnosis and deciding on the best course of treatment, or nontreatment. Sometimes, it is best to follow Law XIII of *The House of God:* "The delivery of medical care is to do as much nothing as possible." If internal medicine isn't as exciting as surgery, there are also fewer moments of sheer panic. If internists don't make as much money, they don't have to work such long hours or assume as much risk. I decided I would just have to put up with some melancholic colleagues. But unlike many internists, I am not mad at surgeons.

The glumness that I noticed among internal medicine residents twenty years ago was mild compared with the black cloud that hangs over the entire profession now. One of my colleagues feels that she is in mourning for her beloved profession, which is dying. Family practice and internal medicine residencies (still the most severely affected) have difficulty filling positions that were once coveted by the nation's top medical graduates.

Many people seem to believe the common stereotype: Doctors are all rich, and they all spend their time playing golf at the country club. One congressman, author of legislation to reduce doctors' fees, stated that doctors are whining because they won't be able to buy their second BMW this year.

For the record, I think of an eight-year-old car as "new." I have never belonged to a country club. I can't afford it, but it doesn't matter because I have no desire to join. Golf is boring to me. I would rather play chess with a five-year-old (at least I have a chance of winning). The earnings from my medical practice have been negative for the past two years. That means I lose money on it and have had to find another source of income—serveral other sources.

If I had survived teaching in the public school system, my financial status might be better, I think. Medical school was four years of expenses instead of modest income, so my time there cost at least eight years of a teacher's income. Residency was three years of subsistence wages—at best, a teacher's total pay for three times as many hours of work. I did make about $50,000 per year working at the VA—the most I have ever earned from the practice of medicine. My gross has been higher than that in private practice, but more than 50 percent of the gross is needed just to pay overhead. My earning *capacity* is higher than a teacher's because of my degree, but to reach that capacity my office would have to become an assembly line: five to ten minutes per patient. Alternately, I could market a high-priced gimmick or learn to do a quasi-surgical procedure or go into administration.

I am not asking for the reader's sympathy, because very few readers could possibly be as fortunate as I have been. I am not "in mourning," and I never regret having received a medical education.

What most people think about doctors who don't make very much money is that they must not be very good. It's a Catch-22. If you do make a lot of money, they think you are mercenary, but they still want an appointment, at least if their insurance will pay for it.

One reason my fees have always been low is that I accept money only from patients, not from insurers. (Patients may submit their own claim to an insurer.) This means I have to charge a fee that the patient will think is reasonable. Another reason is that I got caught in the Medicare fee freeze starting at a very low level, and I have not been willing to charge young working people more to compensate for it.

But let's say that I am definitely not typical. Do other doctors earn too much money? Maybe some of them do. But to say that most doctors earn too much you also have to say that they work too hard. One study showed that surgeons earn about $38.80 per hour of actual, not necessarily billable, work and internists about $33.90.[1] It adds up because they work such long hours—87.8 and 70.6 hours per week, respectively. Of course, some specialists earn a lot more than this.

Some doctors do indulge in conspicuous consumption—fancy, tax-deductible cars, vacations in the Virgin Islands, expensive homes, and so on. So do some lawyers, congressmen, and athletes, but they are not criticized for it. There is a double standard. Doctors are believed to profit from human misery (which they help to relieve), unlike lawyers and congressmen.

Today, doctors may *have* to earn a lot of money to pay off the debts they accumulated in medical school. Some people think that doctors *deserve* to make a lot of money because of enduring the arduous years of medical school.

Neither of these reasons applies to me. In the 1970s, it was possible for a family of moderate means to pay for a medical education. Although I attended one of the most expensive private schools in the country (Columbia), I was graduated without debt. I had savings from a couple years of teaching, and my parents paid the rest. Tuition and living expenses were much less, even considering inflation, than the amount my sister paid to send my nephew to a private college. There were even luxuries: Grandma bought me an airplane ticket every time I had a chance to come home. My sister and her husband put $750 in a savings account for my "book fund." I was able to give it back with all the interest, even though I bought more books than anybody I knew.

Although medical school is reputed to be very arduous, I had the time of my life. I did have to study a lot, but I am one of those eccentrics who actually likes to study. I thought neuroanatomy and biochemistry and all those basic science courses were fascinating. Also, they were not nearly as difficult as math analysis or physical chemistry. Therefore, I had some time to enjoy the city of New York.

Clinical subjects were much more demanding than basic sciences, in terms of physical endurance if not IQ points. I think the worst moment of my medical school career occurred about 3:00 A.M. one Sunday at St. Luke's Hospital, in the closet where they stored the IV solutions. I realized that I had just stuck an IV into the wrong patient and with great difficulty. Fortunately, he had only received a little salt water, no potent drugs. I had been up for about twenty hours, wouldn't be able to go home for another forty hours, and would probably get very little sleep until then. (Doctors and students on weekend call came in early Saturday morning and went home late Monday afternoon.) Nobody had mentioned this at my medical school interviews! It had never even occurred to me that you didn't get to sleep when you were on call!

Internship and residency were even worse. I never learned to tolerate sleep deprivation. Mercifully, I don't remember too much about those years. I couldn't keep a journal as some interns did. When I wasn't at the hospital or doing the laundry or stocking up on peanut butter and jelly at the grocery store (thanks to which I never missed a meal), I was asleep. Time flew quickly. It was measured by the height of the stack of *The Dallas Morning News* on the living room floor, rubber bands intact. I completely missed out on Watergate, so the situation wasn't all bad.

People don't deserve sympathy just because they have to work hard. The need for hard work is a fact of life, and my family was well acquainted with it. We saw my father do it, and we also heard him whistling every morning as he left for the job at the crack of dawn.

He wasn't going to a nice air-conditioned office either, but might be spending a day working on a roof when the temperature was 120 degrees.

Doctors are not feeling demoralized because they have to work hard. They used to enjoy their work.

And doctors are not leaving the profession because of the inability to buy a new Mercedes every year. They were happier in the past, when they had to travel by horse and buggy or train, even though their financial situation was at times very precarious.

Of course, a forced 50 percent fee cut in one year on top of constant whittling over a period of years is not completely irrelevant. Fees for some surgical procedures were cut this drastically with the institution of the new Medicare Relative Value Scale, which I will discuss in detail later on. Our society often measures a person's value in terms of his financial net worth, and people may measure themselves against this standard. So when they see they have to work harder and harder for less and less, while everyone around them expects an automatic pay increase every year, they tend to become hostile and resentful.

Nevertheless, the main reason for physician demoralization *is not just the money*. Doctors see their authority constantly under attack, as their responsibilities increase. They frequently find themselves in a double-bind situation, with no escape in sight. If doctors feel harassed, it's because they are. I did not make up the examples in this book. There are many more that had to be deleted for lack of space.

The overall situation faced by doctors could have come from my college psychology textbook on how to induce stress in experimental subjects:[2] (1) disruptions of physiologic homeostasis (e.g., sleep deprivation); (2) distractions, razzing, or time pressures; (3) real, contrived, or anticipated failure, as due to impossible standards; (4) social conflict; (5) conflicting clues; (6) realistic threats to one's safety or well-being.

So why am I not mad at the world?

For a time, I was. I worked at a VA hospital for over four years. I was a staff physician in the ambulatory care department and also an assistant professor. I did enjoy making rounds with a retinue of medical students and residents. And I liked the veterans, especially the ones who really did fight in the war and were not just there to get prescriptions for free aspirin. But there were drawbacks.

One problem was the bureaucracy. One of the nurse practitioners came up with an excellent suggestion about how to make more effective use of time spent at our monthly administrative meeting: Place a tape recorder on the table to play the tape of the previous meeting and go to the canteen for a cup of coffee.

Another problem was the incentives. You didn't have to be very bright to notice that your paycheck was the same no matter how much work you did. If you scurried around taking care of patients while other people were on a two-hour lunch break, you got tired, and you got blamed for all the problems that occurred. You did *not* get a larger paycheck or a nicer office or a promotion to associate professor. The patients tended to be short-tempered after sitting in the waiting room for many hours, and they usually weren't very pleasant. But then, neither was I.

I had two choices: adapt to the system, or escape before the golden handcuffs got too heavy. I noticed that I was beginning to adapt by developing a civil-servant attitude.

At a crucial moment, a Tucson physician retired and asked me if I'd like to buy his equipment. I cleaned out my VA retirement account (about $10,000) and borrowed more money from my youngest sister. Another sister put up money to buy an office building. I hired the retiring physician's nurse and went into business.

Within a couple of months, I had an office and some stationery. I was a private doctor. I intended to do things my way, without having to fight with people. I was available to those who wished to consult me. Those who didn't want to see me didn't have to. As it says in one of my favorite cowboy songs, "Them that don't like me can leave me alone."

Of course, the biweekly paychecks stopped. Nevertheless, I was able to pay my bills on time and to repay the family loans within a couple of years. There were some nice bonuses: homemade dill pickles and jelly; wonderful Christmas cookies; homegrown cabbages, beets, and radishes; some delicious trout; and excellent tamales. (I have never gotten a chicken, only part of a cow, and that's a long story in itself.) The secret was to keep the overhead down.

My practice is possible because it is a family enterprise. Except for a part-time nurse, who was well past retirement age when we started and who worked for me until her vision and health failed, I have never had an employee. I have volunteers.

My mother immediately volunteered to be my office manager, receptionist, and all-around helper.

My father volunteered to be the charter, keyed charperson. (Unlike *chairman* or *human*, *charwoman* refers to only one sex. My father said he was not a woman, and he'd never heard of a charman, so he would be the charperson.) The charperson takes care of the trash and any maintenance jobs and keeps up on the news by chatting with the gardener. My office is the first stop on his way to whatever building project he is working on. I don't pay him, but there are perquisites. He gets to the Dumpster every morning before Waste Management does. When the church next door bought a new organ, they discarded the packing crates, from which my father built about twenty laminated bookcases. One day he found a perfectly good refrigerator. There was also a nice doorjamb with three hinges. He finds lots of firewood. It is possible that he recovers from the Dumpster almost as much as he contributes to it. Or at least he did before recycling became politically correct—the market is now glutted and doesn't pay enough to buy gasoline for the trip to the junkyard, I mean recycling center.

People frequently stop by the office to offer us money-spending opportunities. But we don't need them. We don't need a billing service, because we send very few bills—patients usually pay at the time of service. We don't need an accountant, because there isn't much money to account for. We don't need an investment adviser for the same reason. We don't need a management consultant, because we keep our affairs so simple that even I can understand them. We don't need an insurance clerk, because we have never filed an insurance claim. (We give the patients a "superbill"—a piece of paper with the information that insurers want—so they can file their own.) We don't need somebody to be put on hold to speak to the insurance precertification clerk. Sometimes patients have to take care of that detail themselves, but they're better at it than doctors are. When faced with the prospect of explaining to a prominent attorney why he didn't need a CT scan even though I said he did, the insurer found an easy answer: The patient *did* need the scan after all, so his insurance would cover it.

I do have an answering service, but I don't have a beeper. Some doctors still don't carry one of those hateful pests, and people tell me I am usually easier to find than doctors who do. I can't afford a cellular telephone, and what good does a beeper do if I can't make a phone call? It might cause an accident if it goes off while I'm driving, due to the conditioned hyperreactions that I acquired during residency. And even a cellular telephone wouldn't help patients much in a true emergency. In a true emergency, you need to dial 911.

We receive lots of application forms to sign up with various HMOs, PPOs, and other managed care arrangements. I file them in the trash, unless they are printed on one side, in which case they are good for printing rough drafts. I didn't want to be on anybody's list of preferred providers. I'm a doctor, not a "provider," and third parties prefer never to talk to me. Some of the discounted fees they offered were higher than the ones I normally charge, but not nearly high enough to compensate for having to read their rules, fill out their forms, or risk a visit with a utilization reviewer or other functionary. A neighboring doctor got a visit from such an official, who rummaged through his charts, piled a bunch of them all over the floor, made the receptionist cry, and disrupted the whole day's routine.

Some of the plans—like the one alluded to in the quiz in chapter 5—have a "withhold." They keep part of the doctor's fee and promise to give it back as a bonus at the end of the year if overall costs have been kept down—total costs, not just the ones an individual is responsible for. I first learned about "collective guilt" from my second grade teacher, Sister Francis Mary. Our class didn't get to have a Halloween party because some kids in the class had been bad. All of us were blamed because we hadn't kept them in line. Recently, from my colleagues in HMOs, I have learned about the methods used to keep group members in line: peer group pressure, browbeating, and threats, in addition to failure to pay for honest work.

Besides being collective, the managed care definition of guilt is also backward: The doctor gets rewarded for denying services and punished for providing them. This creates a built-in conflict of interest between doctor and patient. Only a saint could constantly ignore the economic incentives. The continued existence of the plans proves that some doctors are not saints.

Some of the plans offer a capitation fee. They pay something like six dollars per patient per month, no matter what you do or don't do. If you sign up for enough patients, you could pay your overhead without necessarily having to do any work, providing you honed your "buff-and-turf" skills. "Buffing" the chart and "turfing" the patient was the method used by interns in *The House of God* to get gomers off their service. On the other hand, if somebody got sick and you were conscientious, you could lose big.

I didn't have to think twice about this. Whatever the capitation payment was, it wasn't enough. No way was I going to subject myself to 3:00 A.M. requests for treatment authorizations or advice on diaper rash, much less to the more serious risks, in order to save money for the plan or to fulfill *their* advertised promises of twenty-four-hour service. Nor was I going to put myself in an automatic conflict-of-interest situation with a patient who could benefit from medical care but could have it only if I paid for it.

In case my determination ever wavered when I looked at the summary page of my ledger, there was the ultimate deterrent:

"If you sign up for any of these scams, I am going to quit," said my front office.

So we remained independent of any third-party chains, even as the "market penetration" of the HMOs in Tucson reached levels rivaling Minneapolis, where many of these plans began. Some of our patients left us for the doctor they "had to" see because of their employers' decisions about medical benefits. Some came back for things they couldn't get from their HMO (like an early appointment to see a doctor). But the effect on our income was simply irrelevant. We thought the third-party contracts were both unethical and intolerable, and that was that.

My income has gradually declined over the years, partly because of my refusal to "participate" and partly because we have not aggressively tried to build up the practice. For one thing, I had other work to do. For three years, about half my time was spent editing a textbook for medical students called *The Art and Science of Bedside Diagnosis*. That was an expense, not a source of income. The biggest financial disaster struck in September 1990. That was when Medicare started requiring physicians to file claims for all Medicare beneficiaries. As far as we were concerned, the Stamp Act had been passed.

There are many practical reasons for not filling out the new Medicare claim form, HCFA form 1500 (which is *much* worse than a VA 1010). One is that they are printed in pink ink and have dozens of tiny boxes. We can't even *see* the printing without great effort. The questions are mostly irrelevant, and some are unanswerable. It would take me more time to fill out the form than it usually does to see the patient. (My front office, of course, has refused to touch them.) The form is a minefield of opportunities to make an error that *could* be punished with a $2,000 fine at the whim of a bureaucrat.

For example, one could write down the wrong ICD-9 (International Classification of Diseases) five-digit diagnosis code. The ICD is a useful system for institutions that do clinical research; it enables them to retrieve records of all patients who had a certain diagnosis, and they hire experts in coding for their medical records office. But what use is it for processing Medicare claims for office visits? The payment for all "intermediate office visits" is exactly the same regardless of the diagnosis. I would guess that 25 percent of patient visits to an internist are for reasons (such as "I just don't feel good") that don't have a code, not even a symptom code. And there is no diagnostic code for "I don't know, at least not yet." The only reason I could see for spending my time with these codes was that Medicare would deny my patient's benefits if I didn't. The only outcome I could see for myself, besides frustration and wasted time, was possible punishment. I was certainly not allowed to charge anyone for this required but useless "service." There was a constant threat that somebody would audit the charts and find one in which *she* felt the ICD-9 code was not justified by the record. My hatred of that book was starting to generalize to my feelings about seeing a Medicare patient.

Probably the most serious error is to write down the wrong CPT-4 (Current Procedure Terminology) code for the service. Physicians have received demands to repay as much as $50,000 to $100,000 from Medicare because of this. This fact was all I needed to know, but I'll explain more about the codes later.

Once you fill out the form and mail it to Medicare, that is still not the end of it. You have to file a copy somewhere so that you can find it again several months later. If Medicare loses it, you have to send it again. But you had better not send it again if Medicare *didn't* lose it. Thus if the patient doesn't get paid for months on end, you have to try to determine what the reason is, and this can take all day and still be unsuccessful. Even if Medicare does receive the form, they frequently send it back to be done over on some pretext or other, especially if it is cluttering up somebody's desk on a Friday afternoon.

Putting all this paper in the patient's chart is still only half the problem. Someday you might need to *read* the chart in order to figure out what is going on with the patient. The useful nuggets of information are probably buried in a pile of Medicare clutter. Who knows what important things have been missed as a result. I *hate* covering for doctors who participate in Medicare for this reason. When a patient of mine shows up in the emergency room, I can get all the pertinent information in a few minutes from my front office. If it's somebody else's Medicare patient, I really cannot rely on his secretary's effort to extract the wheat from the chaff.

All of this could make a person very depressed and irritable. It makes Franz Kafka look like a perceptive observer rather than the crazy man I once thought he was. But it doesn't bother us at all. Not anymore. We look at the procedure as disinterested spectators. The reason is that we have yet to file our first HCFA 1500. We don't need $21.35 that badly. However, I do keep up on the regulations in order to write a newsletter, one of my other jobs. I need to keep my readers informed of pitfalls they might have missed while they were busy taking care of patients.

When the new Stamp Act passed, I put a notice in the newspaper that my practice would be restricted to private medicine and that my services were not covered under Title 18 (Medicare). I became a superfluous woman, who provides only unnecessary and unreasonable services (about this, too, more later). We sent a letter to all our active Medicare patients, and we provide an explanation to all new patients who call to ask for an appointment.

Some patients are not the least bit understanding. They want their $21.35, and I am supposed to get it for them, even at the risk of unfunded liabilities that could put me out of business overnight. If they needed the money that badly, I'd rather just give it to them, but then they would be insulted. If I don't file their claims, they will see somebody else who will. Actually that somebody else will probably go to a coding seminar and learn how to collect about $335 on "assignment" for doing less than I did for $35. ("Assignment" means that the government pays the doctor instead of the patient.) The patient may think that he got a tremendous deal—$335 worth of service for nothing, or for at most $67, the 20 percent copayment.

If patients really want to see *us*, we do the best we can. If we suspect a patient of being Medicare eligible, we don't send him a bill or any other paperwork that he (or a family member) can send to the government. Sometimes patients or their families tell us after the fact that they *are* a Medicare beneficiary and want to file a claim. If they send it in themselves, the government could fine us $2,000 for not having done it for them. We'd rather refund their money than file a claim, and if patients complain we send them a check and refer them to a doctor who will send in the claim for them.

A message to any agents of the federal government who might be reading this book in search of a self-incriminatory statement: We do not knowingly provide any Medicare-covered services to Medicare-eligible patients, even though under the U.S. Constitution and the Medicare Act it is still perfectly legal to contract privately with a Medicare-eligible patient.

Our income has decreased, but so have our aggravations. No more denial-of-benefits letters to answer! No more need to be polite to bureaucrats who write inflammatory letters to our patients! (I never actually "participated" in Medicare, but before September 1990, some of my patients submitted claims.)

Although I had to answer *their* letters, the bureaucrats usually didn't answer mine. The only reply was the return receipt. You have to send the mail certified, return-receipt-requested, because failure to reply is comparable to failing to file your tax return with the IRS. Maybe the carbon copies I sent to my congressman and senator and patient helped prevent further troubles. Wounded HCFA bureaucrats moan and cry about such carbon copies in letters to medical newspapers, but I have never been moved to sympathize with their plight.

I am not the only doctor who has dropped out of Medicare. Other doctors who have done so said they felt as if they had been born again or that a tremendous burden had been lifted from their shoulders, even though they expect to earn less money.

It is better to not get paid for not working than to not get paid after working very hard, especially when the nonpayment is accompanied by abuse. I didn't need to see a psychiatrist to treat the problems with my head—I just had to stop beating it against a stone wall.

We don't really understand why doctors put up with nonsense, but probably they do it from fear, or from sheer economic necessity. They may have an army of clerks in their front office filing those forms, and the clerks have to be paid. They probably also have children in college.

And maybe they can't think of another way to earn a living—a number of the medical school applicants that I interview have no idea what they will do if their application is rejected again.

Whenever I look at my ledger, it is clear that I would be better off financially if I just closed my clinical office altogether. Maybe Sir William Osler was right—medicine is only for people who are independently wealthy. But I don't want to give up; it might be impossible to start again if I quit entirely. Maybe things will get better. Also, my family and a group of patients have come to rely on me. When you're sick, you need somebody who knows how things get done, even if she can't do all of them herself. And every once in a while, there are satisfactions that more than compensate for the drudgery and frustration. The day after I wrote this draft, I think I may have saved a patient's eyesight by making a prompt diagnosis of temporal arteritis.

Staying in practice has been my intention. But since I started writing this book, still more administrative threats and more "reform" proposals have appeared, which may make solo practice impossible.

By the time you read this, all the independent doctors may be "out."

As Senator Ted Kennedy said, "Those who want to be outside the stadium [where the managed care gladiators compete] will be there."

....

7

THEY SWORE AN OATH, DIDN'T THEY?

....

You may think you know what the Hippocratic oath says, but you probably don't, and you should learn about it before they do away with it entirely.

ON A PBS television special called *Borderline Medicine*, a pregnant Medicaid beneficiary claimed to have called about seventy-five physicians without being able to get an appointment. None of the doctors were willing to accept patients on MediCal, the California Medicaid program.

"They swore an oath, didn't they?" the frustrated and indignant patient asked.

Apparently, she thought the oath meant that doctors were supposed to take care of all comers, regardless of circumstances. Certainly they were supposed to take care of *her*.

What about this oath? What do patients have the right to expect from physicians? Do they have the right to whatever treatment they want, regardless of circumstances (such as payment arrangements or the lack thereof)? Do they have the right to the physician of their choice, regardless of the physician's wishes? And if the Oath of Hippocrates doesn't guarantee them these things, should we substitute a different one?

VOWS THEY *DIDN'T* TAKE

Very few American medical graduates under the age of forty have taken the Oath of Hippocrates in its original form. Only 6 percent of

American medical schools used a literal translation in 1977, while 42 percent used a modified version. The Geneva Declaration of the World Medical Association was used by 28 percent, the prayer of Maimonides by 10 percent, and some other oath (often a new one) by 15 percent. About 6 percent of U.S. medical schools and 37 percent of Canadian schools did not administer an oath of any kind. A recent innovation is to have the oath chosen by a vote of the students.

The new oaths are not mere redactions to update the terminology and modernize the literary style. They reflect a fundamental change in philosophy, as we shall see.

Before discussing what the oaths *do* say, let us note that *none* pledge the physician's service to all prospective patients under all conceivable circumstances, as many people (who have not read the oaths) are inclined to assume. Only religious vows come close to making a total self-effacing commitment such as that.

In modern times, physicians seldom take monastic vows of poverty, chastity, and obedience. In medieval times, such vows frequently bound those who cared for the sick. Selfless monks and nuns served with unquestionable dedication but dubious medical effectiveness, easing their patients' passage into the next world—the usual outcome of admission to a hospital.

All of the monastic vows were important, but especially chastity. Family obligations inevitably dilute a person's ability and desire to give unlimited service compensated only by accumulating jewels for a heavenly crown. And once a person acquires property (not allowed to a person who has taken a vow of poverty), he usually feels inclined to protect it (for example, against judgments in lawsuits).

Actually, very few people advocate reviving vows of chastity or even settling for a promise of childlessness. They will usually agree that physicians ought not be forced to live in dire poverty. Whether physicians should be permitted to live in affluence might be a point of contention. But quite a few people seem eager to have their physicians obedient to an authority. Even an authority that, like a religious superior, might turn out to be the doctor's inferior in terms of knowledge, experience, and responsibility.

Should we demand that physicians, in return for the "privilege" of a medical license, take the equivalent of one or more monastic vows? Are we *sure* we want them to?

People might like to be served by a selfless monk, at least if he promised not to preach. But it is doubtful that they truly want medieval medicine. Can they have one without the other? In particular, can they have medical progress if physicians are compelled to be subservient to a designated medical authority?

Without deciding at this point what should be required of physicians, let us read the oaths to see what they *do* require.

OATHS THEY *MIGHT* HAVE TAKEN

The oaths are printed in the appendix. Let's compare and contrast the Oath of Hippocrates with the others. Obviously, those who wrote their own oaths intended to correct deficiencies in the original. Louis Lasagna, for example, the dean of Tufts University Sackler School of Graduate Biomedical Sciences and professor of psychiatry and pharmacology, wrote his oath because he felt that some parts of the 2,000-year-old oath "sounded outdated and irrelevant to doctors living in a postpantheistic, postslavery age." Louis Weinstein, professor of obstetrics and gynecology at the University of Arizona, also took it upon himself to update the oath to reflect modern circumstances.

The Ultimate Authority

The Oath of Hippocrates is the only oath that is actually addressed *to* somebody—Apollo, Aesculapius, Hygeia, and Panacea. Some revisions delete the names of the Greek gods, but substitute God or whatever the swearer holds sacred. This assumes that something or somebody is sacred, an ultimate lawgiver and law enforcer. Hippocrates thought that there was a law of medicine—an absolute law, not made by human beings and not to be altered by them. Violations of the law had consequences. Adherence to the law meant enjoyment of life and the respect of all men in all times, and violations meant the reverse.

The other oaths are addressed to nobody in particular, and say nothing whatsoever about the consequences of violating the oath. The Geneva declaration alludes to the "laws of humanity." Does that refer to laws made *by* humanity, through some political process, and presumably *enforced* or *amended* by humanity? Does this mean that the legislature can overrule the physician's conscience? The text does not say.

For Whose Good?

The Hippocratic physician has responsibilities to the gods, the profession, and the patient, and these responsibilities are not in conflict with one another. The gods require the physician to take proper care of his patients. "I will prescribe regimen *for the good of my patients* according to my ability and my judgment and never do harm to anyone," and again "in every house where I come I will enter *only for the good of my patients.*"

Notice that the Hippocratic physician does not promise to go into *any* house where he might be called. But if he does go into the house, he will behave honorably and work for the benefit of the patient.

The other oaths introduce another responsibility, one that transcends and may conflict with the physician's duty to his individual patient: responsibility to society, humanity, the health of mankind, or even to a political agenda. For this reason, some consider the new oaths superior to the Oath of Hippocrates.[1] Some ethicists believe that the Oath of Hippocrates may actually be *harmful* to society:

> To say that the physician must do the best he can for each patient is likely to pit physicians' loyalties to particular patients against the rights of those who have no one to serve as their loyal advocate. The uninsured and underinsured "belong" to no physician, and a growing number of persons with AIDS cannot claim one physician's loyalty.[2]

The Declaration of Geneva states that the health of the patient is to be the *first* consideration. Does that mean it may not be the *only* consideration? Certain things are not allowed to intervene between doctor and patient: religion, nationality, race, party politics, or social standing. But no such list can be exhaustive. Does the fact of enumeration imply that some other considerations might override the welfare of the individual patient?

The Soviet Oath refers to the physician's "responsibility to the people and to the Soviet state." This might well intervene between doctor and patient. What if the people's welfare requires sacrificing the individual? (Some people would dismiss any discussion of the Soviet Oath on the grounds that it is history. And maybe in the former Soviet

Union, it is. However, as recently as 1985 it was compared favorably with the Oath of Hippocrates in the *Journal of the AMA.*)

Lasagna declares that physicians have "special obligations to *all* [their] fellow human beings, those sound of mind and body, as well as the infirm." Does this imply that sometimes the sick are to be sacrificed for the benefit of the healthy? Rationing schemes such as the Oregon Basic Health Services Program are designed explicitly for that purpose, as we shall see later.

What if care of the sick interferes with the "preventive approach to the problems of mankind, including the social ills of malnutrition and poverty" (see Weinstein's oath) or with efforts to prevent nuclear war (see the Soviet Oath)? Before 1989, certain groups of physicians actively fought against improvements in the treatment of disaster victims because they thought preparedness might somehow increase the risk of nuclear war.

Only the Hippocratic physician promises to do no harm. Is that an oversight by the others? Or may it sometimes be necessary and morally acceptable to harm an individual patient in the name of a higher purpose (cost-effectiveness, social responsibility, or saving the environment)?

These issues will be discussed in detail later. Keep the questions in mind, including this one: Which oath do you want *your* doctor to take? If medical students can vote on which oath to take, shouldn't patients have a say in it, too?

Prohibitions

The Oath of Hippocrates specifically and absolutely proscribes abortion, euthanasia, "cutting for stone," the seduction of patients, and the betrayal of confidence. The modified oath as actually used generally omits reference to abortion and operations for stones. Note that cutting for stone is not altogether forbidden; it is to be "performed by specialists in this art." As to confidentiality, the wording is strict: "all that may come to my knowledge . . . , which ought not to be spread abroad, I will *keep secret and never reveal.*"

The Declaration of Geneva prohibits two things: allowing extraneous matters such as religion to intervene between doctor and patient and using medical knowledge "contrary to the [unspecified] laws of humanity." It exhorts the physician to *respect* human life from its (undefined) beginning and also to *respect* patients' secrets. There is no strong language like that of the Oath of Hippocrates ("to please no one will I prescribe a deadly drug, nor give advice which may cause his death"). Perhaps the physician, under the Geneva declaration, may end a patient's life, as long as he does so with dignity, and may *reveal* patients' secrets as long as they are *respected*.

The Soviet Oath says nothing at all about respect for human life.

In Lasagna's oath, the physician promises to "tread with care in matters of life and death." Taking a patient's life is specifically *not* forbidden; but if done, it should be with humbleness and awareness of one's human frailty.

Weinstein's oath explicitly *allows* the physician to terminate human life, under the proper conditions, and even commends it as an "act of supreme love," again under the right circumstances.

Physician Autonomy

Possibly one of the most controversial aspects of the Oath of Hippocrates is the implied "standard of care," which is still the law in most U.S. jurisdictions although increasingly threatened, as we shall see later when we consider "practice guidelines." The Hippocratic physician swears to act according to the best of "*my* ability" and "*my* judgment." *Not* the judgment of the U.S. Department of Health and Human Services, or the American Medical Association, or the managers of a managed care plan, or the consultants who drafted a set of guidelines.

Other oaths say nothing about the primacy of a physician's own judgment. They exhort the physician to humility, a virtue to be sure, but one that can easily be confused with subservience. The Soviet Oath does specifically state that the physician must be subservient, at least with regard to the conditions of his work: The physician must "work in good conscience *wherever* it is required by society." If *wherever*, why not *however*?

THE ANSWER TO THE QUESTION

Returning to the Medicaid patient at the beginning of this chapter, here is the answer to her question:

Maybe they swore an oath, and maybe they didn't.

Even if they did, *none* of the oaths guarantee her an appointment.

If she wants the "right to medical care," it will have to come about by some means other than the physician's oath. The non-Hippocratic oaths may in fact make it *more* difficult for patients to get an appointment, if caring for their needs happens to be a lower priority than some other service to humanity.

HIPPOCRATES AND WESTERN HISTORY

Who Is Sovereign?

The Oath of Hippocrates is basically *Western* in its premises, although free institutions were only in their infancy in ancient Greece. The worth of individual human beings is axiomatic to Western civilization.

The replacements for the Oath of Hippocrates deny the sanctity of the individual, which is at the heart of Western political philosophy. Thus they set the stage for an entirely different era in history—a non-Western era.

In non-Hippocratic medicine, neither physician nor patient is autonomous. There is always the abstract higher good of society to consider. However, abstractions do not make real nuts-and-bolts decisions. People do. Humankind or society must speak with the voice of an interpreter.

And who is the interpreter?

The answer to that question is usually in accord with the Golden Rule: He who has the gold makes the rules.

In medicine, the patient used to pay most of the bills. Certainly this was true in the time of Hippocrates. Now the bills are usually paid by somebody else—the third party. Sometimes, the third party is an insurance company. Increasingly, it is the government. Medicare and Medicaid together paid 28 percent of medical bills in 1990. And if "tax subsidies" for insurance are included, the government's share of medical spending reached 53 percent in the early 1990s.

There is another type of medicine in which *all* the bills are paid for by someone other than the patient—veterinary medicine.

Animals, of course, cannot pay bills. Sick or injured animals receive medical assistance only if their owners provide it.

Do farmers and pet owners have the animals' best interests at heart? They may think that they do. But leaving aside the question of whether a farmer can possibly think like a sheep in order to perceive the sheep's best interest, it is obvious whose interest will prevail in the event of a conflict. Who would choose medicine for the dog, even a beloved pet, over the bare minimum of food for his own table?

Will the decision makers at the Health Care Financing Administration or Blue Cross put the individual patient's interest first? They cannot. Can patients trust physicians to fight the payor on their behalf if ever there is a conflict? They had better not. (How far can animals trust the vet?)

But surely patients are not owned by society, are they? People owned by other people are called slaves. It is said that there is no more slavery in our enlightened age, except possibly for children allegedly sold into bondage to carpetmakers in India. One reason why Lasagna wanted to edit the Oath of Hippocrates was to delete mention of slaves.

WHICH THEORY IS CORRECT?

Some Other Greeks

In science, theories are ultimately judged by their results. Do they agree with observations of the real world?

A Greek named Aristarchus had the idea, 1,700 years before Copernicus, that the earth revolved around the sun. Rejected in his own time, his idea was reborn in Europe centuries later, when Copernicus "turned back the clock."

Copernicus, of course, was persecuted as a deviant because the views of still other Greeks were in ascendancy. To reconcile the observed movements of the heavenly bodies with the incorrect assumption that they all revolved around the earth, the Greeks invented celestial spheres and epicycles. As inconvenient data accumulated, ever more complex systems had to be elaborated. The virtuoso of epicycles and eccentrics was Ptolemy, born in the second century A.D. in Ptolemais on the Nile. Of his astronomy it has been said: "Wheeling and whirring in Rube Goldberg fashion, the Ptolemaic universe could be turned to predict almost any observed planetary motion—and when it failed, Ptolemy fudged the data to make it fit."[3]

The very complexity of a theory is a clue that something may be wrong. Einstein said, "God always does things the simple way"—a statement that seems incompatible with special and general relativity, but that's another story. As Edward Teller put it, "Science is the search for simplicity."

The rules and regulations of Medicare, along with other increasingly desperate efforts to "make the system work," remind me of the epicycles of Ptolemy. They *can't* make the system work very well, if the system is fundamentally wrong. And even if the system manages to accomplish some basic tasks, the wrong assumptions could destroy the potential for significant advances as surely as Ptolemaic astronomy would be an insurmountable barrier to space travel.

Complexity, however, is just a clue. It is not a proof that the theory is wrong. Disproving a theory requires seeing how it actually works in practice—without fudging the data to make it fit.

A look at the actual results is what much of this book is about.

Let's start with a question asked by another patient.

Is You the Doctuh?

In the emergency room at Parkland Memorial Hospital, the ambulances discharged what some considered to be the human effluent of the city. The triage nurse had a stamp for the most common presenting problems: OD (overdose), SW (stab wound), GSW (gunshot wound). The patients were mostly poor, unwashed, illiterate, and "low sick" (seriously ill). But one such patient, who had been seen by a parade of staff, had a question more perceptive than those usually asked by many a tenured bioethicist.

"Is you the doctuh?"

He wanted to see somebody with the responsibility and the authority to do something about his problem. Not a lady with a clipboard. Not a committee. Not a patient advocate or representative. Not a professor or department chairman. And not an alternative health care provider. He was waiting for the doctor.

Most patients, like this one, have the idea that doctors can diagnose the problem, write a prescription, perform an operation, or at least give them some advice. After Doctor has spoken, they do not expect to have to await a decision by a committee.

Is You the Patient?

The Parkland resident (who was no doubt very tired) fielded the question expertly, by asking another question: "Is you the patient?"

Today the answer is no longer so obvious.

It was formerly thought that "the patient is the one with the disease" (Law IV of *The House of God*).

The logical inverse of this idea is cited in three different places in the Greek Testament: "They that are whole hath no need of the physician." Is this one source of the "disease orientation" deplored by critics of Western medicine?

Spokesmen for organized medicine declare in prestigious journals that *everybody* needs a physician. Physicians are to broaden their vistas beyond tending the sick and the injured, not just to preventing disease but to enhancing wellness. And not just the wellness of the person who finds his way to the doctor's office, but the wellness of society as a whole, or further still to planet Earth itself (herself?), and maybe even the cosmos.

In the light of this broader perspective, the Parkland resident's question revealed an appalling narrowness. Of course, the man in the examining room was *a* patient, but he was not *the* patient. The socially responsible physician always has an infinite number of patients, all at once, and all with competing needs. The awesome nature of the balancing task will become apparent when we review the work of the rationing committee that produced the Basic Health Services Program.

So what is the physician to do? Is he to put a single patient in the center of his universe of concern, as Hippocratic medicine would seem to require? Or does something else belong in the center (the community of all patients, society, planet Earth, the government, you name it)?

Whose name does he write at the top of the prescription? And whose on the signature line?

8

RIGHTS, PRIVILEGES, AND NECESSITIES

When politicians say you have the right to medical care, this is what they really mean.

MEDICAL CARE is sometimes a necessity—to prevent untimely death or disability or to relieve pain. The *right* to medical care is a necessity—for all politicians trying to get elected.

There was an upset senatorial election in Pennsylvania, which scared the politicians to death. Former U.S. Attorney General Richard Thornburgh was the overwhelming favorite before the election. Then Democratic incumbent Harris Wofford said if every criminal in America has the right to a lawyer, shouldn't every working American have the right to a doctor? Later events showed these were not necessarily magic words. The Wofford formula was tried in Texas; Kay Bailey Hutchison defeated it with consumer choice.

Long before the Wofford election, I had discovered a reliable way to make a politician squirm (it works with both Democrats and Republicans). I pointed out to a congressman that the supposed right to medical care was like a postulate in geometry. If you started with the wrong postulate, your entire geometry would be wrong. And there would be no way to fix it unless you changed the erroneous assumption.

The politician was not dumb. He knew very well that (1) proclaiming a right to medical care created endless problems and (2) he was offering my colleagues and me to the public as a political plum without our consent. He also recognized an opportunity to commit political suicide when he saw it. So he skillfully evaded the question.

The question, however, will not go away. How shall we answer it?

Shall we take a vote? Will it be Hippocratic medicine, or non-Hippocratic medicine? Medical care as a right would have to be non-Hippocratic, as I shall explain. A vote would give us an answer, but not necessarily the right one, especially if we asked the wrong question.

The method of science and logic is to carry the alternate assumptions to their conclusions and look at the result. *Before* taking any votes.

Let's assume that there is a right to medical care, and see what happens.

The most obvious result is that costs and spending go through the roof. There is no limit to the potential need or desire for medical care. There are a lot more people who might need or benefit from medical care than there are criminals in need of a public defender. Also, criminals need a lawyer only for the trial, not for the rest of their lives. Immediately, the right has to be limited to "basic" care involving only "medically necessary" and "cost-effective" services. The right to a lawyer is limited, too. Poor people can have a lawyer if accused of a crime but not necessarily if a victim of a civil wrong. Contingency fees work only if the defendant has a deep pocket and the potential judgment is large enough.

As a former geometry teacher, I know about undefined terms, for example, *point* and *line*. People have an intuitive grasp of what those things are. Their intuition might be wrong, but inescapably you have to start somewhere.

Things like *medically necessary* and *basic* are undefined terms, of which people are assumed to have an intuitive understanding. But in the real world, they *must* be defined somehow or other. Let's look at some of the definitions.

A Superfluous Woman and a Necessary Phantom

Early in my practice, I was confronted with a very challenging patient. Call her Mrs. A. She was an elderly woman with numerous complicated medical problems who developed a pancreatic abscess. She could have died. Younger, healthier people often die of this condition. She probably would not have survived repeated major surgical procedures to drain the abscess, but thanks to modern technology, surgery wasn't necessary. The radiologist can now produce a good enough image to direct a thin needle right into the abscess and aspirate the pus, without ever making an incision.

Taking care of this patient still was no simple matter. I couldn't stick the needle in the abscess—that was the consultant's job. But he couldn't check on her heart, her state of mind, her blood pressure, her family problems, her serum electrolytes, and numerous other details. That was the attending physician's job. Mine. It took at least one hour a day for more than a month. I had to drive to and from the hospital (where I had no other patients), see the patient, read the chart, check the laboratory results, look at the x-rays and electrocardiograms, write orders and progress notes, and at last dictate the summary. Besides the time that I actually spent at the hospital, I had to answer frequent telephone calls from nurses, consultants, and the patient's family, at all hours of the day and night.

For this type of work, one really does need three years of internal medicine residency. I felt I had done good work and performed a necessary and beneficial service—exactly the type of personal service people say they want. Mrs. A. seemed to think so, too. After all, she recovered and did well for years.

After Mrs. A. was discharged from the hospital, I sent her a bill for my services. It was the largest bill I had ever sent to any patient, for about $1,200. (I understand this is a very modest sum in comparison with most medical bills.) In due time, Mrs. A. submitted my bill to Medicare. Instead of a check, she got an Explanation of (non)Benefits, stating that most of my bill had been disallowed.

I was shocked. I asked some of my more experienced colleagues about this. "Oh, yes," they said. "This happens to internists all the time."

Especially general internists. If they find it necessary to request consultation from a subspecialist, say a gastroenterologist who is also an internist, Medicare is likely to deny payment for one of the bills. Usually, the one to be denied is the general internist, even though the specialist charges a lot more. This is not a deliberate effort to destroy general internists. (Medicare is probably just mindless, not malicious.) Consultants usually submit their bills first, before the patient leaves the hospital. They sign off the case when they feel they are no longer needed. The general internist, the patient's personal attending physician, stays with the patient until the end and is therefore the last to send a bill.

My colleagues had some advice for me. "Play the game," they said. That means to be careful in wording the diagnosis to be sure that it is different from the one used by the patient's other physicians. For the general internist or family physician, this is difficult. The different subspecialties each lay claim to one organ or system. By the time they have finished dividing up the patient, there may not be much left for the one who takes care of the whole person. There's nothing in the ICD-9 diagnosis code book for the whole person.

Mrs. A. was also dismayed by this situation. It meant that she was personally responsible for my entire bill, which was not a trivial sum to either of us. So we appealed to the Medicare carrier—Aetna, the insurance company that handles claims in Arizona. We both appeared before the "fair hearing" officer with photocopies of a very thick chart. On many days, I was the only physician to have written a progress note or an order. But somebody had already been paid for those days. I call him the phantom cardiologist.

Although Mrs. A. did have a history of cardiac problems, she did not have any trouble with her heart during this illness. That may have been the only system that wasn't a problem. Therefore, I had never requested a cardiology consult. I checked the patient's heart daily myself.

Even though he never left a trace of his presence in the chart, Dr. Phantom materialized in the patient's room each day. He was in the hospital for some other reason and dropped by. The patient was pleased to have the attention of her personal cardiologist. And she didn't mind the expense because Dr. Phantom "takes assignment," which means he sends the bill directly to the government. Better still, he doesn't bill her even for the copayment. Medicare considers this to be "fraud and abuse" on the theory that the total fee is inflated to begin with (and maybe it is). But many physicians have been doing this with impunity, at least until recently, and they can still justify it in cases like Mrs. A.'s on the basis of the patient's financial hardship.

Dr. Phantom's claim was promptly paid. Therefore, the work of caring for the patient—my work—had been paid for. Therefore, Medicare didn't owe the patient any more money. The hearing officer (who incidentally was being paid by the agency that denied the claim in the first place) denied the patient's appeal. He didn't even have to give her an explanation.

The patient made monthly payments of $5 or $10 for a long time until I finally wrote off the remainder. As far as I know, she didn't have to skip any meals to do it. But even though she never complained that I hadn't earned my pay, Dr. Phantom is now her personal physician, and I am a superfluous woman. Medicare probably told her that if she had only seen a participating physician, who takes assignment on all cases, she wouldn't have had to pay me anything, even if the government paid me $0.00. Actually, she didn't *have* to pay me in the legal sense. The obligation was a moral one only.

Recently, Congress has come to the aid of people like Mrs. A. They passed a law to "protect the beneficiary." This is Newspeak for "protecting congressional incumbents." There are a lot of Medicare beneficiaries, and a lot of them vote. If they can see that Congress is cutting their benefits, they get mad. Congress has decreed that patient payments for "unnecessary, covered services" have to be refunded, under pain of a $2,000 fine, unless the patient signs a waiver form in advance. They want the waiver form to be submitted with the claim—an invitation to deny it? along with the specific reason the physician thinks the claim might be denied. "Medicare is arbitrary and capricious and might deny any claim for reasons I can't figure out" is not an acceptable reason, even though it is true. It has to be something like "Medicare doesn't usually pay for more than x number of visits in a month." This is hard to find out because the review criteria are kept secret on the assumption that physicians will try to game the system. (They do. The secrecy just drives up the price of the "inside information" offered by entrepreneurs who give seminars.)

I did have patients sign waiver forms when they came to the office. No one ever declined to do it. After all, if they chose to come to the office, it was hard for them to say that the service they sought was of no value and shouldn't be paid for unless a Medicare clerk okayed it. But one cannot present a waiver form to a patient who is lying in a hospital bed. The patient can't walk away, and neither can the doctor.

After this experience, I had some questions.

Is it necessary for a patient with a potentially fatal illness to have an attending physician?

If it might be deemed unnecessary, is it a right?

If the service is of *no value* to the government or other insurer, is it still a right?

It's true that my problem in this case was caused by the phantom cardiologist, who was engaged in behavior rewarded by the system but surely did not deliberately deprive me of payment for my services. However, Medicare has also denied payment for my services in other cases in which I had *requested* the cardiology consultation.

If the service is of no value, how do you get someone to provide it? Doctors give billions of dollars worth of pro bono services that they judge to be necessary and worthwhile. But charity is voluntary; thus it cannot be relied upon to provide service that is a right. But if that service is unnecessary and worthless, how can you justify the use of force to ensure access to it?

Here is how the government has handled the conundrum with Medicare and Medicaid: They entice doctors to volunteer for a kind of lottery. The doctors won't know ahead of time how the paying agency will classify the service, but chances are pretty good that they will be paid in any given instance, and they can improve their odds by sending their office managers to coding seminars. So far, this has worked. It works so well that private insurers are doing the same.

WHAT IS "MEDICALLY NECESSARY"?

One example does not make a definition of "medically necessary." It could be that my case was just a glitch that I think is important mainly because it happened to *my* patient and me. Here are some other determinations by Medicare and other insurers. The reader's job is to use inductive reasoning to derive a definition of medically necessary and medically unnecessary that will be comprehensible to a clerk with a high school education.

• Necessary: a $750 technetium scan of the heart (that turned out to be normal) in a patient with no evidence of heart disease. He didn't think he really needed it, but it was nice to know that his heart was okay, and the insurance company was paying the bill.

• Necessary: a $365 ultrasound study of the gallbladder, and a $320 study of the liver, along with a $383 study of the pancreas in a patient who occasionally has a stomachache. Yes, those organs are close together, and you can see all of them on one study, even if you can see gastric hyperacidity, which is what the patient probably has, only on television commercials.

• Necessary: periodic cholesterol checks, and if the cholesterol has not gone down, lectures from the doctor about the importance of eating less fat and taking every single dose of your ion-exchange resin (that's one kind of medicine). The lecture does not need to include information on the margin of error in the laboratory test, which might well be larger than the change in the patient's reading.

• Unnecessary: an electrocardiogram (EKG) on a patient in the ICU who had just had an episode of ventricular fibrillation (an "acute dying spell").

• Unnecessary: a visit to an eye doctor, because the patient saw a second eye doctor on the same day. The first one diagnosed the retinal tear and sent the patient immediately to a retinal specialist who was equipped to treat the problem and saved the patient's vision.

• Unnecessary: a nursing home visit to treat acute congestive heart failure, because the doctor had just seen the patient a few days previously for the routine checkup required by the nursing home. The heart failure didn't happen until afterward.

Maybe you are having trouble with these definitions. But Medicare clerks have no trouble at all. It is easy to get the computer to spew out denial letters.

I have come up with my own definition: *Nothing* is medically necessary, and I am a superfluous woman.

I arrived at this conclusion by process of elimination. Consider the possibilities. Could something be medically necessary if it prevents death? This question was answered by another question that someone once asked me: "What is your mortality rate?"

"It depends on the length of follow-up," I said. "Ultimately, 100 percent."

What about postponing death? Is something medically necessary if it postpones death?

This definition is better but still not very good as a guide for insurance coverage. It would eliminate a large number of medical treatments that are widely believed to be beneficial. Some treatments, like total joint replacements, may sometimes hasten death by subjecting the patient to the risks of anesthesia and surgery but make life much more tolerable. Also, one can ask how long the reprieve has to be. Is it medically necessary to resuscitate a person with a terminal disease so that he can die one week later? Six months later? And what if a treatment is likely to postpone death but doesn't work, and the patient dies anyway? Or what if the patient might survive the disease (pneumonia, for example) even without treatment but is somewhat more likely to live if he receives an antibiotic? Is the antibiotic really necessary?

By this definition, I would estimate that at least 95 percent of my work has been medically unnecessary. My sickest patients died of their disease despite everything I could do. Most patients don't have a fatal disease when they see me. Many of them would get better even without seeing a physician, although I can sometimes help speed recovery or prevent a complication. Frequently, reassurance is all I can provide. Sometimes I feel completely useless. If a patient tells me he had a cold but is getting better, I tell him he should have come to see me sooner so that I could take the credit.

Is a treatment medically necessary if it increases the quality of life? Most of the things that increase the quality of life—a loving family, interesting work, decent living conditions, and so on—are not medical interventions. They have not yet been declared to be a right, and the quality-deprived cannot receive them through a federally funded program. And how much of a quality increase is required and from what starting point? Is it *necessary* to increase from good to superb, or from abysmal to very poor, or from bad to tolerable?

Medical necessity is a new issue. Several decades ago, the odds that a patient would benefit from visiting a physician were less than 50:50. In the heyday of bleeding and purging, some poor people survived longer than their richer cousins because the poor could not afford to call the doctor.

Today, modern medical care does more good than harm on balance, although sometimes the treatment is still worse than the disease. Modern medical care often prolongs life, although public health measures such as sanitation are much more important. Unquestionably, modern medicine can relieve pain and prevent or mitigate many disabilities. This is beneficial. But is it *necessary?*

In the early days of Medicare, when costs were not of great concern, "necessary" meant "ordered by a physician." Now it means whatever a person with authority says it means. That is probably as good a definition as any, the term being undefinable.

Now the discussion is shifting to a different, also undefinable, term: *basic.* Basic medical services are the ones that everybody in the civilized world is to have by right, even if they are unnecessary. Many of them *are* unnecessary by almost any definition: for example, if they are designed to "prevent" a disease the patient wasn't going to get anyway. The state of Oregon has taken the lead in trying to define this term.

THE OREGON BASIC HEALTH SERVICES PROGRAM

The state of Oregon has designed a system of "health care priorities" that is supposed to "contain costs" (i.e., put a lid on expenditures) while enabling the state to expand Medicaid eligibility. The idea is widely praised because it forthrightly uses the R word: *rationing.*

The system's author, John Kitzhaber, M.D., states that it is a first step. Once applied to the poor, it can later be extended to everybody else, making the allocation of medical resources at last rational and fair. The system is a scientific one: They propose to try it on the dogs first, not on themselves.

The Oregon project starts by listing all currently known medical procedures; there are 714, unless it has changed by now. The next step is to rank all the procedures in order of priority, based on social value. Then the legislature will draw a line, based solely on budgetary considerations. Procedures above the line will be funded under the Medicaid program; those below the line will not. In this way, Medicaid eligibility is to be expanded to a number of persons who previously didn't qualify, without increasing the drain on the state budget by more than a few million dollars.

The ranking is accomplished by a consensus process. About 20,000 hours were volunteered by citizens to express their feelings about various symptoms and the quality of life, weighting factors like mobility, physical activity, and social activity. A Quality of Well-Being (QWB) scale was devised for assigning numerical values to these feelings.

Citizens with a diversity of interests participated, but they all had something in common. As far as I can tell, none of them needed a kidney transplant or a prosthetic hip or open heart surgery or any of those other high-cost procedures they were evaluating.

The list offers something for everybody. Well, almost everybody. Certainly everybody who can vote.

Near the top of the list (#167 for adults and #143 for children in 1991) are preventive medical services that are of some proven value, at least in the collective sense. Everybody can be screened and treated for hypertension. Although it costs about $175,000 to save one life that way, nobody knows which life it will be, so all can enjoy a theoretical benefit. Also, everybody can get well-baby checks, cholesterol screening, and abortions (#322) for unwanted pregnancies. The last might yield a net cost saving, assuming that all babies who are unwanted by their mothers at the time of the abortion would consume more over their lifetime than they produce. But if the well-baby check reveals a congenital dislocation of the hip (#522), we'll have to see where that line is drawn before we recommend surgical treatment. Ditto for children with cerebral palsy (#434) or cleft palate (#376). Very few people can benefit from operations for these conditions.

Eye surgery to prevent blindness in patients with glaucoma or diabetes is ranked around #325, while sterilization procedures are #161 (male) and #162 (female). If some of the rankings seem strange from a subjective standpoint, remember that they were arrived at by an objective (fair) method. For example, visual impairment has a QWB (Quality of Well-Being) weight of −0.244, while trouble with sexual performance has a QWB weight of −0.255. Treating impotence is thus more valuable to society than preventing blindness.

Applying the test of common sense to the Oregon list led to some remarkable observations: Thumbsucking was near the top of the list because it is easily treated at relatively low cost and affects a large number of people. It was way ahead of cystic fibrosis, certain types of arthritis, and impacted teeth. When this was pointed out, advocates of rationing howled with righteous indignation about "cheap shots." They issued a revised list after "cleaning" the data. Some of the results (which continue to be revised) are listed above. They fixed some details without questioning the underlying assumptions.

To reiterate the key underlying assumption: It is benefit to *society* that is important in arriving at the rankings, not the individual physician's judgment about what will benefit his individual patient. The Oregon plan legislates non-Hippocratic medicine.

At first, the plan could not be put into effect. It did not meet federal Medicaid requirements and was denied a waiver because it discriminates against people with disabilities. But the Clinton administration granted the waiver.

IF IT'S A RIGHT, CAN YOU GET IT?

The right to medical care is supposed to mean universal access. But every discussion about universal access almost immediately turns into a discussion of rationing, which means *restricted* access. That means denial of care, even if the care is available. Denial of care means that you have *no right* to that care. As a former geometry teacher, I would be inclined to stop here. The right to medical care leads to a contradiction. Q.E.D., the assumption is wrong. But for those who do not follow Euclid, there's more, much more.

In the real world, the right to medical care means something very different from what people think. For example, people may think that U.S. Medicare gave senior citizens the right to the medical care of their choice. Not so. Robert Bork, when he was solicitor general in the U.S. Department of Justice, stated very clearly what Medicare really does mean: Its beneficiaries have the right to *whatever the government sees fit to provide*:

> Patients whose medical care is provided by public funds have **no constitutional right** to whatever care [their physicians] using "the highest standards of medical practice" . . . may "judge necessary" . . . or to obtain that care "from a physician of their choice."[1]

If the government pays for it, the government has the right to regulate it. But what if the government doesn't pay for it?

Medicare carriers have told physicians that if Medicare patients do not *completely disenroll* from Medicare Part B (thereby becoming uninsured for physicians' services, since no alternative coverage is available), government restrictions apply to *every* medical transaction the patient makes, except for a few services such as cosmetic surgery that are clearly not covered and arguably not "medical." This means that if the government doesn't pay for it—if it isn't a "right"—then the patient *can't have it*, unless he can find a physician who will perform the service without payment. This resembles the law of physics or of Communist economics: Everything that is not compulsory is forbidden.

Because this is the United States of America, patients find it difficult to believe that they are allowed to spend their own money to buy a yacht, or a Caribbean cruise, or dinner at a restaurant, but *not* to see the physician of their choice. In fact, the Medicare law doesn't say that.

Five Medicare patients and their physician, Dr. Lois Copeland of New Jersey, took the government to court. In a court of law, the U.S. attorney denied responsibility for statements by the Medicare carriers. Therefore, the judge decided that HHS had no "clearly articulated" policy against private contracting. He doubted that HHS could lawfully sanction physicians who did contract privately with their patients.[2]

Unless Congress changes the law, Medicare patients have an escape hatch from government restrictions, but only if they renounce their claim to *any* Medicare reimbursement for a given service. And only if their physicians are unusually courageous, since carriers and HHS bureaucrats continue to issue threatening statements. They say that patients and physicians may enter into a contract but that the government won't recognize it. In their view, the physician may be bound by his word but the patient isn't. If the patient wants to complain about the physician not filing a claim (even though the patient said he didn't want one filed), Medicare *may* try to punish the doctor.

In other words, the government is threatening to punish doctors for doing something that is perfectly lawful! Indeed, it is inviting patients to violate agreements and snitch on their doctors. Is there a better way to destroy the patient-physician relationship, which absolutely requires mutual trust?

Over the next few years, the United States may decide this question: If necessary medical care is a right, is access to unnecessary or non-approved medical care a privilege that can and eventually will be denied?

IF IT'S A RIGHT, HOW DO YOU ENFORCE IT?

Governments exist to protect citizens' rights, or so our Founding Fathers thought. And how are rights enforced? Necessarily by the use of force. Sometimes deadly force.

If someone threatens your rights, you have a right to defend yourself or to call upon the government (the police) to defend you. For example, if you are convinced that a person is about to kill you, you have the right to shoot him, because your life is yours by right. Your continued existence is not just a privilege conferred by Congress. Of course, you may have to convince a jury that your weapon was fired in self-defense, and this may be more difficult in New York than in Texas. That's because the person you shot has rights, too. He forfeits his right not to be killed *only* if he has first threatened *your* right not to be killed.

Questions about violations of absolute, negative rights, like the right not to be murdered, require a jury, not a resource allocation committee.

The right to life is one right that can be interpreted only in a negative way. Human beings are not able to confer life on something that is not already alive, not even if they have a medical degree. The most doctors can do is try to postpone death. Or they can put a living egg and a living sperm together and hope that a new person eventually results—an unpredictable new person, not necessarily the one they want.

What about the means for maintaining life or for making it seem worthwhile? What about liberty and property? Do people have an absolute right not to have their liberty or property forcibly taken from them if they have not been convicted of a crime against the liberty or property of others?

There is a moral absolute related to this question: "Thou shalt not steal." I think this must be a natural law, because very young children instinctively understand the meaning of "mine." That's one of the traits that makes them human. Teaching them the meaning of "not mine" is one of the things that makes them civilized.

While visiting Williamsburg, Virginia, I attended a dramatic reenactment of a trial that occurred in Colonial times. A young woman was accused of the crime of stealing a silver spoon. The sentence was death by hanging.

The woman had an excellent excuse for taking the spoon. I don't remember exactly what it was, but it would have melted the hardest heart. The woman was desperately poor even though she worked from dawn to dusk, and her sick mother had to have medicine immediately or she would surely die. Something like that.

Nevertheless, in those times the law was the law. Even then, people might have thought that the penalty was too harsh. But few doubted that the woman had committed a crime and deserved to be punished.

In Moslem countries, even today, penalties for stealing are still extremely harsh, such as amputation of the thief's right hand.

In a story I once read, a young Moslem girl was accosted by bandits, who intended to steal her shoes.

"No!" she screamed at them. "I will not allow you to steal my shoes. Here, I will *give* them to you."

Allah's punishment for stealing was so severe that the girl did not wish even these bandits to incur it on her account.

Did the woman in Williamsburg need the spoon? Did the bandits need the shoes?

Did they need these things more than the owners?

If so, were they really stealing?

Few would be willing to legalize burglary or banditry by individual citizens, though many argue for excusing the people who commit it out of need.

But we have a problem. The voters are not satisfied with mere negative rights. To say they have an equal, absolute right not to have their property or labor stolen will not suffice. They want economic rights, not moral rights. They want and need food, shelter, and medical care. If they have not succeeded in attaining these things for themselves, then they believe the government should provide them.

The problem is that the government has no access to manna from heaven, and no capacity to provide medical services. To enforce economic rights, it must use force to *take* the money required to purchase the goods and services. Some people think that the government acts as Robin Hood. That is the stated *intention* of many laws: to redistribute wealth from the rich to the poor. In execution, the intention often gets turned around, as I propose to show. The government turns out to be the nobles and the Sheriff of Nottingham, who stole from the poor to benefit the rich and powerful. It only pretends to be Robin Hood, who arguably returned the stolen goods to their rightful owners.

The first step toward guaranteeing positive economic rights is to edit the "thou shalt nots."

The eighth commandment (the seventh, if you use the Catholic numbering system) no longer reads "Thou shalt not steal." It now is taken to mean "Thou shalt not steal, unless thou hast a 'need' for something, and then only by using the force of government to accomplish thy theft."

Robert Ringer wrote these words in his book *How You Can Find Happiness During the Collapse of Western Civilization* as an attack on the income tax. As I see it, the form of the tax is beside the point. Legitimate taxes support the legitimate functions of government. It is the use of government levies as an instrument of social leveling that is at issue. As G. K. Chesterton puts it, "The most dangerous criminal now is the entirely lawless modern philosopher. Compared to him, burglars . . . are essentially moral men." Thieves respect property, Chesterton says—they just want it for themselves. Philosophers wish to destroy the idea of personal possession. In other words, they don't see forcible income redistribution as theft because if there is no personal property there is no such thing as theft. But I digress.

As we have already seen, the positive right to medical care leads to immediate practical problems of (re)distribution. It cannot be an absolute right, only a relative one. Economic goods are *scarce* and cannot be created out of nothing; they can only be distributed. A jury can't do the job; we need committees to determine relative needs and the relative values of the various goods and services, and the hierarchy of rights of consumers to be served and privileges of physicians to serve. The next chapters will examine this process.

....

9

WHAT IS A DOCTOR WORTH?

....

There is a price on our heads; this is how they figure it out.

HOW TO CALCULATE A FEE WITHOUT A COMPUTER

I NEVER had any trouble figuring out what my fees should be, in the days before Medicare fixed them for me. I never used a computer for this purpose, not even my handheld HP 41C programmable scientific calculator.

It's not that I don't know how. But I believe in using the right tool for the job. To do a Fisher's Exact Test or some other statistical test, I wouldn't want to be without my 41C. But figuring out what to charge for my services never required anything more than pencil and paper, or at most an adding machine.

I never tried to calculate a "fair" fee to the nearest tenth of a cent. Plus or minus five dollars or so seemed good enough. And the definition of "fairness" was that both the patient and I were satisfied. As I see it, patients should feel that they are receiving value for money, and I should feel that patients are not taking unfair advantage of me.

The absolute value in dollars is not the measure of fairness. I will do some things for love that I would never do for money. And other things that I will do for money I couldn't possibly do for love. To have the opportunity to do certain jobs, I am willing to underbid almost anyone. To make some jobs acceptable, there isn't enough money in the world. Under one set of circumstances, I would willingly give freely of my time. Other times, I would feel underpaid at $500 per hour.

Some things that do enter into my personal calculus of how much I should charge include the patient's ability to pay and the general vexation associated with his care. The necessity of the service is also important, but my view of it is the opposite of the government's. I feel that the more unnecessary the service, the more I should be paid. If somebody wakes me up at night because of a genuine need for my advice, that's part of the job. But if a good night's sleep is ruined by somebody old enough to know better who says, "I threw up. I *never* throw up. I need a shot or else I might throw up again," I would charge about $500 if there were any hope of collecting it.

Individual patients also place a different value on services that look the same. Something that may seem superfluous and worthless to one patient (say a physical examination) may be highly sought after by another. Some patients may place such a low value on their time that they are willing to wait all day at the VA to get a prescription for free aspirin. Others are quite willing to pay extra for an appointment at a convenient time. Some patients may live in dread of cancer and want to have every possible test done at regular intervals; the reassurance is worth a lot of money to them. Others will refuse to spend $85 for a mammogram but not think twice about the same expenditure at the beauty parlor. Some will be glad to have the mammogram if they don't have to pay for it, though others will avoid it out of fear.

WHY I DON'T EVEN TRY TO CALCULATE WHAT OTHER DOCTORS SHOULD MAKE

I never worry about surgeons making too much money. I do worry that soon they might not be making enough. An alarming number of my most trusted surgical consultants are thinking of early retirement. It is not *just* the money, but the money does have something to do with it. Work involves both direct and indirect costs, such as the loss of the opportunity to do something else instead—reviewing your investments, playing baseball with your son, taking a nap, and so on. The return has to be at least compensatory.

The most important thing I learned about surgeons is how to get them to come when I call. If my patient has a bowel obstruction or a hemorrhage that won't stop or a gangrenous gallbladder, I absolutely need someone who can cut. Say all you want about the importance of a kindly family doctor who will listen to you and hold your hand. If you desperately need an operation, calling the surgeon will be the most important thing your kindly family physician will have to do for you, unless he can do the surgery himself; some old-time family physicians could. Calling a skilled surgeon a "Neanderthal proceduralist," as some proponents of "physician payment reform" do, is a sign that the speaker must never have taken care of real patients.

Since I have been in private practice, I have never had trouble finding a surgeon or a specialist of any kind. In fact, when I first went into practice I was quite surprised to find that specialists treated me with courtesy when I called about a patient.

The reason for my surprise was that in four years as a staff physician at the VA, I never heard a single "thank you" from a consultant. On the contrary, every time I called a resident to admit a patient, I was prepared to take abuse. If the doctor was civil, I appreciated it. All too often he made an insulting remark about my presumed laziness or lack of competence. ("What do you mean, you can't take care of this as an out-patient!" the resident would complain.)

VA residents are on a salary. Do you want *your* doctor to be on a salary so he is not rewarded for doing too much? There's more about the VA later if you're not sure.

Why, with Medicare, You Have to Have a Computer, Although It Doesn't Help

The first time I got out my calculator to figure my fee schedule was around 1987 when Medicare introduced the MAACs. I don't remember what the acronym stood for, but what it meant was the maximum amount that a doctor was allowed to charge, as in "max." They meant business, too; if you charged more than the MAACs, you could be fined $2,000 per *item*. "More" meant about $0.50 more. Our hospital got fined about a quarter of a million dollars because they rounded their charges to the nearest dollar, even though they rounded down as often as they rounded up.

Medicare produced a formula and tables of numbers to be plugged into it. I wrote a little program for the HP 41C. By the end of the afternoon, I had all my MAACs calculated.

I should have saved myself the trouble. In due course, Aetna (the Medicare carrier for Arizona) sent me a list of my MAACs. They were not the same as the ones I calculated. I am sure that I did the math right, but I started with a different set of figures: the amounts that I considered to be my fees. Aetna had used the average charge on claims that my patients had submitted within a certain time period. If no claim for a certain CPT-4 code had been submitted, they used their own numbers. There was no way that I could check their figures, but it didn't matter. Aetna spoke for the government, and the government is right by definition. So I threw out my figures and used theirs. Like everybody else, I used the MAAC as the fee. Why charge less? If you charged less this year, you were going to be stuck with that amount forever after, no matter what happened to your expenses.

Although the MAACs were only supposed to limit the rate of fee increases, they resulted in a substantial cut in some of my fees, because Medicare had received no claims during the chosen three- or four-month period. My fee for a house call, which takes at least an hour including travel time, was to be cut from about $50 to about $35. That didn't cover my office overhead. I decided I could no longer afford to make house calls. Since a nurse's house calls are more valuable anyway (at least Medicare pays more for them), I decided to defer to the nurse. No more claims for house calls were ever again submitted by any of my patients. That is not to say that I haven't done any, but I only do them for love. (Well, once I got bullied into it by a patient's daughter. The patient, who was reasonably affluent, received a whole evening of my time without ever paying a dime for it—but only once. It turned out that she needed a specialist for all her subsequent care.)

The MAACs were only an interim measure. The next step, calculating "fairness," gets into really serious computing. Now we have "physicians' payment reform," or the Resource-Based Relative Value Scale (RBRVS). This revolutionary development has generated millions of pages of computer output.

The most powerful computer in the world cannot, by strong-arm number crunching, succeed in squaring the circle. Can it succeed in calculating fairness, or has it been asked an unanswerable question?

How Many Blood Pressure Readings Are Worth One Hernia Operation?

The American Society of Internal Medicine (ASIM), among others, lobbied hard for the RBRVS. I, of course, agree with them that I deserve to make more money. Family practitioners think they deserve more money, too. Clearly, doctors have traditionally been paid more for *doing* something (like an operation or a procedure) than for talking to patients and thinking ("evaluation and management"). Some people think that's why primary care residencies can't find enough applicants, and rural communities can't find enough doctors. Interest in family practice among first-year medical students declined from 37 percent in 1978 to 16 percent in 1987 to 10 percent in 1988 and 1989.[1]

But simply giving primary care physicians a pay raise was not one of the possibilities. It is thought that we are already spending too much money on medical care. Where was the money to come from? Obviously, from *other* physicians, who are believed to be making too much. But we can't just take from Peter to pay Paul. We need to justify the takings, to make them seem fair.

The RVS is not a new idea. Unfairness, of course, is not new either. In the England of George Bernard Shaw, prizefighters made a lot more money than judges—a scandalous situation, in his view. But he couldn't think up a way of determining how many ounces of judge are worth a pound of prizefighter. Nor could he think of a fair way of deciding how other occupations should be compensated on the basis of merit (or "comparable worth," in modern parlance), especially where "cognitive" and "procedural" skills were being compared.

> Well think it out. The clergyman . . . is able to read the New Testament in Greek; so that he can do something the blacksmith cannot do. On the other hand, the blacksmith can make a horseshoe, which the parson cannot. How many verses of the Greek Testament are worth one horseshoe? You have only to ask the silly question to see that nobody can answer it.[2]

Shaw came up with another solution, which was simplicity itself. He suggested paying everyone exactly the same wage. This had the slight complication that not everyone would be worth what he was being paid. Shaw had a solution to that, too: executing such persons, in a kindly manner, of course. I think he was being serious about this, although with Shaw it is sometimes hard to tell. At least, he did not call this an "act of supreme love," even if the method was "kindly."

Shaw did not have a computer.

The Relative Value Scale in Practice

The RBRVS is based on the assumption that the value of a medical service is the sum of the cost of the resources needed to produce it. Resources include office overhead, the expense of the physician's training, and the time, skill, and stress involved in performing the service.

How does one go about determining the resources needed for 10,000 medical services performed anywhere in the United States? The difficulties were insurmountable; the bureaucrats undaunted.

There were difficulties with even the most straightforward figures. Although real estate agents seem to know about office rents, Medicare bureaucrats "couldn't find" any data. So they used apartment rents as a proxy. Since they didn't know what physicians are supposed to earn, they used earnings for other college-educated persons such as schoolteachers. If they didn't have current data for something, they used data from a couple of years ago. They had a mandate to fulfill and a deadline to meet. If necessary, they just made something up.

The "relative values" of physicians' skills were trickier.

A research group at Harvard, headed by economist William Hsiao, Ph.D. (pronounced "Shau," rhyming with "plow") created tables based on small group surveys of various specialists. These physicians were asked to put an objective number on their subjective opinion about the difficulty of certain procedures. They each took a guess, and HCFA averaged the guesses.

The researchers didn't actually ask about every single service, only about 460 of them. By using "extrapolated data" (i.e., their imagination), they arrived at a total of about 4,000 work units in time for their deadline.

The final rule published by HCFA is a seventy-four-page document containing about 10,000 codes for various services, each with a column for "work RVUs," "practice expense RVUs," and "malpractice RVUs." The formula for calculating a "total RVU" (total Relative Value Unit) looks intimidating, so a consultant will charge you a lot for doing your calculations, although it is actually quite easy to program into your scientific calculator. Or you can buy a manual with your "personalized" fees listed for only $1,595.

The final step is to multiply the total RVU by the conversion factor (CF) that converts it into dollars. The CF is the same in Mississippi as it is in New York or Alaska, and is also the same for optometrists, family physicians, and neurosurgeons.

The Answer Is . . .

The result is that every single fee calculated by this method is wrong. Mathematically, it *has* to be wrong because nobody is exactly average, yet the fee is based on the average of averages of guesses. The fees are also very low.

Practically speaking, the RVS has not achieved its objective of helping the family doctor. I haven't heard of a single one who is not complaining about a drop in income.

Even William Hsiao, author of the RBRVS, admits that the results are unreasonable and the payments so low that applicants will be discouraged from entering the profession. He blames that on the CF and certain technical difficulties.[3]

Dr. Hsiao's belated conclusion agrees with that of about 95,000 others who sent comments to HCFA during the public comment period for the RBRVS rules. U.S. administrative agencies must submit their proposed rules for public comment. The rules are published in the *Federal Register*, and anyone affected by the rule is free to submit a comment within sixty days. Somebody at the agency has to read all the comments and possibly to write a response such as "We disagree."

So what will be done?

The government realized that physicians would not be happy with a substantial pay cut—more than 50 percent for some surgical procedures—and would try to recover some of their income by gaming the system and providing more services. Therefore, HCFA compensated by cutting fees even more. The result is to punish doctors in advance for cheating (or for simply working harder), and to punish them even more severely if they do *not* try to cheat. Those who don't cheat suffer a much greater loss of income than those who do.

Doctors were told that if there were errors not corrected by the comment process, they could be dealt with before the *next* updating of the fee schedule, one year later, if the bureaucrats deigned to listen.

But there is no other recourse. Congress provided in the law that fees could *not* be appealed to a court or even to an administrative board. Not even if the fee for a service is reduced to a level that does not cover the cost of the materials required. Not even if the fee is reduced to zero! Examples include certain new drugs, but also the time-tested methods such as the Unna boot cast used to treat nonhealing ulcers on the lower leg.

Congress need not worry about a groundswell of protest from senior citizens who received higher medical bills. It has also legislated price controls—limits on "balance billing" or billing more than the allowed amount—even more severe than the MAACs After the limits are fully phased in, physicians will be allowed to charge no more than 115 percent of the RVS-determined fee. But 115 percent of zero is still zero, and 115 percent of a nonremunerative amount is still nonre-munerative. Medicare beneficiaries can't be billed for more.

In other words, the answer is this: The nonelected bureaucratic agency that determines physicians' fees is infallible under law, and its dictates are absolute. It is not considered undemocratic, however. A few physician representatives had input into the process, and all physicians had a chance to send a comment to HCFA.

The Bottom Line

After attending a couple of seminars and reading the *Federal Register*, which is even worse than the material in the last section, my conclusion was clear: I can't figure this out. *Nobody can figure this out*. My HP 41C, even my computer with a mighty 386 microprocessor, is of no help whatsoever.

It doesn't even matter what the fee schedule says I am allowed to charge. Before we can begin to calculate the fee for an office visit, we first have to figure out what an office visit *is*.

At the same time that they introduced the RBRVS, HCFA changed all the codes. There are now five different types of office visits for established patients, not six, and you can't just translate an old code into a new one. There is an extremely convoluted definition to distinguish an intermediate visit from a limited one.

I could try to explain to you about the three different axes (key components) that I'm supposed to consider in making (and of course documenting) the all-important code for the visit. But the explanation would probably be obsolete before anybody had a chance to read it, assuming anybody *wanted* to read it.

Keeping up with medical journals is a daunting chore. But there is *no way* I can keep up with the forty- to sixty-page monthly publication from Aetna, most of it full of code lists. Medicare tells me I am responsible for knowing the contents of that publication, as if all my life were to be a sudden-death final exam. The front page of *Medicare News* states:

> The *Medicare News*, together with special bulletins and releases, serve as legal notice to physicians and suppliers concerning responsibilities and requirements imposed upon them by Medicare law, regulations and guidelines. It is very important that the physician and all other appropriate staff members read and become familiar with the information contained in each edition of *Medicare News*.[4]

Gail Wilensky, former administrator of HCFA, acknowledged that it was "difficult" to keep up with the ever changing regulations.

Difficult is not the word for it, Excellency.

The carriers will use education (instead of enforcement) for a few months, until physicians get used to the rules. But the carriers' job is not like that of a math teacher trying to explain the Babylonian number system to seventh graders. The problem is not with the educational maturity of the students or the obscurity of the subject. The problem is that the bureaucrats themselves cannot understand the rules because they are inconsistent and make no sense. The only possible interpretation is arbitrary and capricious.

This is even worse than blackjack. In blackjack, you can only lose all the money you have brought to the table, and it is possible to calculate your odds.

Medicare is even worse than selling naked calls on the stock market—and that can cost everything you have. Calls have an expiration date, and there is a mechanism for bailing out if things start to go wrong. There is a ticker tape so investors can constantly see how they're doing. With Medicare, legions of the inspector general can descend on a physician with no warning, deciding that he's been making mistakes (or committing fraud) for years. A doctor can lose his profession as well as everything he owns. I'll go into more detail in later chapters.

I made my decision not to place bet number one on the RVS before I ever got to what is generally called the bottom line (the fee). But I'll mention some of the fees just to show how far the reality of the RVS departs from its stated purpose. If you think the purpose was to reward doctors for spending time with patients (not code books), think again.

Fees for the five different types of office visits range from about $13 to about $73. The initial evaluation of a sick hospitalized patient, which can take hours, is worth a maximum of about $119, and that includes the telephone calls at night. Treating a dislocated toe is worth about $96, and performing a proctosigmoidoscopy (looking up into the rectum and lower bowel) up to $144. These procedures might take a few minutes.

Why would a person with financial obligations want to do $13 office visits for complicated *persons*, during which anything can happen, when simple, predictable dislocated *toes* pay $96?

THE RELATIVE VALUE SCALE IN THEORY

The Relative Value Scale is basically an application of the Marxist labor theory of value. According to this theory, all prices should be based on the cost of production. This means that the price of a rock should be equal to the cost of digging it up, whether it is a diamond or a piece of common granite. The value to the recipient is supposed to be irrelevant.

The medical moguls who proposed the RVS did not do so out of devotion to the labor theory of value. Most of them probably never even heard of it. They just wanted to right a perceived wrong—to help the ailing family doctor.

When things didn't turn out the way they expected, they complained about HCFA's botching the details.

But the problem is not with the details. The fact that only 100 codes out of 10,000 concerns the evaluation and management of *patients* is not a mere detail. But I am not advocating an increase in the number of codes!

When checking your answer to a complicated math problem, the first thing to do is to see if the answer makes sense. If it is obviously ridiculous, then you probably did the problem wrong. If the procedure for doing the problem resembles the epicycles of Ptolemy, that also suggests a basic flaw in the method.

Should we give the American Society of Internal Medicine and Dr. Hsiao an *E* for effort and a pat on the back for good intentions?

You may, but I won't. The RVS averages things out, just like the bed of Procrustes did. (Travelers who visited the giant Procrustes were forced to fit into his bed. Some people got stretched, and others had their feet cut off.) The RVS is a fundamentally bad idea from the beginning, and its promoters should have known better.

The RVS by its very nature reduces patients to ciphers, important only for their charge centers (dislocated toes, abscessed fingers, skin lesions, etc.). It assumes that all patients are less than the sum of their diseased parts, that all medical services with the same code are exactly alike, and hence that all patients are exactly alike.

But of course the RVS was not really motivated by a desire to help *patients*. Remember that its origin is in a section of organized medicine. It was supposed to benefit certain *doctors*—at the expense of other doctors.

The RVS has to do with filling out a paper, *after* the doctor sees the patient. It gets the questions out of order and overlooks the most important one: *How do you get the doctor to come, to provide the care that you want?*

WHAT'S YOUR ANSWER, THEN?

If the RVS won't solve the problem, then what will? People demand to know. As with many perceived social problems, people will grasp at any solution, however destructive, unless they are presented with a better alternative. They do not live by the Oath of Hippocrates: "First, do no harm."

Why Aren't There More Country Doctors?

Before we apply the leeches to the patient, we need to make the diagnosis. Why won't doctors go into family practice in rural areas?

I can't answer for everybody, but I'll tell you why *I* don't want to do that. I am too scared.

The doctor who is by himself out in the country has to be able to cope with anything. In today's training programs, you don't learn to do that, and the reforms to medical education are making the situation worse.

Where do they send you if you want to go into family practice today? To a rural clinic to see common problems like kids with runny noses.

I never saw a kid with a runny nose when I was an internal medicine resident in Dallas. Yet I felt perfectly capable of handling the first one I saw in my office.

A kid with a routine fracture is another story. I have never reduced a fracture and have only helped to apply one or two casts. This is a hands-on skill that is not properly learned from a book. This gap in my training is enough all by itself to keep me from going into solo practice in the country.

If I did want to go out in the country, I would want to do a rotating internship in a city like Chicago, New York, or Dallas. I would want to be in the place that *receives* the Air-Evac helicopter, not a place that sends one. I would want to learn how to set fractures from skilled orthopedists. I'd want to be at high-risk deliveries with excellent obstetricians. These people wouldn't be available once I got out in the country; I'd need to learn as much as possible from them during my training. I'd also want the opportunity to treat as many seriously sick patients as possible. I wouldn't expect to see too many exotic diagnoses once I'd established my country practice, but I'd sure want to be able to recognize the ones that did come to me.

I don't know whether it is possible to become a well-trained country doctor these days. And even if you were trained to be better than a glorified physician's assistant or nurse, you'd still be treated like one, until it came to a malpractice suit, when you'd probably be held to the same standard as a doctor from the Mayo Clinic.

It's not just the money. Country doctors also get no respect these days. But they do get sued. They also may get targeted by government quality assurance programs. For example, country doctors in Texas were far more likely to face sanctions proceedings by the Medicare Peer Review Organizations than were city doctors. The cost of compliance with increasingly complex government regulations devours a substantially higher percentage of their income. And the same government forces that make life difficult for a family doctor are destroying the rural hospitals that care for their patients.

If we want to have country doctors, this is the Orient prescription:

(1) Bring back the rotating internship. (2) Establish freedom zones in underserved areas, with exemptions from intrusive government regulations, including price controls. Country doctors can't collect outrageous fees anyway. (3) In malpractice litigation, hold physicians to a community standard, not a national standard; in other words, expect no more than a reasonable performance given the real circumstances.

If you are skeptical of the prescription, then try it out first on volunteers. Unlike the RVS, it doesn't have to be imposed on every doctor in the nation to "make it work."

Is the Market Value Fair to Doctors?

Having spent millions of dollars and generated millions of pages of computer output, we are left with the question of whether the RVS is fairer than the market.

Which is more likely to be fair: a price that people accept, even if they'd rather have a higher or lower one, or one that has to be forced upon them?

From a free market perspective, there is only one way to determine the worth of a physician's services to *him:* Ask him. And there is only one way to determine the worth of a service to a patient: Ask him.

Each physician knows what the rent is for his office. He knows how much he pays for supplies, liability insurance, trash collection, and utilities. He knows how much he needs to pay to attract competent office staff. He also knows how much work it is to take care of Mr. Evans, who is not exactly like the forty-five-year-old hypertensive described in a vignette constructed for a coding seminar. The number of complete data sets in his possession is one greater than the number available to any bureaucrat at HCFA, the AMA, or the Harvard School of Public Health. So why shouldn't he set his own fee?

I asked that question once in an editorial. I said that physicians were citizens, too, and ought to have the right to decide what to charge, just as hairdressers, plumbers, and other small businessmen did. They also had the right to include in their charges some allowance for inflation and compensation for spending four years in medical school and three or more years in residency. An irate response in the *Arizona Republic* took me severely to task. I quote it because it shows how well the public accepts the idea of slavery for physicians, which I will discuss in the next chapter.

"I had always assumed that the practice of medicine was mainly for the care and health of the population and was not to be compared with 'plumbers, hairdressers, and small businessmen.' " The writer is insulting plumbers, who are really more important to health than doctors, and the myriad small businessmen, including hairdressers, who care for various needs and desires of *people*, but let that pass. The writer was also irked by the cliché about inflation and long years of training. No one forced doctors to go to medical school, she (or he?) opined. Maybe it's unfair for bureaucrats to cut doctors' pay, she continued, but that's just tough: "Life is not fair." (Now there's a compassionate comment! Apply *that* one to the RVS.)

Another person wrote in response to the outrageous idea that physicians should be allowed to charge what they wish: "Although Ms. Orient has an M.D. after her name, she seems to lack a very important quality for a doctor—compassion." This was under a headline COLD-HEARTED.

You'd think I had proposed to extract a pound of flesh whenever a reasonable payment was not forthcoming—like the government does if you don't pay your taxes or if you make a mistake in complying with their regulations.

I do not think that physicians should be allowed to cheat or steal, or to force people to pay unreasonable charges, or to foreclose on their homes and cars. I also do not think that physicians have any right to prevent someone else from providing a service for less. I do think physicians should be allowed to decide for themselves what they're worth, instead of being forced to submit to the bureaucrats. Is it cold-hearted to oppose the use of force against someone who is himself behaving peaceably? Even if that someone volunteered to go to medical school?

Lots of people think so, although they generally don't express the thought as bluntly as the letter writer did.

Is the Market Value Fair to Patients?

Senator Max Baucus of Montana has said that people will do anything to obtain medical care when they or a loved one needs it.

They might even present their credit card as evidence that they will pay the bill. But is it fair that they should have to?

Some think that it is unfair that people should have to forgo anything else in order to obtain medical services. For one thing, the distribution of sickness seems unfair. Everybody has to eat, but not everyone has to have an operation. (Maybe *nobody* "has to" have an operation, as we discussed in the last chapter, but for the present let's assume we can define "medically necessary.")

Even if we define medical services as a right, some price has to be paid sometime in order to make those services available. It might be paid by "the government," which means the payment will come from the taxpayers and be routed through the tax collecting and tax disbursing agencies. The price to be paid will be determined through some political process, probably involving some negotiations with providers. Whoever else is involved, the patient who will actually receive the services is inevitably left out of the equation. Will the price paid be fair to him as well as to the taxpayers?

Societal calculations are generally based on the utilitarian principle of the "greatest good for the greatest number." So even if the planners do the calculations right, they are maximizing the benefit to *society*—the nameless, faceless masses—not to Mrs. J., who suffers from arthritis and hypertension. The pain, inconvenience, and fears of individuals can't be measured, but even if they could, they would have no noticeable impact on the analysis. Who cares about Mrs. J.'s painful hip when we have the cholesterol of our entire population to worry about?

Mrs. J. cares about her hip. Suppose that she is willing to spend her entire life savings on prompt surgery that might enable her to walk again? Should the government stop her from doing so because the price is thought to be unfair? Not only unfair to Mrs. J., but unfair to others who would also like to have the operation but don't have sufficient savings.

Should society force Mrs. J. (who happens to be a Medicare beneficiary) to do without surgery because the price is higher than we think she should be allowed to pay? Medicare does just that. The surgeon is *not allowed* to accept more than a certain amount, based on the RVS. The hospital is *not allowed* to charge more than the amount provided by Medicare for patients with the same diagnosis as Mrs. J. But if the allowed payment is unacceptably low, Mrs. J. will not be on the operating schedule. Shall we conscript the surgeon and the staff to do the procedure? And make them pay for the hip prosthesis, too? That's the subject of the next chapter.

The rationale for leaving the patients out of the equation is that medical care is just too complicated and too emotional.

It is true that medical care is complicated and emotional. But remember I have a vested interest in your thinking so; it makes my training so much more valuable. Nevertheless, I think that patients are capable of making rational judgments about their medical care and its price, particularly if allowed to avail themselves of the vast resources of our information society.

Patients, in my experience, are not stupid. They may have a low IQ. They may sometimes make perverse and wrong decisions. They may not be paying attention to their doctor because they are afraid or have other things on their mind. But regarding their own medical self-interest, they are usually capable of making as good a decision as anyone else (unless of course they are unconscious or demented or in a confusional state). It may be difficult to get through to them, but it is generally possible.

I have talked to a lot of patients. And to a lot of bureaucrats. I can always tell the difference. In one case, it is like talking to a brick wall.

It is true that there are times when a patient is at the mercy of the system, when price shopping is not possible. There are also times when your car breaks down one hundred miles from the nearest town in the middle of a blizzard. The nearest emergency room or the nearest mechanic may take advantage of you. I don't have an answer for those situations. I do know that the answer is *not* to destroy the entire economy: First, do no harm.

Every patient has a relative value scale, a scale of what is important to him. It may vary from day to day, as circumstances change. It will not be the same scale as anybody else's. It will require no surveys, no computers, and no Harvard economists. It has no one-size-fits-all conversion factor. There is no need for a committee meeting and months or years of delay to make adjustments in the scale. It is a natural phenomenon, and it works automatically and instantaneously.

There is one way and only one way to find out what a value is along that scale: *Ask the patient.* He can tell you how many hours of work he would trade for one hernia operation. Or how many nights on the town he would trade for an insurance policy. Or what proportion of her children's inheritance she would give for a slight chance of surviving another six months. If others come up with different answers than you would, do you think you should try to impose your values on them?

Matching the Relative Values

All doctors have a personal relative value scale, as do all patients. All of these individual scales are different. How can people ever come to an agreement, so that goods and services are traded fairly?

One method is that of central planning. Some authority sets up a Relative Value Scale, which is effectively absolute. The RVS doesn't fit anybody, and the authority imposes it on everybody in the name of fairness. It is fair in the sense that it is unfair to everybody and disagreeable besides.

Or there is the seemingly chaotic marketplace, in which one physician deals with one patient. They either come up with mutually agreeable conditions or they don't, and the patient goes elsewhere. (No, that doesn't apply to emergencies but most medical encounters really are *not* emergencies.)

At the farmers' market in Pittsburgh, there is rarely a need for a policeman or a complaint to the Better Business Bureau. My cousin Louis comes there with a truck full of vegetables. He goes home with money and an empty truck. It is very complicated—there are lots of different kinds and qualities of vegetables. But somehow Louis is able to figure how much to charge for the tomatoes and the squash without using a computer. His customers come with empty shopping bags and go home with something good for dinner. As if by magic, everything comes out even, although every individual at the market has a different relative value scale.

Well, that is a microcosm. There is also the Chicago commodities market, which assuredly does use computers. However, the computers do not set the prices; people in the pit do that by waving their arms and yelling at each other. Everything comes out even there, too, although there are also international relative value scales to cope with.

In all this apparent chaos, there is order. But William Hsiao's seemingly exact and neat Relative Value Scale is creating utter havoc, along with squadrons of medicops to enforce it.

Will central pricing by the RVS have the same result as central planning in other economies? Long lines, empty shelves, shoddy goods, heavy pollution, and prison terms for black marketeers? Is Dr. Hsiao and his mighty computer that much better than all his predecessors? Or are medical goods and services that much different from others?

How much are you willing to bet on the answer?

....

10

SERVICE, SERVITUDE, AND RELATIVE RIGHTS

....

If "society" tries to make doctors do what "society" wants, it will turn doctors into something that you don't want.

WHEN I first discovered that I was a superfluous woman, I thought it was unfair. Then I discovered that I had found an escape hatch from an intolerable bureaucratic system.

Next I became worried that I would soon be prevented from serving my patients under the Hippocratic ethic. Superfluous physicians (those who are independent of a managed care network or of some other contractual arrangement with a third party) may be excluded from practice—by insurmountable financial barriers if not by law.

Now I worry that some physicians may be defined as necessary and required to work as a public utility, even though their services are not worth enough on a Relative Value Scale to get them to work voluntarily.

Am I being an alarmist? I hope so. But why does the Selective Service have a plan to draft physicians (and other medical workers), both men and for the first time in history women, even though there is no general draft, if the president declares a "national emergency"?[1] What sort of emergency could we have that requires no conscripted firefighters, jet pilots, or ground troops, but might require conscripted forty-four-year-old female physicians, nurses, and psychologists?

If we are to enforce the right to have a physician, it will become necessary to abridge physicians' rights to liberty and property. As one of my former patients said, on being informed that my services, while available, were no longer covered under Medicare: "I paid my taxes. Now those doctors should *have to* take care of me." (She wanted a free refill of her medication.)

When asked whether her late husband, a barber, should have been required to give two-dollar haircuts to all comers who met government criteria, she replied: "That's different!"

In other words, barbers aren't doctors, not in the twentieth century. Doctors are a special case. They can be singled out for special treatments that do not apply to other citizens, such as barbers.

Equality under the law is obsolete.

Ensuring "Access"

Not all would-be reformers are as honest as a young woman who spoke on behalf of Citizen Action at a meeting sponsored by the League of Women Voters: "If Mohammed won't come to the mountain, you blow up the mountain and bring it piece by piece to Mohammed."

What mountain did she mean? In context, she meant the private sector, the free-enterprise economy, at least in medicine. That economy is a network of *voluntary* relationships, which need to be disrupted so that the economy can be placed under central control.

"We've got to get control of that health care system—*the whole thing*," declared Judith Feder, Ph.D., political scientist, former staff director of the Pepper Commission (a bipartisan congressional task force on health care reform), and member of President Clinton's transition team.[2]

The control is necessary because programs such as "periods of required practice in underserved areas," "stringent limitations on private profit in the health sector," rationing of expensive technology, and other methods of "ensuring access" are likely to provoke resistance.

As of 1993, many mechanisms that help establish central control have been accepted voluntarily. These were introduced gradually, and employed incentives rather than outright force, although the medical profession frequently hears the not-so-veiled threat: "If we don't do it to ourselves, then *they'll* do it to us." For example, Canadian physicians agreed to a government offer, which allowed the profession time to try to get more young doctors and specialists into outlying regions.

"If they are not successful in persuading some of their colleagues to leave major cities by Jan. 1, 1993, through a system of financial incentives, the government will *force* them out as envisaged in the original reform [emphasis added]."[3]

Incentives induce physicians to sign contracts to participate in Medicare. This means they agree to "take assignment"—take payment *directly* from the government at government-set rates—for *every* Medicare patient they treat, even the very wealthy. Medicare carriers are paid extra if they persuade more doctors to sign up.

The Medicare terminology of "participating" and "nonparticipating" is confusing to doctors and patients alike. Nonparticipating physicians never signed any agreement, but they still have to participate in all the regulations, fee schedules, and restrictions if their patients are to receive any of their Part B Medicare benefits. There is not yet a word for physicians whose services are not covered under the program. "Opted out" is a Canadian term that might serve, although Canadian patients of such physicians can still receive their benefits.

Patients who choose a nonparticipating physician receive fewer Medicare benefits. The fee schedules are deliberately designed that way. Medicare reimburses *patients* of nonparticipating physicians around 3 percent less than it pays the *doctors* who have signed a participation contract.

The advantages of nonparticipation have largely been abolished. Formerly, nonparticipating physicians could save on overhead because they were not required to file Medicare claims; patients could do this for themselves before September 1990. (The forms were a whole lot simpler back then.) Also, nonparticipating physicians can charge patients more, even though the government pays less. The government has now placed stringent limits on this "balance billing."

Balance billing must be distinguished from the copayment. Patients are supposed to be billed for the copayment, which is 20 percent of the Medicare-approved charge. If the doctor routinely waives the copayment, he may be accused of fraud or abuse. Amounts greater than the approved charge constitute balance billing.

Nonparticipating physicians endure many disadvantages, especially more hassles from bureaucrats. Their patients frequently receive letters that say the doctor overcharged or provided "unnecessary" services that did not meet "professionally recognized standards of care." The patients are told that they could save money by seeing a participating physician. Medicare publishes directories of participating physicians.

Nearly half of the nation's physicians have still refused to sign the participation contract.

If incentives don't work, then stronger medicine can be used. The federal government requires physicians to take assignment for patients covered under both Medicare and Medicaid. In Massachusetts, physicians who balance bill *any* Medicare patients may lose their license to practice. Many other states are requiring physicians to take assignment for specific groups of patients, based on "low income" (in Ohio, that means six times the poverty level or $39,720) or coverage by state insurance plans.

Physicians have brought a number of lawsuits against state governments because of such laws. So far, all have failed. It's a privilege, not a right, to have access to the means of earning a living at your chosen profession (that is, to have a state license to practice).

In Ohio, patients are planning to bring a lawsuit. From their viewpoint, the law forces all Medicare beneficiaries who earn up to $39,720 to become, in effect, wards of the state whenever they see a physician.

Is that language offensive? Some patients think the situation is offensive. They are adults who have, through a lifetime of thrift, provided a decent living for themselves in their retirement years. Yet they are told that they are not allowed to pay their doctor more than the government-set fee, even if the government-set fee is so low that physicians don't want to see them. They are presumed to be too stupid to figure out for themselves what they are willing to pay.

At first, it may seem very nice to have the government "protect" patients by dictating the terms of their treatment, down to the second decimal place on the bill. But the ultimate effect is that patients will lose control over the medical decisions that affect their lives.

Patients urgently need to understand this point: An attack on private doctors is ultimately an attack on private patients. They may applaud when a politician insults doctors with cheap shots at their BMWs. Have they heard what Congressman Pete Stark says about patients? He thinks patients are incapable of making choices for themselves. Either they consider themselves "invincible" (when feeling well) or they are "absolutely irrational, brain dead, sniveling, begging, and fantasizing ills and pains." Therefore, he wants the doctors, those evil avaricious doctors, to make all the decisions about what medical treatment is needed.

Obviously, these words are not quoted from a campaign speech. They were an answer to a question from a doctor at a $500-fee conference attended mostly by administrators of managed care plans. If you don't believe I am quoting him correctly, I have it on tape. The condescending tone is not adequately conveyed in writing.

If I am a patient, I don't want the government to be in charge of my medical care. When the government promises to "ensure access," my first question is access to *what?*

As a physician, I don't want to take government money.

WHY I DON'T WANT TO WORK FOR THE GOVERNMENT

No, it's not the size of the government paycheck. Some doctors *do* buy their second BMW with taxpayers' money.

The congressman doesn't get it. Many doctors sign the participation contract because they think they will make more money. And some of us have *not* signed the contract even though we would probably make more money if we did.

Medicare bureaucrats also don't seem to comprehend any motives other than money. When five Medicare patients and their private internist Dr. Lois Copeland sued the government in New Jersey, asking the court for a declaration of rights to contract privately (see chapter 8) without submitting a Medicare claim or collecting a dime from the government, HCFA assumed that the *only* reason the physician could possibly have was the desire to "overcharge," and the only reason the patients could possibly have was an "idiosyncratic, personal" one. Or maybe the patients were weak, stupid, suggestible, and unduly influenced by their physician. The judge asked whether they were certifiably insane.

Dr. Copeland's motive was a desire to serve her patients—say, to call on them at the nursing home when they asked her to—without having to deal with bureaucratic threats. She's willing to accept lower payment in return for freedom from fear.

Here are some of my idiosyncratic, personal reasons for opting out of Medicare. Additional reasons based on my experience as a civil servant are in the next chapter.

My bias against socialism began in grade school. Sometimes we had to work on projects in groups.

A collective group project is not the same as teamwork, in which everybody on the team pulls together, each doing his fair share of the task for which he is best qualified—and he has to *be* qualified, too, or else he doesn't make the team. On a team, there is esprit de corps, but there is also individuality. The quarterback and the fullback are each indispensable, but they are not interchangeable, and they are treated differently. Ditto for the surgeon, the anesthesiologist, and the scrub nurse.

In the collective group projects at school, there was no individual recognition, and the final grade, based on the cooperative effort, was the same for each member.

There was also very little team *work*. What usually happened was that the whole group fiddled around and wasted time during class, and I got stuck with doing most of the work by myself at home. Everybody got a good grade.

Years later, one of my classmates in that school told me about one of her group project ideas. I told her how much I had hated such things when we were kids.

"The intellectuals always hate it," she said.

So they do. But it has nothing to do with being intellectual, and everything to do with being used. Certain situations have the effect of taking advantage of the most conscientious workers. And who wants to be the horse on Orwell's *Animal Farm*?

Then there was Mr. Keith, my seventh grade math teacher. I still remember him discussing the issue of federal aid to education with my mother:

"If you take their money, they'll tell you how wide to make the doors." Was he ever right. I worked at the VA when they were tearing the whole place up to widen the doors to patient rooms, even though those doors had never been a problem. But they forgot about the door to the courtyard. The nurse in charge of bringing the stretcher to code arrest calls in the nursing home unit had to coax it out through the back door of the elevator.

And there's that letter hanging on the wall above my desk, along with an uncashed check. It used to be on the wall above my father's desk, but when he retired from contracting, he gave it to me.

The letter, dated February 4, 1974, reads as follows:

Dear Bill:

According to your government, the powers that be have decided that we have exceeded our allowable profits in 1972 at the rate of 1/13 of 1%. [That's one-thirteenth of 1 percent, or in decimal fractions 0.000769.]

Consequently, we have consented, under a Voluntary Compliance Agreement, to reimburse a total of $789.00, the amount involved, to our 1972 Contractors. We have endeavored to prorate this amount as equitably as possible.

May we take this opportunity to mention that although we have shown a net loss for the fiscal year 1973, it does not have any bearing on the above decision.

Enclosed herewith please find a check to cover the amount due you ($17.90).

Russ of Russ Plumbing had made a fatal mistake. He was low bidder on a government job. He performed the work competently in a timely manner and was paid the agreed-upon amount. Later, the government decided that the amount was too much. After shutting down his business for months while an audit was conducted, the government required Russ to make refunds to other, private contractors as well.

This episode was the death of Russ Plumbing, although the man himself lived for many years on a disability pension.

If you take their money, they can destroy you.

As the late Robert S. Jaggard, M.D., a country doctor from Oelwein, Iowa, explained, when you put out your hand to take the money, you expose your wrist, and that's when they put on the chains. They may be golden handcuffs, but they still have chains. I will now describe some of the chains the government is trying to forge.

ARE DOCTORS A PUBLIC UTILITY?

When Medicare was first initiated, Wilbur Cohen, secretary of Health, Education, and Welfare under President Johnson, reportedly said that the government was very worried that physicians and hospitals would decline to treat the elderly. When this worry turned out to be unfounded, officials breathed a great sigh of relief. The physicians' philosophical objection to socialized medicine (of which Medicare is an example) was not strong enough to overcome their love of money. They liked being paid for services they formerly *gave* without payment.

But what if providers (as the government and most insurers now call physicians) become reluctant to supply services on the government's terms? Do they, unlike Russ, *have* to take a government job now that the profession has been bought and paid for?

The "Antidumping" Law

Under federal "antidumping" legislation, physicians and hospitals are forced to treat any patient with an emergency condition if the hospital has an emergency room and the physician is on call. This was a response to the alleged tendency of private hospitals to do a "wallet biopsy" (to see if the patient had insurance) and "dump" uninsured patients on the county hospital, whether or not the patient might be harmed by a delay in treatment.

It is morally outrageous to delay treatment of a seriously ill or injured patient in order to determine his insurance coverage—or to deny lifesaving treatment if there is no insurance. I doubt that it actually happens very often in hospital emergency rooms, at least in genuine emergencies, as opposed to states of urgent desire for medical attention. What does happen with increasing frequency is that care is delayed while the hospital tries to jump the barriers erected by managed care plans. Also, managed care doctors have incentives to deny care, as we shall see, and they do respond to those incentives. The government wants *more* managed care, not less!

Today people have reason to fear the hospital collectors (who come on the scene *after* the treatment) more than they fear refusal of care. It is said that some public hospitals own a lot of low-cost housing because they took the homes of patients who didn't pay their bills. I don't know whether it is true, but even a rumor to this effect can inspire a lot of fear.

I think that the antidumping laws are mostly motivated by a desire of public hospitals to reduce their bad debt by foisting it onto the private hospitals. It's politically more feasible than raising taxes. And it sounds so morally righteous.

I arrived at this conclusion because I used to work at one such hospital. And there are data to support my opinion.[4]

Parkland Memorial Hospital in Dallas, a leading advocate of anti-dumping legislation, undertook a two-year study of interhospital transfers (which they call dumping). They found that 28 percent of the transfers were unexpected, and 30 patients (1.6 percent of 1,897) reached Parkland in an unstable condition, 17 from facilities that had the equipment and staff to stabilize them. This means that 13 patients arrived from facilities that were not capable of providing any assistance other than a quick dispatch to Parkland. As I interpret the figures, they mean that Parkland, in two years, received 17 transfers that might have avoidably endangered the patients, out of thousands of emergency room admissions.

Referring hospitals make errors of another type as well. Receiving hospitals—such as Parkland or D.C. General—have determined that about 38 percent of patients sent to them do not need admission after all. Because treatment is not necessary—by Parkland's very stringent definition—referring the patient back to Tulia, Texas, population 5,000, or for that matter to the Stemmons Freeway does *not* constitute dumping. When I was a resident at Parkland, interns used to say "put a rock at the front door." When I was medical admitting resident or "pit boss," I had a bad reputation for being a "sieve" known as the Orient Express. Some of the other residents hated me for it, and I responded to this peer group pressure by discharging some patients that I really should have admitted. I hope they did all right anyway, but I'll never know.

Of course, it doesn't matter to Congress how many, or if any, patients are injured by being dumped—by the private hospitals, I mean. The politicians and bureaucrats are riding on their white horse to the rescue. *They* know what an emergency is, even if hospitals in rural Texas often can't tell. To make sure that no episode remains undetected, the Department of Health and Human Services requires the receiving hospital to report suspected dumping within seventy-two hours, under pain of termination of the hospital's Medicare provider agreement. In other words, the hospital that *did* treat the patient also gets punished for not snitching on the one that *didn't* treat the patient, or for not snitching soon enough.

Congressional good intentions notwithstanding, their remedy has side effects. Congress all too often proposes to cut the patient's leg off at the hip because there might be a cancer in the big toe.

Small hospitals and physicians are often in a dilemma. Should they do the best they can for a seriously ill or injured patient, even if their facilities are very limited? Or should they transfer him to a referral center that has a more highly skilled staff and more advanced technology? The first choice may mean a huge bad debt plus a malpractice suit for a less-than-optimal result. The second choice could result in an enormous fine and exclusion from Medicare. Medicare could even stop payment for services already rendered. In other words, if federal bureaucrats disagree with the judgment of the transferring physician, or declare that the rationale for the transfer was not documented properly even if it was reasonable, the hospital could face bankruptcy.

Here is a real case. A Texas physician, Dr. Michael Burditt, transferred a woman in active labor to a hospital more than 150 miles away. The baby was born in the ambulance. According to Dr. Burditt, the facilities of a referral center were needed for both mother and child. The mother's blood pressure was extremely high, and the baby was small. The physician limits his practice to low-risk obstetrics and felt that he was not well qualified to take care of these patients.

Did the benefits of transfer exceed the risk? This is always a judgment call. Unfortunately, labor does sometimes progress faster than a physician expects, and transfers more slowly. This time, Dr. Burditt calculated wrong. But given the information he had at the time, either decision might have been wrong.

The government wasn't sympathetic. For one thing, an important piece of documentation was missing. (They care less about whether the documentation is accurate than about whether it is there.) And while physicians may limit their private practice to low-risk patients, they are not permitted to refuse high-risk patients presenting to the emergency rooms of hospitals that accept Medicare funds (probably all hospitals today, except the VA).

Dr. Burditt lost his case on appeal and is required to pay a $20,000 fine.

Maybe you don't feel sorry for Dr. Burditt because you think he is too rich anyway. I *do* sympathize, because I would have to gross more than $50,000 before taxes and overhead to pay a $20,000 fine, and to earn $50,000 would require about 1,666 office visits at $30 each (20 visits per day for 83 days), assuming that every patient paid. And during those 1,666 visits, I could make some mistake that could easily cost more than $50,000.

Knowing what happened to Dr. Burditt, there is *no way* that I would accept a job in an emergency room in rural Texas. But it doesn't matter because eventually there might not *be* any emergency rooms in rural Texas. The patients will all have to go many miles to Parkland, which may park them in a corner for hours or discharge them but will not dump them because public hospitals don't dump. (Despite all that I have said, I still think that if you are in a serious accident and near death, you should gasp to the ambulance driver "Take me to Parkland" because they save more "elevator cases" there than at any other hospital in the Dallas–Fort Worth area or maybe even in Texas. An elevator case is one that goes straight upstairs to the operating room.)

The ultimate effect of antidumping legislation could be the opposite of the legislators' good intentions, a *decrease* in medical services available to the poor. Congress hasn't found a way of forcing a hospital into existence (or back into existence after it closes) or forcing physicians to work in a particular location. The second challenge, of course, is easier.

Enforcing Other Professional Obligations

Besides lack of payment, other factors make physicians reluctant to do certain types of work. Many physicians, for example, do not wish to treat patients who have AIDS. They may fear infection. They may dislike homosexuals and drug abusers. They may lack the knowledge required to offer optimal treatment for an extremely complex condition.

Physicians are not supposed to allow concern for their own welfare or that of their families to interfere with their treatment of the sick. Nevertheless, some have avoided treating patients afflicted with plague, leprosy, tuberculosis, criminal insanity, sociopathy, and so forth. While it may have been condemned, this behavior generally did not lead to exclusion from the profession. Physicians may have been exhorted but not compelled to serve (except in the military).

Many physicians dislike certain kinds of patients. (I am not supposed to say this because physicians are supposed to be perfect humanitarians, and you don't want to hear it, but it is true all the same.) Some go into pediatrics because they don't like old people. Some choose internal medicine because they can't stand screaming babies. Some choose nonpatient-care specialties such as anesthesia, radiology, and pathology or better still administrative medicine because they don't like patients at all.

Certain personal preferences may be socially acceptable or at least tolerable, but others are not. And a person suspected of harboring one of those intolerable attitudes may be presumed guilty. We have "thought crimes" in post-1984 America.

Physicians have also avoided procedures with which they just don't feel comfortable. Internists may decline to treat a heart attack patient with drugs that dissolve blood clots because they have limited experience with these drugs and fear complications. Given the slightest hint of difficulty, the family physician may immediately try to refer a woman in labor to an obstetrician. A physician who is not a neurosurgeon may refuse point-blank to drill a hole in a patient's head even if he is the only physician available and the patient will surely die if the blood compressing his brain is not quickly removed. This has happened, and the patient did die, according to the neurosurgeon who was trying to help the attending physician by telephone. This neurosurgeon brought a cow's scapula and a brace and bit to a conference at the VA, and all the doctors and nurses on my ambulatory care service practiced drilling holes in bone.

Usually, specialists are more than happy to take over these procedures. In fact, they often try to keep family physicians out of the operating room and the delivery room and internists out of the intensive care unit. They may structure the "credentialing" procedure to be sure that family physicians have no opportunity to learn and practice more skills.

AIDS, however, is different. The family doctor who doesn't feel comfortable with *Pneumocystis carinii* pneumonia or *Mycobacterium kansasii* skin infections or disseminated *Coccidioides immitis* or diarrhea due to *Cryptospiridia* is supposed to sign up for continuing medical education, even if he only expects to see a few cases in his lifetime and has no hope of earning a decent fee from their treatment. The doctor doesn't have to have the slightest interest in weird microorganisms that seldom affect patients who don't have AIDS. He is forced to learn about them anyway. On the other hand, he is not required to learn more useful techniques to treat more common conditions. He does not have to learn how to read an echocardiogram or place a catheter into the pulmonary artery to monitor heart function. Patients who would benefit from these procedures can be—or must be—referred to specialists who charge a substantial fee.

Actually, we have lectures on AIDS quite often at our Tuesday noon conference, and attendance is good. Most doctors really are interested in learning about it, and from the questions they ask, I gather they are treating patients without any government-imposed quota.

Serving the Underserved

The progression has been like this: *If* doctors choose to treat Medicare beneficiaries, then they must do so on government terms, including government-set fees.

If doctors choose to practice in a hospital that has a Medicare contract (essentially, any hospital), then they must accept all patients who show up for emergency treatment while they are on call.

If doctors choose to practice at all, they are professionally obligated to serve patients with certain conditions, although this is not yet a matter of law.

The next step might be like this: *If* a person chooses to obtain a medical education, and *if* there is a patient who needs and is eligible for medical treatment, then the physician is obligated to serve him within the constraints set by society and possibly in violation of his own conscience.

Professor of Medicine David E. Rogers, past president of the Robert Wood Johnson Foundation, describes it this way:

> I have a simplistic view of what we, as doctors, should do. As we move toward a doctor surplus, we should view it as unconscionable that any American in need of care should go without it. That we might trade extra physician capacity for more leisure time or other business endeavors rather than using our expensive skills to care for those in need should be totally unacceptable to us.[5]

What does he mean by that? Is it unconscionable for me to take a weekend off to visit some friends, when there are surely some patients waiting to be served in a nearby clinic? Surely he doesn't mean that doctors should be forced to work until they drop. Or that *every* hour spent listening to music is an hour stolen from a needy patient. No, it's "more" leisure time that he deplores. *Some* amount is apparently okay.

What amount? And who decides?

It's all a question of relative values—always somebody else's relative values—about which, more later.

Do Doctors' Obligations Differ from Involuntary Servitude?

When faced with increasingly oppressive laws and regulations, especially under the Medicare and Medicaid programs, doctors often feel that they are being enslaved. Of course, there has not been an auction, a bill of sale, or literal chains. There is an irrefutable answer:

"You don't have to treat those patients, Doctor."

He is quite right. Doctors do have a choice. They need not treat an emergency patient. They can choose to risk a fine of $20,000 or more for each one they refuse. Or they can stay out of the emergency room, refusing to treat *all* of them.

Doctors do not have to treat Medicare patients. General American Life, the Medicare carrier for St. Louis, explains the alternative: The physician may "surrender his or her license or certificate (in those instances where such a document is required to practice)." Actually, the carriers are wrong. In 1993, doctors can treat Medicare patients outside the program; they just can't accept a dime of government money if they do. But physicians who have become utterly dependent upon Medicare payments interpret the carriers' statements to mean: "You don't have to practice medicine, Doctor. You can do something else instead."

Physicians have a Hobson's choice. To understand its nature, let's apply it to lawyers.

Criminal defendants have a right to a lawyer, but not to the lawyer of their choice, and not necessarily at public expense. If they are indigent, the court will appoint a lawyer: the public defender. The reputation of public defenders is not always the best. Criminal suspects who can afford to pay a lawyer would generally prefer to do so, even if the means test were eliminated.

This situation is not fair. Why should wealthy criminals be able to hire better lawyers than indigent criminals can, thereby improving their chances of keeping their liberty, their property, and perhaps even their lives?

The obvious solution is to require all lawyers to take their turn as public defender, at public defender's pay, regardless of their abilities or interests or the value of their services to other, paying clients. And, of course, all criminal defendants should be required to accept a public defender—the one who happened to be assigned to them.

Lawyers would continue to have a choice. They could relinquish their license to practice.

Would lawyers accept such a choice?

And what about the lawyers' clients?

The United States is supposed to be a society in which all persons are equal under the law, whether they be doctors, lawyers, farmers, or plumbers. It is not supposed to be an *Animal Farm* society, in which some animals (the pigs) are more equal than others. Therefore, it would not be fair to subject doctors and lawyers to different laws simply because of their occupation. However, the lawyers can think of another rationale for the distinction, which would make it perfectly fair.

The rationale is this: Doctors voluntarily *chose* their status, and furthermore it is an elevated, privileged status. (Never mind that privileges are just as unconstitutional as involuntary servitude.) Either they volunteered implicitly by going to medical school, or they did so explicitly by swearing one of the non-Hippocratic oaths or even more explicitly by signing a participation agreement with Medicare.

Suppose that the majority vote determines that physicians have volunteered for the duty of serving under whatever conditions society dictates—after democratically receiving their "input," of course.

Then suppose that some physicians disagree—in sufficient numbers that they cannot be ignored. To guarantee access to their services, society might have to use force.

Would that be involuntary servitude? And if so, would it be justified?

One rationalization for early American slavery was economic necessity. The cotton crop had to be picked, or the planter would suffer.

We don't accept that rationalization today. But medical services are sometimes considered necessary in a higher sort of way. Plantation owners may have felt a need and desire for economic success in their chosen endeavor of producing cotton, but they did not have a right to achieve it, especially not by infringing on the liberty of others. They didn't even have the right to conscript able-bodied men to work for them for a few hours during the harvest, much less to own them entirely. Patients, on the other hand, are said to have the right to certain medical services as a universal human rights, not a mere economic, necessity. They didn't choose to become patients.

RELATIVE RIGHTS

In early America, free men had absolute rights that could not be legally infringed upon unless a person had forfeited his rights by violating the rights of others or had failed to pay his taxes, which are absolute both then and now. Rights were defined in negative terms, "thou shalt nots."

Now we have introduced positive economic (entitlement) rights. These are by nature relative rights. In effect, they give some citizens a claim on a portion of the liberty and property of others, in the interest of redistributing goods.

For example, when does a physician owe a service to a patient, and when does a patient owe a fee to the physician? Must a physician give service without charge to those who are unable to pay? And what does "unable" mean? If the patient is able to buy cigarettes, alcohol, or illegal drugs, is he able to spend at least that same amount on medical expenses? Should he have to forgo a night's entertainment to pay the doctor? Should he have to work an extra shift as soon as he recovers in order to pay the doctor? Perhaps it is unfair to expect patients to give up any of life's small luxuries (including leisure time) in order to pay the physician, since "health" is supposed to be a right, and it is not fair that anyone should be sick.

We must remember that physicians have been granted a privilege by the state—a license, a legal monopoly to practice medicine. Do they not owe society something in return? In my opinion, the answer is to forgo the privilege of a monopoly, but that's another subject.

Just what does the doctor owe? At some point does the doctor himself become disadvantaged? Should he be able to ask people who are richer than he is for payment, even if some of those are teachers or bus drivers? What if he deliberately makes himself poorer by cutting back on his hours of work? Should that even be allowed? Today, Medicare "volume performance standards" have been introduced to prevent physicians from earning too much more by working too much. They could just as well be applied to physicians who work too little as those who work too much.

The calculus of relative justice becomes infinitely complex. I could continue, but surely the reader is already tired. Eventually, the most patient reader will surely say: Stop it, you're being ridiculous.

Precisely. Q.E.D.

When a premise leads to an absurdity, there are two ways out. One, throw out the premise because by the indirect method you have proved its opposite. (The basic premise is the right to a physician's services.)

Two, invoke a deus ex machina, a commission of Harvard economists in partnership with the Health Care Financing Administration to figure it all out on a higher plane. They will simply remove the individual patient and physician from the equation altogether and set the answer by decree, probably after obtaining input from supposedly representative patients and physicians. They will have to have absolute power to enforce their relative values.

Do Patients Want the Guaranteed-Access Doctor?

Patients may think that they want guaranteed access to a physician who will do exactly what they demand, at the moment they demand it, without cost or obligation on their part. Such a physician would, in effect, be their slave. Such a wish cannot and will not be granted. Not even if we repeal the Thirteenth Amendment to the U.S. Constitution.

A slave physician is a contradiction in terms, at least if one means a Hippocratic physician. Slaves follow their master's orders. Hippocratic physicians act according to the best of their knowledge and judgment. A physician can be turned into a slave, but if he is, he will no longer be a physician.

Slaves tend to resent their masters and to rebel in every possible way, unless they develop a plantation mentality, as in the last paragraph of Orwell's 1984: "Two gin-scented tears trickled down the sides of his nose. But it was all right, everything was all right, the struggle was finished. He had won victory over himself. He loved Big Brother."

You don't want to have your life in the hands of a slave. Nor in the hands of somebody who feels as if he has been enslaved (or maybe just robbed), even or especially if you yourself are convinced that he is a fool for feeling that way. You want someone who truly wants to serve you, and not someone who may have been psychologically bullied into *saying* he wants to serve you.

But as I said, literal slavery is not what we're considering here. As to the surreal Orwellian fantasy, do finish the book before dismissing that as pure paranoia. If we turn medicine into a public utility, physicians will be civil servants, not slaves—as in other nations that have national health insurance. Civil servants who want to keep their job. Remember, the patients are *not* their employer. To keep their job, civil servants have to follow the rules and regulations, but they do not necessarily have to help the people they purportedly serve. In fact, they may not be *able* both to help the people and follow the rules.

Experience has shown that governments do not enslave physicians to provide universal access. They don't need to because they don't actually guarantee universal access either; they only pretend to do so. More about that in the next chapter.

For now, I would just like to say that while it is impossible to turn physicians into slaves, it is relatively easy to turn most of them into civil servants and to make them like it, too. Having doctors be civil servants has a lot of advantages.

On a farm that I like to visit, there lives an animal that is simply called The Bull. He is about 2,000 pounds of pure orneriness. The Bull is not evil or malicious, just ill-tempered.

The Bull does whatever he wants. The boys who look after him have learned that it is very foolish to provoke him. It is best to leave him alone. If they inadvertently make him angry, there is only one thing to do: run.

The Bull's mind works slowly, and his massive body has a lot of inertia. That means that if you anger him, you have a head start. You need it because once The Bull is in motion, he can run faster than you, and he can't easily stop either.

There is a certain way to enrage The Bull: slaughter one of his cows. He'll remember that for a long time, probably forever.

It would be easy to solve the problem of The Bull. In an instant, he could be turned into a steer. Steers are placid. They turn grass into hamburger with a minimum of fuss.

Actually, it wouldn't be all that easy to do the procedure now—it should have been done when he was young to prevent the problem in the first place.

In Constantinople, the civil servants were eunuchs. Boys were turned into eunuchs for a reason, and in Byzantium it was not so that they could sing soprano in the papal choir.

On the farm, The Bull is not in any danger—not yet. Not as long as he does his job of defending and increasing the size of the herd. That is something the steers cannot do.

Before we neutralize all the troublemaking doctors, turning them into agreeable civil servants, let's just stop and think whether there are any jobs we still need a doctor to do. An aggressive, independent, recalcitrant, forceful doctor. A doctor whose loyalty is to his patients.

11

SHOULD WE IMPORT A
SOCIALIZED "HEALTH CARE SYSTEM"?

Other countries declare a right to health care, and their people can go to the doctor all the time, but the doctor can't do very much. Access for all means access to nothing.

NATIONAL HEALTH INSURANCE is something they have in every developed country outside of South Africa and the United States of America. Shouldn't we have it here, too?

I have seen this statement about the United States and South Africa in countless articles. Every mother has heard a more general form of the argument: "I want some of what Susie's got."

It doesn't matter very much what the coveted object is. If found lying on the ground, it might be ignored. Susie might actually have gotten *stuck* with it. The attractive feature is that one child has it, and the other one doesn't.

Let's look at the results of the great experiments with medical care—with the same skepticism we use for scientific experiments, keeping in mind that experimenters have been known to paint the mice. One famous scientific fraud purported to show that white mice could be induced to accept a skin graft from black mice. The method didn't work, and the mice rejected the grafts. The experimenter needed a paper, and positive results are much more publishable than negative ones. So he painted the mice. Scientists also have been known to bury inconvenient data in the filing cabinet or to obliterate it from computer tapes.

Most proponents of national health insurance point to a paradise elsewhere. When the flaws in that system become apparent, they find one that is less well known. The British system is seldom mentioned now. The Canadian system has been favored recently, but Canadian television and newspapers cross the border. Since Canadian complaints of a looming crisis have become more widely known, there has been less emphasis on Canada and more on Germany.

We will look at some of these examples. But if you really want to know how national health insurance would work, you probably don't even have to leave town. Just pay a visit to your local Veterans Administration hospital. You can see government medicine in action.

THE HOMETOWN MODEL

The case of Mr. R. came up at a VA committee meeting. His chart was exemplary: a classic example of VA medicine.

Mr. R. first presented himself to the unscheduled clinic with a skin lesion on his penis. The chart had a careful description of the complaint, the lesion itself, the doctor's impression, and the plan for diagnostic tests and follow-up. The doctor suspected that the lesion was a syphilitic chancre, the sore that announces primary syphilis. The diagnostic tests showed that he was correct, as did the subsequent course of the disease.

Sometime later, the patient came to the VA again. His original sore had gone away (the usual outcome for syphilitic chancres) without treatment. This time, he had a rash on the palms of his hands. Again, the physician described the rash accurately, recorded his impression of secondary syphilis, and documented a referral to the dermatology clinic.

The patient was seen several times at the VA by several different physicians, sometimes for different problems, but each physician had duly noted the history and documented the plans for continuing follow-up. But at some point, the patient was lost to follow-up. It might have been on the way to the dermatology clinic. It usually takes months to get an appointment there, and by then the rash would surely have disappeared on its own.

The next known contact with the patient was made at the county jail by the public health officer. A baby was born with the stigmata of congenital syphilis, and the public health officer tracked down the baby's father.

Everybody at the VA had done their job. The documentation—the main product of the VA hospital or of any bureaucracy—was perfect, a textbook description of the patient's disease, recorded in the accepted format. The patient had received referrals to the proper clinics. My memory is fuzzy, but as I recall he had kept at least one of his appointments (unusual for a patient like this).

Nobody had given Mr. R. a shot of penicillin.

That was all he needed. One shot of penicillin. He didn't really *need* a note in the chart, or a darkfield examination of scrapings of the lesion, or an appointment to the dermatology clinic. If the first person to see the chancre had immediately ordered up 2.4 million units of benzathine penicillin, the skin rash would never have appeared. A positive diagnostic test would have been nice to have, but by the time it was reported the patient might have already infected several other people. For lack of that shot, at least one baby was scarred for life. And had it not been for an aggressive public health officer, the patient himself might have eventually developed dementia, insanity, and damaged joints.

Doctors at the VA do know how to treat syphilis. If you gave them a multiple-choice test, they would probably get the answers right. It's just that the patient had shown up at the wrong time or in the wrong department. Giving shots of penicillin was not in the job description of the people who had seen him.

There are some good doctors who work at the VA (also some mediocre ones, and some who are very questionable). But even the best of them are hampered by the bureaucratic system. The main thing the system produces is paperwork. Every desk in a clinic examining room has a file drawer completely filled with one item: forms. All different kinds and colors of forms.

The system is choked by work that doesn't really need to be done, by people who don't need to be there, by rules, regulations, procedures, committees, and forms. The only way to take proper care of a patient, at least an outpatient, is to defy the rules. There is never an appointment available soon enough in the right clinic. If the doctor really cares, he personally has to accompany the patient through the jungle with a machete. One gets tired of it. (One can also get fired for it.) The whole system is geared toward documentation, not action.

For those idealists who think I should've fought to *change* the rules instead of slipping needy patients in through the cracks, read about Don Quixote tilting with windmills, along with the rest of this chapter. The rules are made in that surrealistic city that arose from a malarial swamp on the Potomac. If you think Washington, D.C., is connected with reality, try to find a hardware store there.

One of the reasons for all the rules and regulations is a futile attempt to prevent the abuses that the system invites. The VA was never designed to provide lifelong medical care to every person who ever served in the military. It was supposed to care for veterans who were injured in the course of duty. That's why I always felt that the VA was a constitutional function of the government and a legitimate use of taxpayer dollars. But seldom did I have the opportunity to help an old soldier who had lost a limb or become paraplegic or suffered a burn or some other trauma. The place was swamped with able-bodied persons (mostly men) with sniffles, a chronic stomachache, anxiety, alcoholism, or generalized inability to cope with the world. Whatever the cause of the problems, it probably was not army life or an enemy weapon. Many of the patients had never even seen the enemy.

How could the VA cope with the onslaught of people who manifested the universal human tendency to accept a free lunch? (This tendency is not restricted to the *patients* at the VA, by the way.) I thought the VA should have simply said no. Right at the front door. "Disabled veterans only." All others should have been sent straight to a private facility if they could afford it or to the county clinic if they couldn't. It would have saved the ineligible patients, not to mention the eligible ones, endless waiting and irritation. But this honest approach was not politically feasible. The politicians and administrators didn't want to take any heat. They wanted to pretend to care for all, even though they couldn't. They figured out how to get the doctors to be the bad guys.

The administrators developed a rule. All veterans were eligible for "needed" inpatient care for acute emergencies, or for outpatient care that was needed to prevent "imminent" hospitalization. That may sound simple, but it was an infinitely elastic definition, a subject for discussion at many prolonged, inconclusive meetings.

I may have thought that I was at the VA to teach students and residents, to take care of patients, and to do a little clinical research. But the real reason the government was writing me a paycheck for

$50,000 a year was to enforce that rule. I might have been called a provider, but my function was to deny or to do the bare minimum, which was generally easier than delivering an outright denial and not much more expensive.

The schizophrenic nature of my position ultimately proved intolerable. I escaped from my VA job, but the essence of the VA system is following me. The private sector equivalents of the VA ambulatory care staff physicians are called gatekeepers by managed care plans. And Medicare doctors are more and more like VA doctors except that they have to pay all their own expenses.

The most tragic thing about the VA is the shabby treatment received by disabled veterans, who tend to get lost in the shuffle. The money poured into the VA could be spent on developing better prostheses, better surgical techniques, better treatments for tropical diseases. Instead, a lot of it gets poured into the salaries of people who deny or limit medical care: my successors and the clerical workers who support them.

CALL IT SOCIALIZED MEDICINE

According to Webster, socialized medicine is "complete medical care, made available through public funds, for all the people in a community, district, or nation." That is what they have in all those developed countries except for the United States and South Africa.

Medicare is socialized medicine if "community" is taken to mean a defined group of persons, such as all those over the age of sixty-five and those with qualifying disabilities. Beneficiaries do pay a premium for Part B, but the cost is heavily subsidized by public funds. Working people pay about 75 percent of the cost of Part B insurance. They are not the beneficiaries of that insurance. They hope that they will someday receive medical care paid for by the *next* generation of workers, if Medicare lasts that long (an increasingly dubious proposition).

Socialized medicine was the high school debate topic when I was a senior, in 1964. It is a major political issue in the 1990s, although its proponents don't like to use the S word, which reminds people of socialized agriculture (collective farms) and the resulting disastrous famines and chronic shortages.

National health insurance is a Newspeak term, which sounds like something that has traditionally been considered a prudent investment. (*Single-payor system* is another version.)

National health insurance is indeed nationalized—the opposite of "privatized." The rest of the world is now trying to privatize its nationalized industries—not an easy or altogether peaceful process. It might not even work because some of the industries, especially in Eastern Europe, may have been damaged beyond repair.

However, national health insurance is *not insurance,* and it does not buy health, which is not available for sale at any price.

Insurance is a method of sharing the risk of a catastrophe. It is not a comprehensive method of paying for things you need or want, such as food, shelter, transportation, or routine medical care, except to restore something that has been lost. You don't expect your car insurance to provide all your transportation needs or to pay for preventive maintenance on your car. And you couldn't afford it if it did.

Furthermore, you don't expect State Farm to fix your fender. It is an insurance company, not a body shop. The body shop fixes the car, you pay the bill, and then the insurance company reimburses you (not the repairman) for whatever portion of the cost that it has contracted to cover.

Socialized medicine, along with many private plans that call themselves insurance, is a payment mechanism for medical services, often combined with a method for actually providing those services. Physicians and other medical personnel may be directly employed by the government or by the "plan," for example, by the VA or the British National Health Service or "Group Health of Yourtown." Or they may seem to be in private practice, even though all their payment comes from the government, as in Canada. This arrangement is called a monopsony, for a single buyer, compared with a monopoly, in which there is a single seller.

People might have second thoughts about putting an insurance company executive in charge of their auto repair shop. How about having politicians and politically appointed bureaucrats in charge of their hospitals and clinics? An insurance executive is just as well qualified in mechanics as politicians are in medicine.

Although socialized medicine is sold by appealing to people's fears of serious illness, the system in operation ends up being inundated by people in search of checkups or a prescription for cough syrup. There is supposed to be easy access to a doctor. What this really means is easy access to a spot on the assembly line. The doctors end up having to see huge numbers of patients every day, spending an average of just a few minutes with each, including time spent completing paperwork.

Today, American patients complain when they get short shrift from the doctor, even if they have a condition that really does take just a few minutes. It could be that they are most unhappy about the wait and the bill. British and Canadian patients are reportedly well satisfied, at least if they are not very sick.

Socialized medicine has always been much more popular than socialism in other areas of the economy—farming, for example. The main reason is that medicine is not nearly as important as food. The human race had an extremely precarious existence before the development of agriculture, but thrived for millennia without the benefits of modern medicine. Everyone suffers when there is a famine, except possibly the elite. Only sick people suffer when there is a shortage of medical care. Note that I said *medical care*, not public health measures such as immunizations to prevent epidemics. And the influential people who could change the system are not obliged to live under it. Margaret Thatcher goes to a private hospital when she needs surgery. Senator Kennedy does not have to sit in the waiting room of an HMO. Socialized medicine, in the view of the elite, is for the masses— the dogs.

Another reason is that people are much more knowledgeable about food. They know the difference between rotten cabbage and steak. They may *not* know the difference between the capabilities of the local GP and the university medical center. They might believe that kidney failure dooms one to death at age fifty-five (or whatever the politically determined cutoff is), unless someone tells them that dialysis works perfectly well in older people, too. If the doctor is obliged by the system to tell them they can't have dialysis, he generally does not wish to tell them it would give them years of productive life. Patients may not know about the latest drug that could save their lives if only the government would spend money to buy it for them. The main thing they will notice is whether or not they can go to see the doctor—some kind of doctor.

This lack of knowledge is not inevitable. It may be partly the legacy of generations of socialized medicine. An American neurosurgeon who worked for some years in Britain said that British patients seldom asked a question, but Americans were different. An American patient may on one day learn the term *cerebral arteriovenous malformation* and the next day ask the surgeon if he is going to use a laser to fix it.

Socialized medicine is based on the same set of assumptions as socialized agriculture. It's supposed to take from each according to his ability and to give to each according to his needs. Management by the state is supposed to be both fair and efficient.

The theory sounds eminently humane and is very familiar to religious people, who believe that God will provide for our needs and expect us to perform on the basis of our abilities. From those to whom much has been given, much is expected.

But the theory is a disaster when implemented by anyone who is not God on this side of Eden. There are two problems: inadequate information about needs and abilities, and human nature. Under socialized systems, needs multiply and means diminish. People try to evade the system—they have to in order to survive—and the only way to stop them is by using force.

The socialization of agriculture exacted a heavy price: "To make an omelet, you first have to break some eggs." "Breaking some eggs" meant starving some 11 million people to death in the Ukraine. And the "omelet" meant low, state-controlled prices for nonexistent or shoddy goods, after hours of standing in long lines or, alternately, extortionate prices on the black market. The price for socialized medicine may not be as high.

The perceptive reader will surely observe that I am making an assumption: that medical goods and services are governed by the same laws of economics as food, shelter, transportation, and other things that meet human needs. That goes contrary to the popular wisdom that medical services are *just different*. Because medicine is supposed to be different, people assert that a free market will not work in medicine and that socialism will.

But let's leave theory aside and look at some specific results.

THE BRITISH MODEL

If we had to have socialized medicine, the British model is the one I would choose, for several reasons: (1) It is the most honest. Doctors are civil servants, employed by the government. There is no charade about a National Health Service (NHS) doctor being in private practice. (2) It wastes the least amount of money. It does waste a tremendous amount (for example, it pays for about 17 million ambulance rides per year for purposes such as picking up a prescription at a pharmacy),[1] but it diverts the smallest proportion of the GNP to the socialized medical sector. (3) It permits private medicine. Some people call it "Fleet Street medicine" for the very rich. But private insurance is enjoyed by many others, too. Labor unions consider private insurance to be one of the most important benefits of employment. Private GPs say that the majority of their patients are people like taxi drivers and shopkeepers, who place a monetary value on their own time and therefore think private medicine is less expensive.

One problem with the NHS is that general practitioners are paid on the basis of capitation. They get paid the same amount per patient no matter how much or how little they do for him. In effect, they are punished for being conscientious and rewarded for being sloppy. But both patients and physicians can escape into the private sector, at least when it really counts.

Britain has the lowest medical expenditures of any Western country: about 5.8 percent of the GNP. But patients pay a price. Nearly a million patients are waiting up to four years for treatment.[2] Every year, rationing denies renal dialysis to 9,000 patients; cancer chemotherapy to between 10,000 and 15,000 patients; coronary artery surgery to between 4,000 and 17,000 patients; and hip replacement to 7,000 patients.[3] It's not just the total funds available, but the method of allocation that causes these shortages. If the NHS charged patients the full costs of their sleeping pills and tranquilizers, enough money would be freed to treat 10,000 to 15,000 additional cancer patients and save the lives of 3,000 additional patients with kidney failure.[4]

One thing Britain does not suffer from is a shortage of bureaucrats. The bureaucrat-to-doctor ratio increased from 1.07 in 1965 to 2.01 in 1976. During that decade, the number of hospital doctors increased 29 percent, while the number of administrative staff in NHS hospitals increased 134 percent.[5] Between 1948 and 1988, despite huge investments, the NHS lost 60,000 hospital beds, although the number of administrators increased by 70,000.[6]

Dr. Vernon Coleman, a British physician, asserted that "people are suffering and dying because too many NHS employees have forgotten that it exists to look after patients, not to provide a cushy living. . . . The system is so inefficient it costs $60 to change a light bulb in most NHS hospitals."[7]

Some assert that the NHS is really very efficient, with administrative costs of only 4 percent. Others assert that the impression is false; the 4 percent figure includes only the cost of health authority headquarters, and no one knows the total costs, even though bringing them under control was one of the principal goals of Thatcher's reform program.[8]

Despite its problems, the NHS is probably safe from any serious reform efforts. Attacks on it are politically suicidal in Britain. However, American politicians have little enthusiasm for importing it and have turned their attention to Canada.

THE CANADIAN MONOPSONY

Although it is also called "medicare," the Canadian system is quite different from American Medicare. The latter is a contributory, limited-benefits program available only to senior citizens and certain others such as the disabled. In Canada, medicare is a universal, compulsory system with no deductibles or copayments. Theoretically, it provides equal access for all citizens to the medical treatment of their choice— whenever or if ever it is available under the "global" budget (see glossary).

Theoretically, the Canadian health care system is controlled by the provinces. However, the provinces do not receive the federal government's share of the payments (about 40 percent) unless they follow certain central mandates. The government permits no opposition to its mandates. Private insurance is not allowed, and physicians and patients, with a few exceptions such as opted-out doctors in some provinces, are not allowed to contract privately for services—at least, not within Canada. The Canadian private escape hatch is the U.S. border, and patients can buy insurance to cover services rendered outside Canada. In general, if the government doesn't pay for it, nobody else can either.

The promises made by the Canadian system have a strong political appeal. According to opinion polls, the majority of Americans favor importing the system, even though they admit to knowing almost nothing about it. The majority of Canadians like it, too; only 1 percent of their population is on a waiting list for a surgical procedure.

American reformers like the idea of universality combined with cost-containment. Canada spends only 8.7 percent of its GNP for medical care ($1,683 per capita in 1989) compared with 11.8 percent ($2,354 per capita) for the United States. Canada has the second most expensive system in the world.

Additionally, some reformers believe that the Canadian system is more efficient than ours. They say that tremendous, virtually painless cost savings could be achieved by shifting from the pluralistic American system to a single payor. In the United States, there are about 1,500 insurance companies and over 100 million individual patients who pay medical bills. Estimates of the savings from "simplified adminis-tration" have ranged from $3 billion to $241 billion.[9] Estimates must be speculative because they cannot account for the off-budget hidden costs in public programs. Some believe that these hidden costs exceed the measured overhead costs of private insurance, and that this is not surprising since "monopoly public insurers have weaker incentives than private insurers to minimize overhead borne by patients and provid-ers."[10]

The least attractive feature of Canadian medicine is the need to wait for diagnostic tests and surgery. Television specials—especially those produced in Canada—show the plight of individuals who have had their coronary artery bypass repeatedly delayed. Proponents of social-ized medicine dismiss the fate of individuals and cite statistics to show that a lot of medical care is unnecessary anyway. They assert that emergency treatment is quickly available in Canada; only elective procedures are delayed. (The definition of "emergency" is elastic and depends partly on the political influence of the doctor and the patient.) They say that Canada is not glutted with advanced technology. Right. It has very little. Hospitals place advertisements in newspapers soliciting charitable contributions to buy technology such as a defibrillator, the basic device that is absolutely required to resuscitate someone whose heart has stopped.

Hospital beds continue to be closed due to lack of funds for staffing them; 2,900 of Toronto's 15,000 acute-care beds were closed between 1989 and 1990.[11] Yet about 250,000 Canadians are now awaiting major surgery.[12] Most provincial health ministries do not collect data on queues for hospital procedures. Here are some sample figures from questionnaires returned by 145 specialists in British Columbia in 1990. The average number of *weeks* waiting for hand surgery was 12.4; for hysterectomy, 16.3; for colonoscopy (a diagnostic procedure that might find a cancer), 6.2; for hernia repair, 24.6; for cholecystectomy (gall-bladder removal), 31.7; coronary artery bypass, 23.7; other open heart surgery, 21.4; prostatectomy (which relieves difficulty in urination and often finds treatable cancer), 30.9; cystoscopy (often done to diagnose cancer), 23.6.[13] The costs of waiting in terms of lost productivity and patient suffering are not entered into the explicit cost calculations.

Despite the waits, statistics on medical services are often interpreted to show that Canadians receive more medical care than Americans do—when they're not very sick. In the two years immediately after the implementation of universal health insurance in Quebec, doctors' office visits rose by 32 percent. But at the same time, physician time per visit declined by 16 percent and telephone consultations fell by 41 percent.[14]

One way of looking at the figures is to say that Americans can have immediate access to a CT scanner to diagnose a brain tumor (there were 5.7 scanners per million population in the United States in 1979 versus 1.7 in Canada).[15] Canadians will have to wait months for an "urgent" scan, but in the meantime they can have as many free doctor visits as they want to obtain free medicine for their undiagnosed head-ache. It *might* be a tension headache, and it might be a brain tumor.

Most headaches are tension headaches. But some are more suspi-cious than others. In a free economy, you can choose how to spend your money. How much is it worth to relieve your anxiety? That may depend a lot on the nuances of your particular headache and your doctor's opinion about the odds in your individual case, not the set of all cases of headache. If patients ask questions and I am not forced to see them in three minutes or less, we can make a reasonable decision together. In Canada, the options are foreclosed.

There is one group of patients in Canada that do (or did) have prompt access to CT scanners during off-hours. These are *not* patients who have a right to necessary CT scans. Such patients are not allowed to pay a fee, and the government can't afford to pay technicians for an extra shift. However, for *veterinary* patients, who have no right to the service, the facility can, and does, charge a market price. Dog owners pay, and the scanners run at night. Or at least they did until the fact was publicized.

The proposed solution to the problems of Canada's "disintegrating health care system" (a term used by Canadian news media) may sound familiar: "a comprehensive national strategy, a major resetting of priorities, a reallocation of funds, better management." A British Columbia royal commission on health care made 650 recommendations, the majority requiring the government to expand bureaucratic control through thousands of additional regulations.[16]

One suggestion is to inform patients of the cost of the services they receive. A physician interviewed by *The Journal*, a Canadian television program, said that patients just have no idea how much their care costs.

Actually, they know exactly how much it costs *them*. Care costs them nothing at the time of service. The cost is paid through inflation, high taxes, and a national debt that is twice as high as the U.S. debt on a per capita basis. Medical services now devour one third of the provincial budgets, and the proportion is rising inexorably. Even if they are aware of the connection between high taxes and generous social benefits, Canadians correctly conclude that they will pay the same taxes whether or not they forgo their share of the benefits. The most expensive treatment for one individual, even a heart transplant, is but a drop in the bucket compared with the provincial budget. Individuals really don't count.

If government programs have great difficulty in estimating their *current* costs, they are still less capable of projecting the costs of new programs. At the outset, government economists tend to be very optimistic about low costs. For example, when the free prescription drug plan for seniors and the indigent was introduced in the province of Ontario about twenty years ago, the government experts said it would cost about $1 million in the first year, and would *never* exceed $10 million annually. By 1975, it cost $45 million, and in 1991, it reached $916 million for that one year alone![17] (The maximum estimate was too low by a factor of 91.6.)

It took almost twenty years after the introduction of socialized medicine in Ontario for the politicians to grudgingly acknowledge that "health care spending is on a collision course with economic realities."[18]

And what has been the effect of the system on doctors and their patients? Have the doctors been transformed into selfless, caring patient advocates now that the economic incentives have changed? Here is the opinion of a Canadian ENT specialist, Dr. William Goodman of Toronto, a prominent critic of the Canadian medical system who has been "on strike" since the act that forbade physicians to directly bill their patients:

> The emigration or early withdrawal from practice of many of our best physicians has left large gaps in the medical, hospital and university hierarchies. What's even more disturbing is the indefinable loss of the sense of vocation by our older doctors, many of whom can hardly wait to quit; and the total absence in most of the younger practitioners of what used to be a feeling of almost religious dedication to medicine. Where medical practice was once a calling like the ministry, it is well on the way to becoming a 9-to-5 trade peopled by practitioners who are civil servants in everything but name—with the same tremendous commitment to excellence and service which characterizes other civil servants. This change has not been lost on our young people, the college students who might have become the doctors of tomorrow.[19]

If you don't believe Dr. Goodman, ask an expatriate Canadian physician. You can probably find at least one nearby. Or buy a subscription to a Canadian newspaper, such as the *Globe and Mail*.

THE GERMAN KRANKENKASSE (SICKNESS FUND) SYSTEM

What the Canadian system is losing in popularity among American would-be reformers, the German system is gaining. Key congressional health experts have visited Germany to learn about its reputed "uncanny ability to control medical spending without rationing care."[20] Germany allocates 8.2 percent of the GNP to medical spending.

The Krankenkasse system—a descendant of the system started by Bismarck—is funded by a 12.2 percent payroll tax. Like the British and Canadian schemes, the system is *not* insurance. There are no deductibles or copayments, and coverage is comprehensive, including even a two-week visit to a health spa. Doctors are closely monitored on the basis of detailed practice profiles, and doctors whose usage of services is more than 50 percent above average may have their pay cut. Also, physician associations monitor every prescription that is written, and if a doctor writes more prescriptions than is deemed appropriate, he may have to pay the Krankenkasse in cash for the overage.

Most hospital-based physicians are paid on salary. Payments to office-based physicians are based on a relative value scale, similar to the one recently adopted by U.S. Medicare. Balance billing is not permitted. The only way for a physician to maintain his income is to see large numbers of patients. One group of five physicians reported seeing 250 to 500 patients per day, for an average of three to five minutes each.

Could I see 50 to 100 patients per day? Certainly, if most of them just needed a shot or a blood pressure check, which could be done by a nurse. I have seen that many in a day when I was a resident in the Parkland minor medicine section of the emergency room. To expedite the type of medicine that is practiced under such conditions, the VA hospital thought of removing the chairs and desks from the examining rooms and just having a shelf where the doctor could write something while standing up. The only reason the idea fell through was that the desk drawer was needed for the rainbow of indispensable forms.

Would I put myself in a situation that required seeing 50 to 100 patients a day? Only if I were desperate for money and could not find another job. I would have to give up any illusions of practicing good internal medicine.

Unlike Canada, Germany does permit private insurance to be sold, and physicians can also bill patients outside the system. In some German practices, nearly a quarter of the revenue comes from private insurance. German physicians can earn much higher incomes than physicians in many countries (physician income is 4.28 times the average in Germany, versus 3.47 in Canada, 2.01 in Denmark, 2.39 in the United Kingdom, 1.80 in Sweden, and 5.12 in the United States).[21] However, to achieve this income, they, like their American counterparts, work brutally long hours.

OTHER SYSTEMS

Since every country except the United States and South Africa has socialized medicine, it is not difficult to find another example. Sweden has a fully socialized medical system. It is known for its particularly low level of productivity; only half the doctors and other medical personnel are actually working at any one time.[22] There are also other problems. One study showed that only 43 percent of the patients saw the same doctor on two clinic visits in a row. Waits for a routine visit to an orthopedic surgeon could be up to three years.[23] Sweden is considering market reforms.

In New Zealand, 25,000 people are waiting for surgery. In Japan, there is a way around the queue. An illegal "gift" of $1,000 or $3,000 can get a patient admitted sooner and ensure treatment by a senior specialist at Tokyo University Hospital.[24]

In a college debate, the affirmative is supposed to have the burden of proof. Why don't we ask the advocates of socialized medicine in this country to point to a socialized system elsewhere that is fiscally sound, not plagued by waiting lines, and not experiencing a crisis in its own perception?

This example does not exist, but it doesn't matter to many reformers. The experimental results are not important because the controversy is not about science. However, advocates of socialized medicine will tirelessly claim better health outcomes—for the community, if not the individual. And when problems persist and multiply, they will, like the British and Canadians, call for still more emphasis on improving health rather than treating sickness.

So let's look at the statistics.

We need to remember the words of Mark Twain ("There are lies, damned lies, and statistics") and Stalin ("Let's put statistics on socialist rails"). But statistics are an indispensable tool of science.

DOES SOCIALIZED MEDICINE PROVIDE BETTER MEDICAL TREATMENT?

In asserting the superiority of socialized medicine, infant mortality is the most commonly cited measure.

In comparisons of infant mortality in various Western countries, the United States does not look especially good. About 8.9 out of 1,000 babies died before their first birthday in 1991, the lowest rate ever, and about half as high as in the early 1970s. However, the United States ranks only twenty-second in infant mortality rates, and the Japanese rate is half as high.[25] Some but not all differences are explained by how long a baby has to live to be counted as a "live birth."

Infant mortality is strongly correlated with low birthweight and prematurity, which are strongly correlated with the mother's receiving prenatal care. Advocates of national health insurance argue that spending more money on preventive prenatal care would not only correct a national disgrace but also would save tremendous amounts of money now spent on neonatal intensive care.

Would it?

A study was done. The result: Expanding Medicaid eligibility to cover more prenatal visits had no effect on birthweight or infant mortality.[26] The editor of *JAMA* didn't like the implications. He explained them away by asserting that insurance was "necessary, but not sufficient." He could be right. Or it could be that lack of prenatal care does not *cause* premature babies but is correlated with maternal factors that *do* cause prematurity.

The raw data for this study did show a positive correlation that the investigators chose to disregard. Married women had healthier babies. The correlation is independent of race, age, or education, and has appeared in other studies also. Infant mortality is almost twice as high for illegitimate babies.[27]

So why don't we bring back the shotgun wedding?

Shotgun weddings might do much more to lower the infant mortality rate than Medicaid ever did. For one thing, the prospect would be a strong deterrent to the conception of an illegitimate child. Enforced marriage would not be the total solution, of course. Preventing pregnant women from smoking, drinking alcohol, or using illegal drugs— by random drug testing and incarceration if necessary—might also help a great deal.

I'm not proposing that we do these things. The end doesn't justify the means.

Marital status and drug consumption are examples of confounding variables. In making comparisons between countries, all the confounding variables—not just the presence or absence of socialized medicine—must be considered. Probably the most important variable is genetics. Descendants of the Vikings have a lower than average incidence of prematurity, and blacks have a higher than average incidence, and not very many blacks live in Sweden. This factor alone could explain Sweden's lower infant mortality.

The most closely matched groups I have ever seen discussed are Native American populations in Canada and the United States. Their infant mortality is twice as high on the *northern* side of the border, and life expectancy for men is five years shorter.[28]

Narrowing our focus to high-risk infants, there is no doubt that their chance of survival is greatest in the United States. At any given high-risk birthweight, both black and white babies did better in the United States than in Norway or Japan, the frontrunners in the overall infant mortality rates.[29]

The United States also takes the lead in other conditions in which modern medical treatment makes a difference. Patients with cancer, heart disease, or chronic renal failure live longer in the United States. American medicine takes better care of the sick and the injured than nationalized medicine does. Proponents of socialized medicine have to look at other measures to make their case.

DOES SOCIALIZED MEDICINE LEAD TO BETTER HEALTH?

Faced with their inability to meet all the demand for expensive treatments to sick people, those who promise a right to health care shift their emphasis to prevention. When the British NHS was instituted, its proponents thought that expenses would decrease once the backlog of unmet needs was cleared away. Instead, the backlog kept growing. Canadian health ministers avidly promote prudent diet, exercise, and healthy lifestyles as a solution to the crisis there. And Americans invented the Health Maintenance Organization.

Prevention sounds wonderfully appealing. I like the abstract concept myself, and have thought of establishing Jane's Aerobics Center. When I drive down Speedway early in the morning and look through the display windows of a new gymnasium, I can see hundreds of people working out on exercise machines. Unlike people who engage in bricklaying, who demand that *you* pay *them* for their exertions, these people are willing to pay *you* to subject them to the punishment of Sisyphus.

Prevention is a good thing. However, it is thoroughly dishonest to say it is the solution to the fiscal crisis in medicine. On the whole, it does not save money, particularly when the entire population rather than a known risk group is targeted.

Two of the most cost-effective preventive measures are mammography and the treatment of hypertension.

Mammography doesn't prevent breast cancer, but it can discover it at a much earlier stage, when treatment is more likely to cure it. A patient can buy a mammogram for about $85. If the mammogram is positive, she may have bought twenty years of life for her $85. If it's negative (as most are), she has bought some reassurance. Is it worth it? In a free market, each patient would have to answer that question for herself.

Cost-benefit questions today are not generally asked that way. Rather, the government asks: "Is it worth it to *society* to spend *society's* money to buy every woman a mammogram?"

If so, it is *not* because mammography is a great money saver. "Society" had to spend $80,000 in 1975 dollars (more than $180,000 in 1990 dollars) to avert one death from breast cancer by means of mammography. That amount of money could buy about four coronary-artery bypass grafts, each one of which could be lifesaving. And remember, a lot of women could easily afford to pay $85 themselves, whereas very few people can come up with $50,000 for open heart surgery.

The control of hypertension does prevent some strokes, some cases of renal failure, and perhaps some heart attacks. Surely that is worthwhile. But it is not a money saver. Only 20 to 25 percent of the costs of hypertension screening and treatment are recovered in the form of savings from illnesses that are avoided. Per fatality avoided, hypertension control cost $75,000 in 1975 dollars ($175,000 in 1990 dollars).

Cervical cancer screening cost about $25,000 per life saved in 1975. Due to increased federal regulation of Pap smears, the cost of a Pap smear has at least tripled. Correcting for this as well as inflation, the cost is about $175,000 today, perhaps somewhat less due to an increased incidence of abnormal Pap smears. (That means that there are more lives at risk so you don't have to look as far to find someone to save.)

The publicity campaign about cholesterol is having a tremendous effect. Almost all my patients are worried about "their numbers," including eighty-five-year-old women who desperately need the calories and calcium that come with the fat in the foods they are avoiding. Patients are extremely impressed by laboratory results. They are prone to worry about differences so small that they are within the laboratory's margin of error. It can be very difficult to reassure them.

Unquestionably, the level of serum cholesterol is correlated with risk of coronary artery disease, at least in younger men. The risk to older women is unproved and doubtful. What is it worth to lower the serum cholesterol and how much does it cost? There are many variables, including the patient's other risk factors. Extending life by *one year* by altering serum lipids with cholestyramine treatment may cost between $36,000 to $1,000,000.[30]

Screening tests and preventive interventions may be wonderful for my business, the laboratory business, the industry that produces low-fat foods, and the patients. But they cannot bring fiscal soundness to socialized medicine. Socialized systems don't use them much in any case.

In Britain, a 1989 study suggested that half the patients with diabetes remain undiagnosed, while 5 percent of the diagnoses are made at a late stage by an *optometrist*. British patients receive far fewer preventive services than Americans do, even though they see a general practitioner four times as often. In 1976, only 8 percent of eligible British women had a Pap smear (compared with almost 46 percent of Americans). Canadians are not entitled to receive routine cholesterol checks and often experience long waiting times for Pap smears or mammograms.[31]

Besides the benefits of prevention, there is the benefit of treating common diseases at an early stage. Sometimes prompt treatment can be lifesaving, but the benefits are often exaggerated. For example, a young, confident consultant for the Arizona Medicaid substitute (the Arizona Health Care Cost Containment System or AHCCCS) told the Medical Services Committee of the Arizona Medical Association that our wonderful $600-million-plus program treated colds before "they went into pneumonia." (Obviously, that's better than being able to make a hundred $6 million men!) There were more than a dozen physicians in the room, and not one of them said a word. I confess that I, too, was left speechless.

I like to remind my patients about the cartoon that says: "I'm sorry to tell you that you have the common cold, and there's no cure for it. But cheer up, you may get pneumonia, and we know what to do for that!"

I have overheard people in the supermarket complaining that their cold "went into their chest" because the doctor didn't give them an antibiotic. People come to the office frequently because they want to go on a trip and they have to get over their cold fast. Hope springs eternal, and it's good for business.

Every physician is taught that antibiotics do not cure viruses. Indiscriminate use of these wonder drugs causes the emergence of resistant bacteria, so that if the patient does get pneumonia it may be harder to treat. All drugs have side effects, some of them fatal. Patients have died from a shot of penicillin for a cold it wouldn't have helped. So why do doctors prescribe antibiotics for colds? Well, maybe the patient has something else that an antibiotic will help, and besides, he'll complain if he doesn't get a prescription.

Could I decrease the number of serious illnesses in my patients by seeing all patients every time they got the sniffles? No way. Maybe I would cause *more* serious problems. And the office would be so swamped that I might miss diagnosing the next case of tuberculosis.

Is Socialized Medicine Equitable?

As Dr. William Goodman explains, paraphrasing Winston Churchill, "The inherent vice of the American health care system is the *uneven* division of *blessings*; the inherent virtue of the Canadian health care system is the *even* division of *misery.*"[32]

Michael Walker of the Fraser Institute puts it more strongly: "Rather than throw a group of drowning people life preservers, the government sinks a yacht so they can cling to the wreckage."

Nonetheless, Canada still has a two-tiered system. The small uppermost tier can go to the United States. But even in the lower tier, the wreckage is not evenly distributed. There are striking differences in the services received by rich and poor or urban and rural populations in Canada, Britain, Sweden, and New Zealand.[33]

American Compromises

It is clear that the promises of socialized medicine have been elusive. Americans have been reluctant to go all the way and adopt the systems tried elsewhere. Yet they have not been able to renounce the tempting ideal. The result has been a mixed economy, a patchwork of fixes, a Band-Aid here and some baling wire there.

At various times, someone points to what is supposed to be a shining example—today, it's Hawaii. Dr. Raymond Scalettar of the AMA referred to Hawaii as a model during testimony before the one public meeting of the president's Task Force on Health Care Reform chaired by Hillary Rodham Clinton. Hawaii has a state-mandated package of benefits and requires employers to purchase coverage for all workers employed more than twenty hours per week. Because Hawaii has so many part-time workers, and because dependents may not be covered, there are still uninsured, the majority of whom are covered by the State Health Insurance Program (SHIP).

Some physicians have told me that Hawaii is a disaster but that physicians will not say anything negative about it in public because their paychecks are controlled by the dominant insurers, and it is harder to leave Hawaii than California. (About 57 percent of the population is covered by the Hawaii Medical Service Association, the Hawaiian version of Blue Cross/Blue Shield, and 18 percent by Kaiser Permanente.) Some physicians complain that the insurer tries in some instances to enforce substandard medical practices, such as treating diabetics with insulin only if there is sugar in the urine, rather than routinely checking blood sugars, a far more sensitive measurement.

Outside the silent island paradise, many physicians complain bitterly that the present system is so dreadful that things couldn't be any worse, not even with socialized medicine.

Things can indeed get worse. The next chapters will explore the "fixes" that we are adopting, piece by piece, at an accelerating rate. Some of them are called market solutions, but they are definitely not *free*-market solutions. None of them are called by the discredited S word, even if based on the same principles. They do maintain a pretext of private ownership but under central bureaucratic control. They might be able to do certain things very efficiently—perhaps they can, so to speak, make the trains run on time.

. . . .

12

"MANAGED" CARE

. . . .

Managed care is about preventing medical care in order to make money for third-party payers or save money for the government.

WHAT IS MANAGED CARE?

IN THE old days, "management" of a patient's problem was a task for doctors and patients, especially if the problem was an incurable disease like rheumatoid arthritis or an inevitable condition like old age. A family doctor taught me about it. Sometimes, you couldn't make the patient whole again, but somehow you and the patient "managed," one day at a time.

Today, managed care is a system of providing medical service *by* the managers and *for* the benefit of the managers, but generally not *of* the managers—the majority of them go to a private doctor.

There are a lot of variations on the theme of managed care, which are often called "alphabet soup." There are Health Maintenance Organizations (HMOs), Preferred Provider Organizations (PPOs), and Independent Practice Associations (IPAs). They differ in the degree of independence retained by the network of member physicians and the degree of choice available to member patients. They also differ in management, which is often revolving.

A better term for managed care would be prepayment for the rationed consumption of medical care, with constant attention to the bottom line of the managers. This is the way it works: Subscribers, or more often their employers, hand over a large fee (erroneously called an "insurance premium") to the plan, and the plan doles it out for the medical care that it approves, by the doctor and in the facility that it "prefers" (has a contract with). The patient who thinks he has a skin cancer can't just call up the dermatologist and get an appointment to have it removed. He has to see the "gatekeeper" first. If the care is unsatisfactory, the patient can't just pick another doctor or hospital, not without a big financial penalty. Some plans have "open season," during which subscribers can hunt for another plan. But what frequently happens is that the employer picks another plan based on the company's financial considerations, and the employees have to change doctors whether they want to or not.

The government now encourages the masses, especially the elderly, to sign up with managed care plans, and has created a variety of favorable conditions for such plans. This way, the government can put a lid on expenditures while delegating the bad guys' job to the managers, who delegate it to the doctors, just like at the VA. The multimillion-dollar scandals involving some plans have not deterred the government from supporting the general idea, despite the concerns expressed by the late Pennsylvania Senator John Heinz about his own legislative progeny: "What was intended as an exciting *choice* for thirty-one million aged and disabled under Medicare too often functions as a costly *chance*."[1]

Managed care plans work like Canadian medicare in that they have a "global" budget. Their patients can escape from a plan's constraints more easily than Canadians can (at least they don't have to go to a foreign country), but at a price. Some managed care plans do cover emergencies away from home, and some cover a small portion of expenses incurred outside the plan.

Managed care plans differ from Canadian medicare in that they are managed by private-sector bureaucrats instead of government bureaucrats. They also purport to introduce one feature of a free market: competition. This kind of competition is not a civilized contest in which everyone plays by the rules and the winner is the one who can provide the best service in the most economical way. Rather, it is competition with other managed care entities, of the sort engaged in by Roman gladiators. The nongladiators had better stay off the field.

Competition between individual Hippocratic physicians and managed care colossi would be like competition between the Christians and the lions.

The theory behind managed care is that (1) a lot of medical care is unnecessary, and (2) less would be necessary if people got preventive maintenance.

The first part is true, as I have explained. The trick is in defining *which* medical services are unnecessary. You can't trust doctors and patients, say the managers. With this type of funding you *can* trust the *patients* to be oblivious to costs, and copayments are frequently added to help ease the congestion in the waiting rooms. Therefore, there are clerks and committees.

The second part about preventive maintenance is a fallacy, as I have shown. But in any case the managers don't seem to think that health maintenance includes consulting a physician when you think you may have a problem. Inability to get an appointment with the plan doctors is one reason why my former patients drift back to see me.

Managed care plans do spend less on medical services, largely because of the methods they use to induce cooperation by physicians (more details follow).

So are managed care plans cheaper?

Not much, especially not when you consider that sick people don't like HMOs, and hence avoid them. Most plans achieve savings in the first year, but the rate of increase after that remains unchanged.[2] Many corporations have been very disappointed.

Managed care achieves cost savings by decreasing hospital stays and lowering doctors' fees. But there are also increased costs: for billboards, high-pressure salesmen, and television ads. The plan also needs teams of utilization review nurses to descend on hospital nursing stations to tell doctors how to get patients out of the hospital twenty-four hours after they have had prostate surgery. And of course it needs managers with cellular telephones to approve service denials.

One thing the managers do is "transmit the risk to a lower level" (their expression). That means that they place the doctors at financial risk if their patients happen to be sicker than average.

I asked one manager what happened if the company miscalculated and didn't shed enough risk. "Well, we just won't be here anymore," he said. He was not visibly distressed by the prospect. It's the company's assets that are at risk if the company goes bankrupt. Not his. His salary and perks come off the top.

Managed care plans often take bankruptcy. In 1986, the latest year for which I can find these data, 71 percent of HMOs faced deficits.[3] They may be bought out by other entrepreneurs after they are relieved of part of their liabilities.

One way they dispose of their liabilities is by not paying their outstanding bills to doctors and hospitals. The hospital administrators know that a substantial share of their accounts receivable is owed by entities that are in financial trouble. The administrators worry when payments become delayed. But they don't worry enough to stop signing those contracts. They don't want to lose market share.

Physicians are often left holding the bag when the managers bolt. Many of them signed a "hold harmless" clause. They can't bill the patients, they can't abandon the patients, and they have no recourse against the insurer.

So much for the doctor and the hospital. What does managed care mean for the patients? For one thing, it means the destruction of unmanaged care. That could be one reason why, after nearly twenty years, only 15 percent of the U.S. population was enrolled in an HMO, although the percentage continues to increase.[4]

AN EXAMPLE OF UNMANAGED CARE

This is the story of a patient who was an "outlier" (her care cost much more than average) and a failure of the health maintenance system. There was no way that her immediate problem could have been prevented. It was caused by diabetes and the effects of her previous (lifesaving) cancer treatment.

The patient was a seventy-something-year-old woman I'll call Mrs. C. She came to my office one day with leg pain, accompanied by very subtle redness and swelling, along with a fever. My mother saw her first. Fortunately, she had no protocol or list of criteria to go by, only her infallible clinical instinct. She probably saved my patient's life.

"You'd better see Mrs. C. right away," she said.

I don't know whether Mrs. C. would have gotten past the utilization review nurse these days, but back then there was no such barrier in the admissions office. Mrs. C. was in a hospital bed about half an hour later.

The next day she was in the intensive care unit. Even though she had been promptly started on intravenous antibiotics, her findings were no longer subtle. Two days later, she had a huge, draining surgical wound, and an especially nasty concoction of resistant bacteria was growing from the pus.

Mrs. C. was a long-term survivor of radiation therapy for cancer, and probably an infection had tracked into the soft tissues of her leg from the pelvis, due to the scarred, broken-down tissues. A recurrence of the cancer was of course a consideration and would have made her prognosis far worse. It turned out that she didn't have cancer, though we didn't know that at the time. She just had a deep soft tissue infection. Diabetics are especially susceptible to such infections.

Mrs. C. made almost daily trips to the operating room. Almost as soon as she was breathing on her own after one anesthetic, it was time to intubate her again for the next operation. Finally, she was just left on the ventilator. So she looked like the ICU patients in the horror stories—she had tubes everywhere. Her wound became more and more gruesome. The surgeons kept removing more muscle tissue, cutting away the infected parts in the hope that the healthy tissue could heal. But the infection kept progressing; they couldn't stay ahead of it.

I was mostly a superfluous woman. Mrs. C. had several surgeons, an anesthesiologist, and an infectious disease consultant. Her diabetes was pretty much on autopilot. Still, I came to see her every day. And one day I came twice.

I don't know why I visited one Sunday evening. I had been at the hospital that morning. The patient had been to surgery, so the surgeon was really in charge. I had not been called about any special problem. Surely Medicare would have considered my visit unnecessary and inefficient. But I stopped in, said hello, and looked at the intravenous solutions, as I automatically do. For some unknown reason, I asked the nurse about the one that I *didn't* see. Not that it would necessarily have been there, because antibiotics are given over a short time and then the bottle is taken down.

The antibiotic had been canceled due to an automatic stop order from the pharmacy, a cost-saving measure. Sometimes surgeons forget to cancel the prophylactic antibiotics, and patients receive a few unnecessary doses. So the pharmacy decided to help out by stopping the medication automatically in postoperative patients, unless the surgeon thought to write a T next to his order. T is for "therapeutic," while P is for "prophylactic," and apparently the latter is the default option in postoperative patients. Calling the doctor to confirm the stop order, or even notifying him, was not part of the protocol.

I did take the trouble of going to a meeting of the Pharmacy and Therapeutics Committee to tell them what I thought of their automatic stop-order policy, months after the fact. I don't know whether they changed it; I don't go to that hospital very often. Committees can change mistakes they have made. But it takes months, and some disaster usually has to occur first.

I restarted Mrs. C's antibiotics immediately. A delay of a few more hours could conceivably have cost her her life. We'll never know. We cannot conduct a controlled experiment.

After a number of operations, the patient's family was discouraged. Although they were very devoted, they wondered if it wasn't about time to give up, to stop the heroics.

"I would be lying to you if I said the outlook was good," I told them. "But I can't honestly say there is no hope. If her heart stops, it might not be worthwhile to try to start it again. But it's not time to give up altogether." I wasn't feeling very hopeful myself, but the patient had one very important thing in her favor. She hadn't given up the fight.

Even though I had seen to it that the patient was getting her medicine, it didn't seem to be doing the job. The surgeon said there was only one more thing to do: to disarticulate her leg at the hip. He said her chance of surviving the operation was about 50 percent.

At this point, the job of the superfluous woman was a small one: obtaining the patient's consent for the surgery. I explained the situation to her as best I could. She had a tracheostomy tube connecting her to the ventilator and couldn't talk. But she seemed to understand. And she signed the consent form.

The next day, there was nothing for me to do but wait for the bad news and be thankful I didn't have to be present at the operation.

The news came sooner than I expected.

"We didn't do the amputation," the surgeon said. "When we got in there, we saw that she was getting better. The wound was starting to heal."

The patient went to the operating room a few more times. Eventually, the enormous gaping wound granulated in with healthy tissue. A skin graft was needed to close the wound completely. But the patient walked out of the hospital on two legs.

Three years later, she was still doing well. Of course, if she had died, she would have contributed to the awesome statistics on how much money we spend on people who are in their last six months of life. These oft-cited figures prove that people often get sick and receive medical treatment right before they die. The reason for quoting the figures is to make a case for limiting care to people who are about to die. The problem is in knowing for sure who is about to die. One patient like Mrs. C. destroys a lot of faith in prognostications.

ECONOMIC CREDENTIALING

Taking care of Mrs. C. today could have ended my hospital career, especially if the managers couldn't hold me personally responsible for paying her bill.

Managers don't want patients like Mrs. C. in the hospital, especially not under the care of an unmanaged doctor. Economic credentialing is one way to discourage such admissions.

In the words of a manager, "efficient use of health center resources will be an important consideration" in reviewing applications for staff privileges.

One patient like Mrs. C. would ensure that I didn't meet the statistical criteria for efficient use, because my hospital practice is very small. And the managers are looking for reasons to remove private doctors from the staff. Private internists like me are blamed for much of the 10 to 30 percent of medical care that they deem to be unnecessary. According to the management experts, 41 percent of our patient days are unnecessary in contrast to only 14 percent for doctors in closed-panel HMOs (who may only use consultants who are on the panel).

The reason, they say, is that private doctors can bill patients for hospital visits whereas HMO doctors have a "dual negative incentive." If they have a patient in the hospital, they have to work harder, but they get no more payment. (How would you like for *your* doctor to have a dual negative incentive to take care of you, i.e., an incentive to *not* take care of you?)

Additional negative incentives can be provided, for example, by increasing the paperwork required to order a laboratory test. Many laboratory tests are unnecessary. And if you define a test to be unnecessary every time the results are normal, *most* lab tests are unnecessary. The reason they are ordered is because the patient with the abnormal one might die unnecessarily, and you don't know whether the test is normal until you do it.

When I order a test, I'm playing the odds. Managed care plans want to change my criteria for placing the bets. But remember, under managed care the person who is saving the money by forgoing tests is not the one taking the risk to life or health.

SELLING MANAGED CARE TO THE DOCTORS

One Saturday, our hospital sponsored a day of lectures about managed care. After I sat through an entire morning of lectures, the truth finally emerged at lunch. I sat next to one of the speakers and asked him a question about the doctors' involvement with the plan.

"Of course, you realize there is a certain amount of prostitution involved here," he said.

One way of getting the doctors to cooperate while control of the hospital is being preempted by managers is to give them a "discretionary job," for example, utilization review.

"But remember," the manager cautioned, "you can't buy them; you can only rent them." The going rate for utilization review runs around fifty dollars per hour. Many doctors net less than that from seeing patients for an hour.

Another is to get the most respected members of the staff involved in the process. For example, protocols are not implemented until the staff has participated in frequent long meetings to discuss them. They have massive, tedious "input" into the details. The only thing that isn't on the agenda is the possibility of junking the whole idea. It reminds me of the definition of Chinese Communist democracy: Everybody has the right and obligation to attend the meeting and agree with the plan. I learned this from a seventy-year-old man who had spent most of his life trying to emigrate from Communist China.

A third way is education. One method is to provide physicians with an economic profit report, to show them how their practice compares with that of their colleagues, to get them to discuss conformity, and to strive to bring their practice to the average. I don't necessarily object to statistical reports that might help to improve care or to help patients make decisions. Economic coercion based on misleading samples is something else.

Finally, there is economic credentialing: a 1989 survey showed that about 42 percent of 500 hospital chief executives believed that within five years their hospital might be using economic data in deciding whether to grant admitting privileges.[5]

What will happen to patients like Mrs. C.? Perhaps they can be persuaded to cooperate, too. There is the Patient Self-Determination Act, a subject for the next chapter.

Selling Managed Care to the Patients

It is not easy to sell managed care to patients. In fact, I don't think that patients are actually sold on the idea very often. When patients have left me to go to an HMO doctor, they generally have said, "I have to do it because my employer bought this plan, and you're not on the list." They feel that they can't afford not to get their care under the plan. After all, they have paid for it in advance one way or another, usually by a deduction in the wages they would otherwise have received. It is not my fee that is the main problem. It's the fact that tests or drugs or consultations that I order will not be covered either. All of those things require the approval of a gatekeeper who has a contract with the plan.

The details of that contract are generally kept secret from the patients, and for good reason. The contract might forbid the doctor to make derogatory comments about the plan. It will set forth the financial incentives that the gatekeeper has for denying or restricting care. It will delineate the barriers that the gatekeeper will have to overcome (phone calls, forms, committee meetings, etc.) in order to obtain approval for any unusual procedures he wants his patient to have.

HMOs spend a lot of money on billboards and television ads, which show smiling, attractive people bursting with health. These people are actors, and patients know that. Most patients know better than to expect an HMO to be anything like the trusted family doctor who has been with them through the crises of their lives. They know, or will soon discover, that the doctor they see will usually know nothing about them except what he gleans from a few harried minutes of skimming their record. They are an identification number, a diagnosis, a cost center, a liability, and one unit of a quota of work that must be processed in a certain period of time. The reality of HMOs and other managed care entities bears little resemblance to the billboards.

One of the new guarantors of quality: a simple consumer report card, to hold doctors accountable for results.

If you don't like the new system, you could just give it a bad grade.

Giving a student a bad grade does not in itself make him any better. Giving the new system a bad grade doesn't bring back the old one.

Why not build on the strengths of the present system of personal, individualized, unmanaged care, and try to expand its benefits?

13

THE RIGHT TO DIE

The right to die could turn out to mean the necessity to die sooner than you otherwise would.

WHY NOW?

WHEN a patient comes to a physician with a complaint that he has had for twenty years, the physician's first question should be, "Why now?" Is this complaint really the same old headache, or is there something new? Did the patient's wife leave him? Is the patient suing someone, seeing the chance to collect compensation for his malady? Or has he developed a brain tumor? (Patients with chronic migraine are not immune to tumors.)

Why the Patient Self-Determination Act now, in the 1990s? This federal law requires that all institutions receiving Medicare or Medicaid funding ask every patient whether the patient has executed an advance directive or a living will. If the patient has not done so, he is to be provided with information and forms. Signing the forms is not required—at least not yet.

Why are hospitals (even Catholic hospitals) now quoting a 1990 Supreme Court decision that stated "the timing of death, once a matter of fate, is now a matter of human choice"?[1]

The fact is that our choice concerning the time of death is the same as it always was. A number of ways to kill a person have been available since the beginning of the human race, all equally effective, though some are quicker or kinder than others.

What about our ability to thwart death? We now have more so-phisticated means of replacing or substituting for failed organs, in-cluding bone marrow destroyed by heroic cancer therapy. Some diseases such as leukemia, that were once invariably fatal, can now sometimes be cured. But our ability to keep people with *untreatable* conditions alive with tubes and other artificial means of life support has really not advanced much in the past twenty years. Defibrillators to shock the heart out of a fatal rhythm and ventilators to breathe for an unconscious patient have been standard equipment for nearly two decades. I saw people living in a coma (now called a "persistent veg-etative state") or lingering near death with multiple tubes when I was a medical student. There may be more of them now, and they may live a little longer.

What is really new?

We are not having a sudden outbreak of humanitarianism as a reaction to decades of overly aggressive, futile medical treatment.

Some people think that doctors have traditionally seen death as the enemy and have felt compelled to fight off the Angel of Death with every possible weapon to the bitter end. Maybe there are a few doctors who are determined to do every possible billable procedure while the body is still warm. But I don't think there are many. Surgeons definitely do not like patients to die on the operating table. Most doctors bring a sense of humane perspective to death and dying, especially after they have been in practice for a few years.

Personally, I have always been reluctant to do invasive things to dying patients. It might be the vivid memory of the old woman who died while I was inserting a feeding tube. She had suffered a left-sided stroke on top of an old right-sided stroke, and I think her death was coincidental to my ministrations. But a bystander could have gotten the impression that I killed her by sticking a tube in her nose.

Most of the time, doctors, patients, and their families are able to come to agreement about what to do, and without any help from a lawyer or other third party. You seldom hear about those cases; I'll tell you about one.

When I was a resident at University Hospital, one of my patients, a very old woman with multiple complications of diabetes, went into kidney failure. There hadn't been a reversible precipitating event. It was one more step in the relentless progression of age and disease. I explained the situation to the family haltingly, as their English was not perfect and my Spanish is miserable. They asked about dialysis.

This is how I think about such questions: Is organ failure a step in the dying process and a consequence of dying, or is death the consequence of failure of a particular organ in an otherwise viable patient? I thought the first was the situation with this patient. Dialysis would have been a nightmare. Maybe it would have slowed down the patient's dying, but it might also have speeded it up. I didn't recommend it, but of course the final decision was up to the family. I would have called a nephrologist (kidney specialist) if they had asked me to. I did make another recommendation, whether or not they decided to have the nephrologist: to call a priest.

I was no longer a Catholic at the time, but the patient was. I remembered about the importance of the last rites from my sixth grade education. The family appreciated the suggestion, and because they were far from home, I called the priest from the church across the street.

He came, and so did the whole family. It was a large Mexican family. There was noticeable commotion on the floor as they all filed in to say goodbye to Mama.

Some of the nurses were upset with me for disrupting their routine. I thought the scene was a lot less disruptive than a code arrest, during which nearly a dozen people run to the bedside, a heavy cart in tow, and try to restart a patient's heart. For one thing, the family members, although they were not as quiet as we would have liked, did not swear or throw bloody objects on the floor, the way doctors sometimes did.

It occurred to me that sometimes a code arrest was the medical equivalent of the last rites. But the medical type is bloody and violent and in cases like this almost always ends in defeat. Even if you don't think that religious last rites are a prelude to final victory, they do remind the staff that the decrepit-looking person in the bed is somebody's great-grandmother, and that somebody will miss her when she is gone.

In 1976, we somehow got by without advance directives or living wills, in which people attempt to spell out ahead of time the circumstances that would cause them to refuse medical treatment. And while the idea of ethics committees was around, nobody had much experience with them. We did have code arrest teams and had come up with the idea of "no code" orders all by ourselves. If we thought a patient was near death and should be allowed to pass on without needles, tubes, and cardiac massage, we wrote an order *not* to call the code team when the patient was found without pulse or respirations.

Ethics committees really are distinctly different from what we had before. When I was an intern in Texas, in the Bible Belt, our public hospital permitted chaplains. You could call them if you wanted to, but it was easy to avoid any contact with them whatsoever if that was your (or the patient's) preference.

If I had a patient who was seriously ill, I generally asked if he wanted to see a chaplain (or if the family did), and called if the answer was affirmative.

The chaplains were invariably helpful. Whatever their denomination, they did the same basic things. They prayed and comforted the patient and family. They discussed sticky issues, especially autopsies, if the doctor or the patient or the family wanted them to. I always felt as if they spoke with authority. Whatever other sources of authority they might claim, some of it was derived from the respect accorded them by the patients.

Ethics committees might have some ordained persons as members, but they are dominated by ethicists, or bioethicists. The ethicists' credentials consist primarily of an academic degree, and their authority derives from an official or quasi-official stamp of approval. If they ever read sacred scriptures, or pray, or believe in God, you couldn't necessarily tell by listening to them. Their discourse is secular and academic. They relate to doctors and other professionals, *not necessarily to patients*.

If you see a man in a Roman collar or cassock coming, you are forewarned and can run away if you like. You are free to reject everything that he says, no questions asked.

Not so with bioethicists. They are very hard to escape. They may present themselves as mere facilitators, but their opinion would probably carry a lot of weight in a court of law, certainly more than that of a priest and possibly more than that of a physician.

Why *now?* I think we have a new type of ethicist for a new type of ethics.

Even an itinerant, illiterate street preacher can understand simple laws like "Thou shalt not steal" or "Thou shalt not kill." And the simplest physician can comprehend the Oath of Hippocrates. These basic moral precepts were once accepted by general societal consensus.

Understanding and enforcing the right to health care and the right to die are a lot more complex. Not infrequently, these concepts conflict with traditional ethics. That is precisely why we get advance directives: to direct physicians to act in a way that might be contrary to their inclinations, or even to their conscience.

There is one major medical development spurring the movement for advance directives: transplantation of vital organs. A healthy person who has been pronounced brain dead can be taken to the operating room to harvest the heart, liver, lungs, kidneys, and/or pancreas for transplant. There's a great and worsening shortage of these organs. The donors are declared legally dead, generally after consulting the ethics committee. After the procedure, they are totally, indubitably dead, and their life-support systems are disconnected without need for further input from the ethics committee.

While organ transplants get more publicity, a more important reason for advance directives is that government programs, which now fund more than 40 percent of all medical care, are bankrupt.

Formerly, the hospital put a Medicare patient on a ventilator knowing that all costs would be paid, courtesy of somebody else, whether or not the patient had a chance of recovery. Now, under the prospective payment scheme, the payment is the same whether the patient lives two hours or two months. In other words, the patient who lingers is a loser. Law IX of *The House of God* applies: "The only good admission is a dead admission"—assuming that the body stays warm long enough to count as an admission and be assigned a DRG (diagnosis-related group). Quick death is the most cost-effective form of treatment.

In presenting the option of the advance directive, the hospital never says, "You might want to sign this because, as a good citizen, we know you wouldn't want to be a burden on your family or society. You might prefer to die and get out of the way, and by the way save our resources so we can use them for somebody else."

Such a statement would be very bad PR, as the truth often is. Instead, the hospital inquires very diplomatically about whether the patient would want to be kept alive if his life were very burdensome, or if he had intractable pain, or if he wasn't aware of his surroundings. Very few patients will say, "I want to be kept alive at all costs as long as possible, even if I am a vegetable." Who would want to be a "vegetable"? Nobody would; the trick is to define the term. And who would want to be in intractable pain?

Is an Advance Directive the Only Option?

Why do we need a new, elaborate, legalistic procedure? Why can't people simply exercise their right to reject medical care, once they decide that it isn't worth it? The fact is that they *can*—I think we're just afraid that not enough of them *will*, unless we encourage that choice.

Usually, it is easy to reject medical care. You just don't go to the hospital, and above all, you don't dial 911. (Paramedics are required to resuscitate patients; they are *not* in a position to make decisions about withholding care.) Dying patients can often be cared for at home, if they have a dedicated family willing to undertake a sad and demanding task. I have seen men and women from a variety of unlikely occupations turn into outstanding nurses when a family member needed them. No one could have done a better job in caring for their loved ones. Their patients probably lived both longer and better than would have been possible in an institution, despite or perhaps because of the lack of aggressive medical intervention.

If patients who have a terminal disease such as cancer can no longer be cared for at home, the best option may be a hospice that provides adequate pain medications, pleasant surroundings, and good nursing care. Patients in a hospice don't usually need a doctor except to perform functions designed by a bureaucracy (signing orders and filling out forms) or to prescribe new medications. They do need a good nurse. They understand upon entering the hospice that advanced life support is simply unavailable. Unfortunately, hospice beds are in short supply. In our city, hospice nurses who make house calls help to fill the gap.

When patients spend mostly their own money for medical care, they may choose not to call the doctor because they prefer to use their money for another purpose or to save it for their heirs. There is the problem that heirs might skimp on caring for their mother if they have control over her money. But the answer is not to make it easy for people to shirk their familial responsibility and impose it on other people's children and grandchildren. A confiscatory estate tax, another possible answer, has the side effect of encouraging conspicuous consumption instead of building for the future. The best answer, in my opinion, is for older persons to keep control of their own money as long as possible.

Some people think it's horrible to have to choose between medical care and some other good, especially if one doesn't have very much money. That is the rationale for appropriating other people's money for the purpose, without the other people's consent. People *do* give consent for this use of their money when they voluntarily purchase insurance or make a charitable contribution. One can argue that they also give consent to be taxed for that purpose, but people seldom vote knowingly to have their own taxes raised. The extension of Medicare to catastrophic expenses was repealed immediately when the intended beneficiaries found out that *they*, rather than the rich or the younger generations, would have to pay for the benefit.

The bitter economic truth is that goods and services have to be paid for somehow. If payment is not forthcoming, the goods or services aren't available. We have assumed that it is more humane to ask an ethics committee to unplug the machinery, all the while asserting that the patient has the right to choose treatment, than to ask a family to pay something or to apply for charity to continue treatment. But patients need to realize that if other people pay the money, other people eventually *will* make the choices.

Sometimes, of course, other people *have* to make the choices because the patient is not capable of doing so. Situations like that are the rationale for the advance directive. Just remember though, when considering the hard cases, that Representative Pete Stark thinks that *all* sick people are "brain dead."

THE HARD CASES

Problems arise when an unconscious or mentally incompetent patient is in a hospital. Hospitals are designed for aggressive, death-delaying treatments, and they dread litigation by families. The institution and physicians could exercise good medical judgment and simply decline to administer treatments that merely prolong dying. And patients and families could exercise their best judgment to choose physicians and facilities who will treat them as they wish to be treated and demand a change of physician or transfer of the patient if they are dissatisfied. But can we trust doctors, patients, and families with such responsibility?

If not, how can we trust them to execute advance directives?

The main problem with advance directives is that people truly don't know how they will react when facing death or severe disability. The normal human reaction is to struggle to live a little longer. When patients with a terminal disease have given up the struggle, they usually die rather soon, without any artificial help. A semantic note: "Artificial" is seldom used as it is here, to refer to "aid in dying," such as lethal injections. It is generally reserved for means of sustaining life, such as food and water, as in "artificial nutrition and hydration."

Ordinary people tend to recognize that they might change their minds about a situation once they are in it. When 150 patients on chronic dialysis were asked how much leeway they wanted their surrogate to have in overriding their advance directives if they felt it to be in the patient's best interest, 31 percent said "complete leeway," 11 percent said "a lot of leeway," 19 percent said "a little leeway," and only 39 percent said "no leeway."[2]

Patients with terminal diseases seldom commit suicide. The main reason they might wish to hasten death is intractable pain. But for pain, there are a number of effective therapies, of which the most important are narcotics and radiation treatment for metastatic cancer.

Radiation treatments require highly trained technicians and expensive equipment. In societal cost-benefit analyses, they do not yield a high return on investment, except possibly in curable cancers affecting young patients. Therefore, radiation therapy is at the bottom of social priority lists, even though it can make the months of survival much more comfortable. In Canada, radiation oncology departments suffer a serious shortage of staff, and patients may have to wait for many weeks. In the Oregon Basic Health Services Program, cancer patients with a less than 10 percent five-year survival are at the bottom of the list, along with those who need transplants to survive.

Narcotics are controlled substances, and there's a war on drugs.

The diligent efforts of the Drug Enforcement Administration, medical licensure boards, and resource allocators might have the presumably unintended consequence of increasing the number of patients with intractable pain. Then, advance directives may help to ease the burden, especially when combined with the next logical step of "aid in dying."

WHY NOT A "GOOD DEATH"?

We have not come to the point of implementing George Bernard Shaw's offhand suggestion to execute in a kindly manner those who don't earn their keep. But it could happen sooner than we think.

If we were to administer a "good death"—euthanasia—to patients who choose in advance not to live under certain circumstances, we could use the resources saved for another purpose. Instead of buying rice or potatoes or other nutrients to put down feeding tubes, at a cost of at least $100 per year, we could buy condoms for teenagers, asphalt for roads, and salary increases for public school teachers. The possibilities are endless. Many object to the idea that *individuals* should have to forgo anything else in order to buy basic medical care (at least if they pay at the time of service rather than on April 15). But why should society forgo useful projects in order to provide medical care to those who didn't want to live—or to the useless, or even to the unwanted?

In the early 1990s, California and Washington had ballot initiatives to permit voluntary, "active" euthanasia. Both were defeated. The key sticking point was "lack of consumer protections."

Active euthanasia is not promoted as a means of improving universal access. Rather, euthanasia is supposed to protect the patient from fates worth than death: pain, indignity, and a sense of being a burden. But do the promoters tell the whole story?

Euthanasia is supposed to be purely voluntary on the part of the patient. It is unlikely that people would vote for it otherwise. However, experience in the Netherlands suggests that it won't stay that way. Between 5,000 and 10,000[3] people are euthanized in Holland each year, of the 128,000 persons who die. The ratio of involuntary to voluntary euthanasia is about 2.5 to 1,[4] and it is not known how many volunteer for a lethal injection in response to social pressure. Some Dutch patients carry a card saying "Please do not euthanize me." For perspective, about 5,000 children were killed in the Nazi euthanasia program.[5]

Society might not be ready for involuntary euthanasia. But the situation can change. Ten years ago, society wasn't ready to consider euthanasia at all.

EVOLVING BEYOND HIPPOCRATES

Readiness changes with societal mores, and also with perceived needs. Thirty years ago, society was not ready to legalize abortion on demand. Twenty years ago, society may have been ready for abortion on demand but was not ready to compel physicians to perform the procedure. But now a shortage of providers is threatened.

Between 1976 and 1985, there was a 22 percent decline in the number of obstetrics and gynecology residency programs that offered training in first-trimester abortions. In half of the programs, the training is optional. In 1987 and 1988, 83 percent of U.S. counties had no abortionist. Only 34 percent of obstetricians and gynecologists are willing to perform the procedure, and of those who do not perform it, 71 percent cited moral or religious reasons.[6] What should be done?

The American Public Health Association responded to the shortage by passing a resolution stating that residency programs in obstetrics should be *required* to include training in abortions. The American College of Obstetrics and Gynecology still talks about incentives rather than compulsion. One program, at the University of Washington, does not require residents with religious objections to actually perform abortions, but does require participation in the "counseling training to learn to speak sensitively and nonjudgmentally to women about their options."[7]

Medical ethicists are pondering whether physicians who are morally opposed to abortion should be permitted to receive training in perinatology (maternal-fetal medicine). "Is there such a thing as a pro-life perinatologist?" they ask. "[Does it make sense] for doctors to enter a specialty if they deem it immoral to perform one of the specialty's common procedures?" For now, the conclusion is that pro-life perinatologists should not be excluded from patient care, as long as they are careful to "avoid complicating their patients' decisions" about a "difficult" question and are willing to refer patients promptly to an "appropriate and competent" abortionist.[8]

What if someday society legalizes euthanasia but experiences a dearth of euthanasia providers? "What would we do about physicians who consider physician-assisted euthanasia to be immoral?"[9]

At a meeting of our hospital's medical executive committee, the nurse in charge of implementing the Patient Self-Determination Act mentioned that in the past, physicians with objections to living wills could simply recommend that the family find another doctor. Now the burden has already shifted to the physician to find someone willing to do that which he considers immoral, although as far as I know there have been no compulsory counseling training sessions. This means that physicians may be legally required to become an accessory to an act that they consider to be a crime. The Washington ballot initiative provided that if the physician was unwilling to carry out a euthanasia directive, he was to be obligated to make a good faith effort to find someone else to perform the procedure.

Physicians can always follow their consciences. A few brave physicians at Auschwitz refused to do "selections" (the process of sending some Jews directly to the gas chamber as they emerged from the train). But most performed their assigned task, obnoxious as it might have been, knowing that if they didn't do the job, somebody else would.

Today's physicians may also ask why they should incur society's punishment (even penalties not as severe as in Nazi Germany) for adhering to the dictates of conscience, especially when it won't make any ultimate difference to the patient. They will receive little moral support from the leaders of the medical profession, who renounce the absolute morality of the Oath of Hippocrates, especially the injunctions not to give a deadly drug, advice that could cause death, or a means of producing abortion. Here are some sample comments by well-respected physicians and ethicists.

"Today we are aware that there are finite resources to support the care of patients, and the decision to prolong one life means that we compromise another. . . . Continuing the historical reluctance to taint 'the healing role' and the economically oversimplified distinction between healing and killing that was so clear to Hippocrates is anachronistic."[10]

"The norms of Hippocrates' time need to be modified to apply to our own."[11]

"Concern that the legalization of euthanasia would be perilous public policy, even if it were well grounded . . . supports the present tyranny of the majority in a matter . . . basic to human existence and personal autonomy. . . . Resisting a rational and urgent request for merciful death in the name of protecting the medical profession reflects the anachronistic values of the Hippocratic oath. . . . "[12]

What about resisting a request for death in the name of protecting *patients*? Do patients want a doctor who knows the difference between healing and killing? Do they want a doctor who has morals and lives by them, even if he wouldn't necessarily do everything they want? How can they rely on him to respect their moral values, if he is willing to compromise his own?

This is a crucial way in which non-Hippocratic medicine resembles veterinary medicine. It is common practice for the vet to put the dog to sleep, out of kindness.

If someone owns a dog, he has a right to dispose of it.

If society owns the resources of its citizens, the better to redistribute them fairly, does it own the citizens and have the right to dispose of *them*?

....

14

PRACTICE GUIDELINES: THE ANSWER
TO COST AND QUALITY?

....

Practice guidelines are the Carter's Little Liver Pills of health policy, except that we may be forced to swallow them.

WHEN it comes to choosing death, self-determination is supposed to be desirable; in fact, it is said to be your right. But you who are presumably capable of making this awesome decision—even in advance of knowing what your actual situation will be—are too ignorant and unsophisticated to make decisions about your own medical care, in the view of the government and organized medicine.

Death ends suffering. It is also cheap and simple. Maintaining life, on the other hand, can be painful, expensive, and complicated. Achieving optimal quality of life involves many complex decisions. Various agencies, including managed care plans, are eager to influence those decisions.

Managed care is one way to narrow patients' options, while permitting government and the managers to talk about maintaining choice. You can, after all, choose a different plan, which has guidelines more acceptable to you, or you can escape altogether to see an independent physician, at least if you can afford to pay twice—once, in advance, for the managed care physician you *don't* see.

To protect (control) both independent physicians and those patients who exercise their right to escape from the constraints of the plan, a broader mechanism is envisioned.

Government and organized medicine (the AMA) agree. The way to contain costs (not to reduce them) and to ensure quality (not to ensure *good* quality or to *improve* quality) is to institute guidelines called "practice parameters." This idea is a central feature of the AMA's sixteen-point plan called Health Access America.

Let's look at some of these guidelines and see whether you will be better off because of them.

THE $850,000 ANSWER TO THE $20 QUESTION

The government has signed a contract to pay $850,000 for the development of practice guidelines for a common medical problem: otitis media.

Ear infections are familiar to every pediatrician, family doctor, internist, nurse, and mother. They are not suspensefully awaiting a state-of-the-art protocol for handling this problem.

Undoubtedly, many hours were spent in expert cogitation over which antibiotic to prescribe. But I am willing to bet a week's pay that the protocol will say nothing at all about what I really need to know.

The most difficult question is: How do you diagnose otitis media? Before you get to that point, you can hardly use the otitis media protocol.

Usually, the mother or the patient does not come into the office with the chief complaint: "The baby has otitis media." ("*I* have otitis media" is not too uncommon as patients become more sophisticated.)

More commonly, the complaint is: "The baby is fussy."

Otitis media is definitely in the differential diagnosis of the fussy baby syndrome.

So how do you distinguish this from the other possible causes—the dog stole the pacifier, or the baby's dinner didn't agree with him, or the baby doesn't like the new babysitter? Or if the baby has a fever and some other symptoms like a runny nose, how do you know it isn't just the common cold?

Obviously, you have to look in the ear. This is where my admiration for pediatricians reaches one of its high points. How do you get the baby to *let* you look in its ear?

My niece Emily used to scream every time she saw me. That's because whenever her mother thought she might have otitis media, she would bring the baby to see Doctor Aunt Jane, who would have to look in her ears. Fortunately, not all babies are as adamantly resistant to otoscopes as Emily was. Emily *hated* to have anybody even try to look in her ears.

Getting the baby to hold still or at least not to squirm too much is only one of the problems. Babies frequently have wax in their ears. But once you deal with the wax and manage to get a glimpse of the eardrum, you have to interpret the findings. If the eardrum is a nice pearly gray, that's normal. But what if it is a little red? Babies' eardrums get a little red when they have been crying. Emily's eardrums were always red, at least every time that I saw them. Sometimes it was because of otitis media, but sometimes it was probably because of coming to Doctor Aunt Jane's. I'd really like to see what that $850,000 protocol has to say about Emily. Not that it matters. Despite the lack of the protocol, Emily never had any complications from ear infections. Also, we are now friends, and that's what counts.

I suppose the practice guidelines will say something about what antibiotic to pick. I'll bet it doesn't say to go look in the cupboard to see what samples have been left by pharmaceutical salesmen. That's what a lot of doctors do. And they admit to it, too, if they're at an informal buffet dinner sponsored by some research or pharmaceutical company.

There are very good reasons for a well-stocked sample cupboard. Certain antibiotics cost a lot of money, thanks to the $231 million[1] worth of testing they have undergone to satisfy the FDA that they work (among other reasons). A high price is surely warranted for those few drugs—about 1 in every 4,000 that undergoes testing on human subjects—that win the prize of FDA approval.[2] Still, Mom is going to be very unhappy if she spends $50 at the drugstore only to have the baby throw up after the very first dose. Of course, she won't care so much about the price if the insurance company paid for the medicine. By the time the next premium increase comes around, the connection with the expensive medicines will be long obscured. But insurance companies have ways of protecting themselves. The new, expensive antibiotics are not on the formulary that the insurance company allows doctors to use, so the questions discussed here might not ever come up between doctor and patient, having already been settled by the managers. The old medicines are probably more likely to make the baby throw up, but the insurance companies don't care about that.

The practice guidelines will probably say something about cost-benefit in the choice of the antibiotic. It is a lot cheaper, for example, to prescribe generic amoxicillin than the latest Cephabug. (Certain classes of antibiotics are proliferating like fruit flies. There are so many types of cephalosporins that I can't remember them all. I hesitate to mention a specific one because it might be obsolete by the time this is printed.) Amoxicillin does work, most of the time. But what if it doesn't?

Bacteria are becoming more resistant to wonder drugs. In some areas of the country, 20 percent of the strains of *Hemophilus influenza*, one common cause of otitis media, are resistant to amoxicillin. That means 80 percent are still sensitive. So the protocol might recommend starting with amoxicillin, reserving the more expensive drugs for resistant cases.

How do you find out whether the patient's bacteria are resistant? One way is obtain a culture specimen from the middle ear. To do that, you would have to puncture the eardrum. Babies like that even less than having their ear looked at—and woe to the next doctor who has to see that baby for any reason! Even if the culture could be obtained without hurting or risking harm to the baby, it would take at least two days for the culture to grow and perhaps another day for the sensitivities to be reported. It would also cost enough to pay for the Cephabug.

Another way is to prescribe the cheaper antibiotic and tell the parents to bring the baby back if it's not better.

The idea of bringing the baby back to the doctor's office is not likely to appeal to most parents. It takes time and costs money—maybe enough to pay for the Cephabug, especially if a parent has to take time off from work. Also, the baby will probably have to be in the waiting room with many other sick children and may catch something else. Worst of all, "not getting better" could mean coming down with meningitis, a rare but potentially devastating disease.

The individual physician, treating a patient he knows well, will take many things into consideration when writing the prescription. What is the incidence of resistant *Hemophilus* in the community? Is the baby in a daycare center where he is more likely to acquire a resistant organism? Has he recently had several courses of antibiotics, making it more likely that he has developed his own resistant strain? Are there any factors that would make him more likely to develop a complication? How sick does he look? How important is the *known* cost of the drug to the parents, compared with the *potential* cost of a slower recovery? How easy will it be to make a change in therapy if it is needed? How do the parents feel about the various possibilities?

The protocol won't have the answers to these questions. The managed care doctor probably won't know the patient and won't have time to ask the questions. (The old-time family doctor would know most of the answers, usually without having to ask.)

And who will write the protocol? Will it be physicians with vast experience in treating otitis media? Will their experience be obtained in a patient population similar to that of the doctor who is using the protocol, or will it be from very specialized referral practices? Will the protocol writers even be physicians at all? The RAND Corporation bids for such contracts, for example. Only about half the panel members for the first protocol, on urinary incontinence, were physicians.

Practice guidelines are already in use in some managed care settings. For example, a certain HMO has figured out that unnecessary tonsillectomies are sometimes done. Their managers have established criteria to determine which operations are justified.

This HMO knows exactly what to do when a doctor requests permission to perform the procedure on a patient who has not had the requisite five episodes of tonsillitis in the past year. They just say no.

It doesn't matter that the child's tonsils are growing together in the back of his throat so that he has difficulty swallowing and breathing. His tonsils are big, but they have not been infected the requisite number of times in the past year.

It doesn't matter that his physician is a specialist in otorhinolaryngology (ear, nose, and throat) and has had many years of experience with tonsils. He knows about the disasters that can result from performing surgery and also from *not* performing it when it is needed. The managers assume that the physician's very experience makes him biased. Besides, he has a vested interest. He undoubtedly expects to be paid for doing the operation and can also expect a long-term benefit from keeping a patient happy. The HMO stands firm. The only thing the doctor can do is advise the family to sue the HMO, unless they want to go ahead with the procedure without benefit of insurance reimbursement. The doctor needs to be very careful, however, about what he says regarding the HMO. Some contracts have a clause prohibiting the doctor from criticizing the HMO.

The doctor could provide his services free of charge, but that doesn't help the patient with the hospital or surgicenter bill, which will be much higher than the surgeon's fee.

In case the reader thinks this is an extreme example: *I am not making this up.*

THE EXPERTS STRIKE OUT

Physicians often say (except when they are advocating practice guidelines) that medical knowledge changes constantly. What is dogma in one generation may be anathema in the next. There is even a famous course on medical ignorance taught by Dr. Marlys Witte at the University of Arizona College of Medicine.

Most physicians can cite examples of how dramatically things have changed within their own memory.

Today, postoperative patients are urged to get out of bed almost as soon as they have recovered from the anesthetic. New mothers go home, fully ambulatory, about twenty-four hours after giving birth. Even patients with heart attacks are out of bed soon after.

Early ambulation (the medical jargon for getting the patient up) prevents blood clots and other complications of bedrest. This commonsense realization came to the medical profession quite recently. My mother was sent home in an ambulance ten days after I was born. When I was a medical student, strict bedrest was enforced for about a week in our heart attack patients.

The medical profession was about 100 years behind my great-great-grandmother, Ellen Hanley. She had the outrageous idea that mothers should get out of bed immediately after giving birth. It is said that she never lost a mother and never had a case of milk leg (thrombophlebitis). Fortunately, there were no practice guidelines at that time, and the medical profession and the government dealt with practitioners like Grandma by ignoring them. There were methods of treatment that were accepted in the medical community, but they were not documented or codified.

When I was in medical school, the treatment of peptic ulcer disease included a regimen called a Sippy diet and various types of antacids. Surgery was common for complications because the medical treatment was not very effective. When patients were bleeding, the site was difficult to determine. Sometimes, a rigid endoscope was passed into the stomach, a difficult and not very satisfactory procedure (though not as dangerous as sword-swallowing). If bleeding didn't stop, major surgery was the only recourse.

Today, we still see patients with Billroth I and Billroth II anastomoses, the ways of connecting the stomach remnant to the intestine after surgical removal of part of the stomach. Most of these were done decades ago, but their complications persist. The treatment of peptic ulcer disease was revolutionized by drugs that keep the stomach from secreting acid. And if patients bleed, they can be easily investigated with a fiber-optic endoscope, requiring only minimal sedation. Sometimes the bleeding site can be treated through the endoscope, obviating a surgical procedure.

These advances are now standard procedure and would surely be included in practice guidelines written today. But what if the guidelines had been written two decades ago? Would Sippy diets and gastric resections still be the standard of care?

Another technology that might have been excluded from practice guidelines, had they been written twenty years ago, was hemodialysis for kidney failure. When I was a medical student, hemodialysis was in use, but not at Columbia-Presbyterian Medical Center. The reason was said to be that Columbia's leading kidney specialist just didn't believe in it.

If a patient at Columbia-Presbyterian recovered from acute kidney failure, that was fine. A patient whose kidneys didn't recover had two options: (1) die or (2) go down the street to Francis Delafield, a New York City municipal hospital, to seek admission to the dialysis program. At that time, the leading kidney specialist's influence did not extend beyond the radius of about one city block. He was not chief of the Technology Assessment Bureau of the U.S. Department of Health and Human Services, with authority to determine what procedures could be done and/or paid for in every hamlet in these United States.

Hemodialysis never underwent a technology assessment. It has provided many years of productive life to end-stage renal disease patients. But the cost has been far higher than the original cost estimates. It might not have been approved in the cost-containment climate that prevails today.

Hemodialysis has now become well entrenched. It would probably be politically impossible to cut off access to this technology. It has an established interest group. However desirable this may be for protecting dialysis patients, it has a downside: an interest in preventing replacement of the industry by a new technology.

THE EXPERTS VERSUS TECHNOLOGY

Stopping medical progress is not a side effect of technology assessment and practice guidelines. It is their purpose.

At a forum sponsored by various managed care plans and congressional representatives from Tucson, a well-respected academician said: "Research is like nuclear war. As John F. Kennedy said, 'The fruits of victory will be ashes in our mouth.' If we don't stop research, care will become more and more sophisticated."

Technology assessment is one part of his answer. As he pointed out, it takes ten to twelve years to bring a drug to market because of FDA regulations. (He didn't mention the $231 million cost.) He would like to set up similar hurdles for devices and procedures.

The second part of the academician's answer is that since we can't afford technology, "we need fewer sick people."

The most cost-effective way to reduce the number of sick people was discussed in the last chapter. So I found his statement to be chilling, regardless of what he thought he meant by it.

While this influential physician is apparently opposed to unlimited research that might lead to technology to turn sick or dying people into relatively healthy people, he does favor research that might prevent certain diseases. For example, he believes we should investigate whether increasing bran in the diet prevents colon cancer.

The reason for preferring research on bran to research on treatment for colon cancer is the presumed cost-effectiveness. But do we *know* that bran research will be the most cost-effective? Certainly not. The conclusions of the study might be negative. Eating huge amounts of bran may have no effect at all on colon cancer. Or maybe it would decrease colon cancer but increase some other disease by the same amount.

On the other hand, research might reveal an effective drug that would help this generation of people who have cancer. Or it might reveal a better method of detecting cancer at a very early stage, when it is easily curable by surgery. Even if eating bran is effective, how do we weigh a potential benefit to future generations who will grow up eating bran against the benefit to people who are alive now, in addition to the future generations? An ounce of prevention may very well *not* be worth a megaton of cure.

What Is the "Standard of Care"?

Technology assessment is intended to determine the "standard of care" for use of, or avoidance of, a particular method or device.

The standard of care is a legal concept used in establishing liability for a bad outcome. To show fault in a malpractice action, the plaintiff needs to show that the standard of care was violated. The standard is supposedly defined by practice in the community, although the trend is to hold physicians to a national standard. But what determines the standard?

The National Bureau of Standards keeps a set of measurements to which all others are compared; for example, the meter or the pound. The very word *standard* suggests the existence of certitude like that which existed with respect to money when the gold standard was in existence. Now the gold standard is purely metaphorical. However, there is no bureau of standards for medicine. The standard of care is what the expert witnesses say it is. Their opinion varies and often seems to be correlated with the source and amount of their payment.

Even though they might disagree with specific practice guidelines, many physicians tend to favor the concept as a way to diminish their exposure to malpractice litigation.

Supposedly, the guidelines would only be advisory. But what would happen to the first dissenting doctor? The Long Island physician who asked that question found out the answer for himself. He lost his county job when he elected to follow his own best judgment in treating his patients (prisoners in the jail) instead of the orders of his administrative supervisor. Another likely possibility is a malpractice judgment. Avoidance of innovation would become very important as a "risk management" technique.

From Square Roots to Abdominal Pain

Sometimes practice guidelines are expressed in the form of an "algorithm." An algorithm is a methodical sequence of steps for performing a calculation, say dividing one number by another or extracting a square root.

Algorithms are indispensable in mathematics. And mathematical concepts are indispensable in medicine. (A lot of diagnosis involves playing the odds.) The branched-chain logic in some published algorithms can be a helpful method of analyzing a problem.

But caring for patients is not a purely mathematical exercise. For one thing, you can't find out if you got the right answer by simply multiplying two numbers together. Sometimes there *isn't* a right answer—as when you're between a rock and a hard place.

We studied some algorithms when I worked at the VA. Did they save money or improve patient care?

The short answer to the question is no. The long answer[3] is beyond the scope of this book.

But the results of our $250,000 study are simply irrelevant. The government is moving rapidly to implement practice guidelines even though it has no evidence that they will help and no evidence that they will *not* actually be harmful.

I did a few other, nonfunded studies when I had access to VA medical records. My conclusions were as follows: (1) A real live clinician, even a VA resident physician or nurse practitioner, makes better decisions than the ones dictated by any of three different protocols for abdominal pain, as determined by clinical follow-up and surgical pathology.[4] (2) The best way to determine whether a patient with chronic lung disease needs to be in the hospital is to *ask him*.[5] I specifically tested the 1983 criteria used by the government Peer Standard Review Organization (PSRO) to approve or deny such admissions. Their guidelines could be rationally applied in only 302 of the 794 visits by VA lung patients that I reviewed and would have resulted in an erroneous decision in 40 percent of those. But it doesn't matter; the PSRO bases its criteria on authority, not data.

Will the government's blue-ribboned experts do better with practice guidelines and technology assessment than I did with my small studies?

At present, the answer must be based on ideology, because there is no science. But if readers would like to make a judgment for themselves, several guidelines are now available. The one on urinary incontinence is described below.

A MODEL GUIDELINE

During a 1992 press conference that announced the unveiling of the second official guideline, on urinary incontinence, James O. Mason, M.D., HHS assistant secretary of health, said that it was a continuation of a "peaceful revolution in American medicine."

Naturally, I opened my copy of the guideline the moment it arrived in the mail. I wanted to see what the AHCPR (whatever that stands for) could accomplish on its "minuscule" budget ($120 million for 1992).

The guideline kit contains a 125-page paperback book, Quick Reference Guides for patients and for physicians, and a toll-free telephone number (800-358-9295). Some of the materials are written to justify the existence of the project. The authors claim that their guideline can save an average of $105 *per episode of stress incontinence* in the outpatient and $535 in the inpatient setting.

Apparently, the authors think that it now costs *more* than $105, on the average, every time somebody leaks when she sneezes.

To bring about the remarkable savings, the guideline makes seven broad-based recommendations including: educate the consumer to report incontinence problems once they occur; improve the detection and documentation of urinary incontinence (UI) through better history taking and health care record keeping; and reduce variations among health care professionals.

The most important and effective treatment for urinary incontinence is surgery for an enlarged prostate (a transurethral resection of the prostate or TURP). It works 97 percent of the time, if an enlarged prostate is the cause of the problem and if surgery has not been so long delayed that the bladder muscle gets too stretched out. (The waiting times in Canada are very important to the outcome in this type of "elective" surgery.)

What do the little boxes and arrows in the guideline say about when to do a TURP? Wisely, the advice is to *ask a doctor.*

However, the guideline *does* have a numbered paragraph describing how to test the ability of a frail nursing home resident to "respond to toileting needs":

This can be assessed by holding up two objects and asking the patient to point to or look first at one object and then the other. Patients are not eligible for incontinence rehabilitation if they fail to respond correctly to the instructions on three separate trials, preferably administered on at least two separate days. This screening must be modified for blind subjects.

There is also a method of demonstrating success or failure:"staff and supervisors monitor with regular checks of wetness/dryness."

Did we really need government contractors to help us figure these things out?

The government contractors do have some suggestions for patients who can't benefit from surgery, estrogen, pelvic exercises, or commonsense modifications of behavior or living space. They deplore routine use of an absorbent product—the mainstay of management in the view of a mere physician. Such unmentionables should be thought of as a last resort, only after a "basic evaluation by a health professional." These things might lead to "acceptance of the condition that removes [the wearer's] motivation to seek evaluation and treatment," encouraging people to remain among the six million who suffer in silence.

What does the guideline have to offer instead? It recommends public education on UI, with public talk shows or interviews, health lectures, toll-free telephone messages, audiotapes, videotapes, movies, slides, slide tapes, film strips, computers, and interactive videodiscs, to teach both men and women about scheduled voiding and proper bladder emptying techniques. It also suggests biofeedback, vaginal cones (to enhance pelvic exercises), sophisticated tests (such as Valsalva leak point pressures and dynamic urethral profilometry), the sharing of experiences in a nonthreatening atmosphere, and trained observations of the voiding process. If all that doesn't work, then the patient can still resort to an absorbent product. (They forgot to mention the washing machine.)

The booklet does contain one genuinely helpful feature: a list of ten drugs that are possibly effective in UI. Only two of the ten are approved for this indication by the FDA. It might be difficult to find out about the other eight from anything other than a government-sponsored publication, because manufacturers are forbidden to talk about such off-label uses (unapproved indications for an approved drug).

To come up with this definitive book, more than 7,000 reports were reviewed by the chosen panel of fifteen experts including doctors, nurses, an occupational therapist, psychologists, a health educator, an administrator, and a consumer representative.

The guideline may have arrived not a minute too soon. After a 50 percent cut in their fee for doing a TURP (as a result of the relative value scale), urologists may go fishing.

Remember that toll-free number: 800-358-9295. Call during regular working hours to receive educational materials.

It's Not Big Brother

Physicians should resist the temptation to pitch the guideline into the trash.

"These guidelines are not Big Brother telling doctors and nurses what to do," says Assistant Secretary Mason. (At least not yet.) "But neither are they idle advice," he adds.

Physicians don't have to follow the guidelines, but they may not ignore them. They need to "document legitimate medical reasons why practice guidelines are or are not being followed," says Kathy Hastings, director of the legal medicine program of the Agency for Health Care Policy and Research (AHCPR).[6]

That's another reason to go fishing. If you must document a *legitimate* medical reason, but what seems legitimate to you is always subject to second-guessing, then you are in a double-bind situation every time you see a patient who is the least bit complicated. The managers assume that you can't do anything right. And, in fact, you can't. You can't exercise medical judgment under these conditions, just as you can't do surgery with your hands tied together.

The patients might as well join the doctors at the lake. Maybe their condition will get better on its own. At least they can avoid a physician who has effectively been given incentives, to do them harm and guidelines to justify such treatment.

15

NEGATIVE INCENTIVES (MEDICAL POLICING)

Most doctors are "going along to get along" because they are afraid.

WHY PHYSICIANS ARE SURRENDERING

IN THE PAST, bureaucratic medicine ran into a formidable barrier: the staunch, organized opposition of American physicians. In the 1990s, physicians have accepted government or other third-party invasions of their offices. Although the majority of them don't *like* managed care or government insurance, they do not resist. They complain in the doctors' lounge, then go back to their offices and "cooperate."

Many physicians are putting in their time until they retire, and many are retiring early. The AMA blusters a little but has no principles that cannot be compromised. In fact, its own journal frequently takes an anti-Hippocratic stance, although AMA officials deny that any of their publications necessarily represent AMA policy.

Why are physicians waving a white flag and abjectly pleading for a "seat at the table" where the terms of surrender are negotiated?

Many physicians have forgotten their principles and their calling. They have no desire to fight against the destruction of their profession because they themselves have abandoned it. Some are even ready for a government takeover of medicine because they say things can't get any worse. The profession is irretrievably lost, they think, but they know that things can get worse for them personally. They still have something to lose, and they are afraid.

They should be even more afraid than they are. Many physicians are oblivious to the implications of the administrative law that is now evolving.

Patients need to be afraid, too. If there are no real physicians, then patients will receive poor medical care. But that's not the worst of the problem.

Society can flourish in the absence of good medical care, although individuals suffer unnecessarily. But it cannot flourish under an oppressive, arbitrary government.

If doctors can be tyrannized, even though they are still relatively high in public esteem (at least compared with lawyers and congressmen), then every citizen is at risk.

THE NEED FOR PUNISHMENT

Modern psychologists talk about "education," "incentives," and "positive reinforcement."

But what does society do when these methods don't bring about the behavior that it wants or stamp out all the behavior that it *doesn't* want? And worse still, what can society do if its own incentives reward undesired behavior? How can it affect the behavior without removing a cherished entitlement such as medical care that appears to be free at the time of service?

Oathing ceremonies don't do the job and could be counterproductive if people take the wrong oath too seriously.

Society—even our seemingly permissive society—demands obedience to the correct code and needs a method of enforcement.

The obvious answer is punishment.

We don't like to talk about punishment. We prefer to call it something else, like "negative reinforcement," "education," "deterrence," "corrective measures," or even an "award" (to the other party). This is not mere squeamishness, as we shall see. Punishing someone in our society is difficult because you have to allow him to exercise his rights.

Just to avoid misunderstanding, let me say from the outset that I do not believe physicians are or should be above the law. But the law must be just. It should treat physicians as human beings, all of whom are equal under the law, not as a special class of scapegoats. And the law's demands must be of a nature that a mere human being can understand and abide.

MALPRACTICE

Tort law is an important quality assurance mechanism.

If someone harms you through malice or negligence, you have the right to sue him under the common law. You have the right to be heard before an unbiased court, unless the accuser has been given immunity as in peer review.

If someone accuses you of a tort, you also have the right to defend yourself before an unbiased court. You have the right to confront and cross-examine your accuser, to call witnesses, and to use legal discovery procedures. You can demand a trial by jury. The trial will be an adversarial procedure, in which both sides have equal rights and rules of evidence will apply.

Conscientious, competent doctors have suffered injustice in medical malpractice cases. One reason is the moral hazard of liability insurance. Another is that the court doesn't really believe what the plaintiff's attorneys love to tell doctors: "You're not God."

Most bad medical outcomes are not under the doctor's control. Even if the doctor does make an error in judgment, the outcome usually results from a combination of factors: the patient's illness, the patient's choices, actions taken or not taken by hospital staff, and sometimes pure chance. But some court decisions seem to mark a reversion to the primitive belief that physicians really do have godlike powers. Given this belief, it was reasonable for the ancients to conclude that a patient's death was the doctor's fault. Liability being commensurate with power, the doctor who lost his patient could lose his life or at least his right hand.

I think that tort law can and should be reformed. However, it would be a disaster for both patients and physicians to destroy the basic adversarial mechanism and to turn malpractice cases into administrative hearings as the AMA would like to do, for reasons I will describe later in this chapter. Individuals must be held responsible for their actions, but they must also have the right to defend themselves.

BEYOND MALPRACTICE:
THE ENFORCEMENT OF POSITIVE OBLIGATIONS

Before there can be a tort, somebody has to be harmed.

The basic Hippocratic obligation is to "do no harm." And every citizen has the responsibility not to harm his neighbor.

However, in non-Hippocratic medicine, in fact, whenever there is a positive right to health care, the physician's responsibility does not stop with avoiding harm to individuals.

Under Medicare, the physician must furnish "health care services economically and only when and to the extent medically necessary and of a quality that meets professionally recognized standards of health care."

What does this mean?

A physician can only say, "You tell me. I don't know."

The government does try to tell him. It produces tens of thousands of rules and regulations. It is literally impossible not to have violated some of them.

So far, not many physicians have been subjected to the draconian penalties that are possible under existing law. Most physicians aren't even aware of what is possible. By the time they are, the mechanism will be solidly entrenched.

The sword of Damocles is being raised. It doesn't have to fall very often to be used as an instrument of terror.

If you think I am paranoid, read on. I would be delighted if you can prove me wrong.

SHOULD PATIENTS CARE?

"If you're not afraid of me, I'll send somebody that you *are* afraid of," said the Blue Cross/Blue Shield (BCBS) investigator sent by the Medicaid Fraud Control Unit of the attorney general's office. So far, they had found nothing substantially wrong, but someone had to find *something*.

The doctor, whose office had previously been invaded by attorney general investigators and the city police, was objecting to an order to read aloud from her patients' charts. Apparently, it was difficult for the investigator to read the charts himself. The doctor thought that might be because she thinks in Spanish, even though the charts are kept in English, as the law requires.

She had overheard the attorney general investigators speaking of her as "that Mexican doctor."

"I am not a Mexican," she told me. "Anyway, I am an American citizen. But you'd think I was living in Argentina."

The doctor practices in the Hispanic barrio of an inner-city ghetto in the United States of America, providing medical care to an underserved population. At least for the present. She thinks the government is trying to drive her out of practice. She sees poor people, and that costs the government money, even if the government doesn't pay her very much for services to her Medicaid patients (a total of $10,000 in 1991). However, she orders lab tests and other expensive diagnostic procedures, and she admits patients to the hospital.

After the attorney general and the BCBS investigators found nothing, the inspector general investigator came. That is someone you have to be afraid of, too.

The doctor was being prosecuted for criminal fraud. The investigators could have chosen to use a civil procedure instead, at their discretion. Possibly, they would have opted for the latter if the doctor had any assets to seize.

One of the doctor's alleged crimes was charging for an office visit in which the patient was not weighed and his blood pressure was not measured. The patient was well known to the doctor, and there was no need to put the patient in an examining room to perform an unnecessary examination, as was admitted by the judge who reviewed the evidence. The service in question was to discuss a prescription for a drug with potential harmful effects. The doctor felt that she was using her training and experience to provide medical evaluation and treatment. She thought that talking to a patient and giving him advice were payable services. So a claim for an intermediate office visit was submitted.

Apparently, there wasn't enough evidence in the medical records to convince a court of the doctor's guilt. So the investigators visited patients, looking for someone to testify against the doctor.

"If she isn't guilty of fraud, then *you are*," some patients were told.

I don't know how the story will end, only that the doctor's ordeal will last for years. She has had to refinance her home to pay her lawyers. Her practice is smaller now because patients (especially her suburbanite patients) are afraid to see her. They don't want any investigators knocking on *their* door. Besides, many people think that the police only go after bad guys here in the United States.

This doctor is accustomed to practice in the ghetto. She was able to take it in stride when a deranged patient showed up in her office with a gun, threatening a member of her staff. But the attack by the government has been devastating.

I think that a jury hearing this case would vote unanimously for acquittal. But by that time the doctor would already have been punished far more severely than the average street criminal.

Who will compensate the doctor for being wronged?

And who, after hearing her story, would want to care for patients in any underserved area? Who indeed would want to invest years and tens of thousands of dollars in a medical education if this can happen to a conscientious, law-abiding physician anywhere in the United States?

Comfortable people, living a safe distance from the decaying inner city, might choose to turn their backs. But the problem is already coming closer to home, as I will show.

WHY DON'T DOCTORS POLICE THEMSELVES?

Some think that all the legal sanctions, from tort law to criminal law the draconian administrative sanctions described later, are richly deserved because doctors don't police themselves. Peer review mechanisms supposedly don't work, because of the "old boy network," or the "conspiracy of silence," sometimes attributed to the fraternalism enjoined in the Hippocratic oath itself.

Of course, other professions don't police themselves so well either. How many unethical lawyers are disbarred? How many corrupt judges are removed from office? How many check-kiting legislators are impeached? And how many incompetent public school teachers are fired? There is a lot of room for more policing of the professions. Maybe methods used against doctors will be tried in *your* profession next.

Before demanding that doctors police themselves—or else—let's ask ourselves what that means and how desirable it is. In fact, doctors are already asking this, and the doctor that *you* might have chosen to see may already have taken up carpentry.

What Policemen Do

Let's start with the definition of a policeman. He is an officer of the law, an agent of the government, invested with the legal right to use force against those who break the law. For all the elementary school propaganda about friendly Officer Joe who helps you cross the street, everybody can see that Officer Joe carries a .357 on his belt. It is loaded, and he knows how to shoot it. (At least I hope he does; he needs to in order to do his job.) Even though we respect the police and would not want to do without them, we must always keep in mind the possibility of abuse of their power. We do have means of policing the police: the police bureaucracy itself, the courts, and the elected officials to whom the chief of police is accountable. These mechanisms are not perfect, as various notorious cases have shown.

Now do we really want to turn every doctor into a policeman, armed not with a .357 or other means of deadly force, but with the power to inflict professional death upon errant colleagues?

The first question is this: If physicians are so evil that they need constant policing by their colleagues, can they be trusted not to abuse police power? True, there are bad doctors, just as there are bad lawyers and bad senators and bad mechanics. But what if the bad guys have the best political skills? Bad legislators often get reelected, term after term. What if bad doctors gain control of the peer review committees? The community might end up with the Titipu solution.

In Titipu, scene of Gilbert and Sullivan's *Mikado*, the emperor (like Ralph Nader) was upset because no one had been beheaded recently. So the community appointed a new Lord High Executioner named KoKo, who was the next person in line for execution for the capital crime of flirting.

Unfortunately, our Titipu solution is likely to lack two features of the original: candor (KoKo was known to be a convict whereas our peer reviewers are above suspicion) and popular assent (in those times flirting was considered to be normal male behavior even if illegal).

Some physicians are eager to assume the role of KoKo, executing judgment against their peers without admitting that they, too, might have been guilty of flirting with the regulations.

James Todd, executive vice president of the AMA, stated: "At all levels we must identify, prevent, or deal harshly with those who would serve themselves at the expense of others."[1] Commenting on physicians accused of Medicaid fraud, Todd says: "What is discouraging is that these physicians did not perceive they had done wrong and would not acknowledge their guilt."

Apparently, it did not occur to Dr. Todd that some persons (even doctors) who refuse to confess might be innocent.

Who are the offending physicians? Like the inner-city physician mentioned earlier, they "typically do not represent the mainstream of American medicine." They tend to be black or graduates of foreign medical schools. Most often, they serve inner-city populations. Their average age is fifty-seven, ten years older than the average for all physicians. Psychiatrists are overrepresented.[2] Some have made themselves quite obnoxious by criticizing their colleagues or the government. They are just the sort of person who might be found on KoKo's "little list of society offenders who might well be underground, and who never would be missed" (by the third parties paying the bills— they might be sorely missed by the patients who rely on them).

The AMA speaks of a "subculture of medical delinquency" comparable to the "subculture of [juvenile] delinquency." Members of this subculture are evidently defined as having a derogatory view of Medicaid, using pejorative terms like *bureaucrat*, thinking their view of how things should be done is more sensible than that of the rightful authorities, claiming to be "trusting people, more interested in the welfare of others than their own salvation," and failing to recognize that "there are other perspectives regarding their behaviors, and that, in the Medicaid program, it is these forces that have the power to define how things are to be done."

There are physicians who are guilty of fraud. They should be defined by their actions, not by their subculture.

If the primary objective is to root out fraud, we should demand that all bills be submitted first to patients rather than only to insurers, and that insurers pay their subscribers rather than providers of medical services. Most fraud would cease immediately, without the need to install an FBI agent or AMA representative in every medical office.

We cannot eliminate fraud by pasting a label of "delinquent" on physicians who might simply be placing their *patients* first instead of the "benefit program."

When we call for doctors to police themselves, we might end up with the worst of them lording it over the adherents to the Oath of Hippocrates.

Why Do We Need More Medical Policemen Now?

The Oath of Hippocrates with all of its alleged faults dates to the fifth century B.C. Why, then, so much furor over the need for self-policing dating from the late twentieth century A.D.?

A smaller proportion of medical students take the Oath of Hippocrates rather than a more "socially responsible" oath. A higher percentage of medical students take a course in medical ethics during their training. We have armies of lawyers eager to champion plaintiffs who seek redress. The programs that are most subject to abuse have far more controls now than they did at their inception in the mid 1960s. Why so much concern over abuses *now*, in the 1990s?

It could be that more abuse is occurring. It could be that our morals are in decline. It *isn't* that it's harder to sue doctors and win judgments in court.

But there is still another possibility. It could be that physicians' behavior is unchanged, but Medicare is essentially bankrupt and private insurance is about to collapse.

The government made promises that it can't keep. Since it is politically impossible to admit to the error, somebody has to take the rap. And somebody has to disgorge money. Lots of money.

Doctors are the obvious scapegoats. Some of them have a high income and valuable assets, and it is easy to use the politics of envy against them.

Doctors do control a large fraction of medical expenditures through the orders they write (even though only 19 percent of medical expenditures are for physicians' services and less than half of that is physicians' personal income, the rest being consumed by overhead). Because physicians are relatively few in number, it is relatively easy to aim cost-control measures at them, rather than at the patients who come to them demanding, and often needing, services. And if the cost-control measures work by decreasing the availability and quality of care, doctors can be blamed.

As doctors are financially squeezed, it becomes easier to enlist their cooperation in a self-policing campaign against other doctors. *Your* doctor might be a target, especially if he provides superior service at a price that his competitors don't want to match.

Medical Police and the Government

The medical police work at three levels: hospital peer review; government-funded peer review organizations; and state licensure boards. The government is involved in all of them, although physicians are needed to consult and lend legitimacy to the process.

The fact is that the government *has* to be involved in police actions, to make them legal. To talk to a colleague in the locker room, or to deny him a certificate from a voluntary agency, or to ask him to come to a meeting of the Mortality and Morbidity Committee is not policing, even though such activities may be very important for improving medical practice. Policing involves compulsion, say, forcing somebody to cease his practice. The use of force *without* the approval of a governmental authority is called "lynching" and "vigilantism."

At present, the political climate favors getting rid of bad apples by increasingly drastic measures. But before we set up any agency tough enough to weed out every last bad apple, we should remember the parable about the man who sowed weeds in his neighbor's field. Yes, it might be possible to root up most of the weeds. But is it worth the risk of losing the wheat, too?

Keep this question in mind.

CRIMINAL LAW

Before discussing peer review, licensure, and administrative law, let us consider the more traditional meaning of the word *police*: to protect against *crime*.

With respect to doctors, the word *crime* no longer has its traditional meaning. Actions that occurred in the course of a normal practice have been prosecuted as crimes. Some were errors of judgment. Some were treatment decisions associated with an unfortunate outcome. And some were minor violations of arcane regulations.

Insurance Fraud

It is certainly true that Medicare and Medicaid fraud occurs: It is simply Sutton's law in action.

When asked why he robbed banks, repeatedly landing in jail, Willie "the Actor" Sutton is supposed to have said, "Because that's where the money is." Sutton's law is widely applied in medicine for deciding what diagnostic tests are most likely to yield the diagnosis or the "money."[3]

Third-party payment mechanisms have created a large pot of money: $700 billion per year, 40 percent coming from the government. The vault is not guarded by closed-circuit television and armed security officers. Fraudulent claims don't say: "This is a stick-up; hand over all the cash." They look the same as any other claim. Medicare is easier to rob than a bank, and there is less risk of being shot.

In the first years of fraud investigations, fraud was discovered. But in order to justify the huge budgets allocated for the purpose, it was necessary to discover more and more fraud. It turns out that this is not very difficult; every physician in the country is probably guilty of insurance fraud. It's just a matter of definition.

When a physician signs an insurance form, he is attesting to its accuracy, including the accuracy of the codes assigned for various diagnoses and procedures. One common form of fraud is coding for a level of service higher than the one that was actually performed— by the insurer's definition.

Many physicians do not even know the technical definition of an "intermediate" versus a "limited" versus an "extended" visit, especially since the definitions were all suddenly changed with the advent of the Relative Value Scale.

Some physicians get into trouble because they are simply ignorant of the requirements. Others try to bend the rules, reasoning that insurers (especially the government) are defrauding them by limiting their fees to levels that prevailed in the 1970s, despite huge increases in overhead. Therefore, they have no moral compunctions about writing down the code that corresponds to the fee they believe they should be paid rather than the one that describes the work they did. This is more convenient for both doctor and patient than having the patient return for multiple, short visits, as doctors in Germany are said to do in order to make enough money.

Some insurance fraud is committed in order to "help" patients or even to satisfy an outright demand by a patient. Most insurance policies do not cover routine office visits, checkups, and so on. But they do cover a visit for an illness. Most physicians therefore write down some diagnosis. Generally, the diagnosis is true in the sense that the patient does have the condition described. Very frequently, however, it is a chronic condition that is not the reason for the visit.

Some people feel that such misrepresentations are completely justified. They have paid their insurance premiums, and they want to get something for their money. They might have signed a contract that specifically excludes routine maintenance. Still, they feel they have been defrauded by the insurer and are thereby justified in extracting from the insurer whatever they feel they should be entitled to.

For a long time, there was little or no risk in shading the truth on insurance claims—only the risk of angering a patient by being too honest. Insurers try to teach patients that the doctor is to blame if a claim is not paid.

For following what was common practice, some physicians have faced accusations that could have landed them in prison for many lifetimes.

To make the case, the fraud squad may resort to a variety of questionable methods. Investigators, carrying hidden microphones and tape recorders, may pose as patients and attempt to entrap physicians. One common ploy is to terminate a psychiatric interview early, then accuse the physician of fraud when he charges for the full session (as psychiatrists customarily do). Another method is to pressure patients to testify against their physicians. This is relatively easy to do if the patients are themselves facing prosecution, most commonly for drug trafficking.

Once an investigation is under way, the threat of criminal prosecution has been used to get physicians to agree to accept civil sanctions, which then can be used as an admission of guilt for purposes of criminal conviction. This method of inducing "voluntary" self-incrimination is *not* placed in the same category as beating a prisoner with a rubber hose, though it may be equally effective.

Even if physicians are eventually acquitted, their reputations may have been ruined by reports of the investigations before they ever reach the courtroom. In addition, their practices can be completely disrupted by the investigation itself. Sometimes, all the physicians' records are confiscated—even records of private patients whose care was never covered under a government program and who never gave consent for their confidential records to be scrutinized by a government agent.

The very possibility that a physician may fall victim to an attempt at government entrapment places a barrier of distrust between physicians and patients. Every patient is not only a potential plaintiff but also a possible spy or informant. I am almost certain that at least one government plant has visited me as a new patient, and this suspicion colors the way I approach every new patient.

Civil Forfeiture

Despite heavy-handed enforcement methods, insurance fraud persists. Like drug trafficking, it pays better than honest work.

The FBI estimates that Medicare fraud might be draining more than $40 billion per year, much of it for diagnostic tests that Medicare is not supposed to cover. The basis for this number is not cited; the FBI could be making it up. But whatever the actual number is, the solution seems obvious: *Quit paying the thieves.* (Again, make the insurance payment to the patient, not to the provider.) But that is seen as "politically infeasible."

The politically feasible course is to subject physicians, clinics, nursing homes, suppliers of medical equipment, and other providers to the same law that is used to wage war on drug dealers or Racketeer-Influenced Corrupt Organizations (RICO). The RICO law provides for civil forfeiture of property.

Under criminal law, there is a certain sequence of events. First, a crime is reported. Then a suspect is investigated. If there is sufficient evidence, the suspect is brought to trial and might be convicted. After being convicted, he is sentenced. And only then is he punished by being deprived of life, liberty, and/or property. If he is not convicted, he goes free. He might have to pay his attorney enough to buy a new BMW. But at least he is allowed to use his money to pay for his defense, and he is not forced to pay the prosecutor.

Under civil forfeiture provisions, the sequence is inverted. First, the suspect's assets are seized, sometimes before there is any certainty that a crime has been committed. Any property that might have been used in committing the hypothetical offense—or any property arguably acquired with the proceeds of the offense—can be confiscated. Somebody has to demonstrate probable cause to a magistrate, but the term is rather loosely defined. After the suspect has been stripped of his property—his home, his bank account, the tools of his trade, whatever—he sometimes comes to trial (and sometimes is not even charged). If convicted, he is likely to lose his property permanently and go to jail besides. If he is not convicted, he is allowed to sue the government to get his property back, without interest or compensation for economic losses, probably years after the seizure. In this lawsuit, he has to prove that the property was innocent, and of course he has to pay his own legal bills.

There are several reasons for promoting civil forfeiture.

The FBI wants local law enforcement to have an incentive to cooperate in the apprehension of suspects. What could be more effective than a bounty? Especially when the bounty doesn't have to be paid by the taxpayer, but by the defendant. Because of this, "the potential of asset forfeiture is virtually unlimited."[4]

Another reason is to keep the defendant from disposing of his property before he is convicted, or from spending it all to pay his lawyer or his creditors or his children's college tuition. One justification cited by a congressman was that in the eighteenth century, sailing vessels were seized for violations of customs laws. Do they fear that a nursing home might set sail for the high seas?

A third reason is deterrence. If punishment is very severe, health care providers won't violate the law, unless they have the right friends in the right places. Not if they can figure out what the law is. One proposed law defines an "unnecessary admission of a patient to a health care facility" as a "federal health care offense," subject to forfeiture laws. And what is an unnecessary admission? It might be whatever a bureaucrat says it is.

This law is indeed a strong deterrent that sends a strong message: If you place any value on your worldly possessions, don't risk them by practicing medicine. Don't bring anything to the practice of medicine that you can't afford to lose.

That may include your life, your health, and your sanity.

Controlled Drugs

Although most enforcement activity related to prescriptions for controlled drugs is carried out by medical licensure boards, as I will describe later, drug laws can be used to entrap physicians into criminal proceedings. Government agents can fake a complaint such as a headache or kidney stones and ask for a pain reliever. One California physician was sentenced to five months in jail for prescribing Tylenol with codeine for two "patients" with headaches who turned out to be investigators. Codeine is a cheap, effective, widely used analgesic agent. The doctor's sentence was rationalized on the basis that he had not done a complete evaluation (including a pelvic examination) on these two patients before treating their symptoms.

If someday you feel you need a strong pain reliever but can't find a physician to prescribe one for you, the reason is much more likely to be the physician's fear of the police rather than any genuine concern that you might become addicted.

"Manslaughter"

Until a Florida case raised this specter, the possibility never occurred to me. A patient's death, unless deliberately hastened by the physician, might occasion a civil malpractice suit, but not a criminal charge.

Breaking new ground, a grand jury indicted a Florida physician for manslaughter in the death of an eighty-three-year-old nursing home resident. The prosecutor stated that the patient died because the physician failed to monitor his diabetes often enough. (I don't know how often is "often enough," as the blood sugar can change drastically within hours.) The physician stated that the patient died of old age. The patient had a history of Alzheimer's disease and several strokes, and his death occurred during a hospitalization for pneumonia.

The manslaughter charge carries a penalty of up to twelve years in prison and up to a $10,000 fine. An additional charge of "abuse of the elderly" could add three years to the prison sentence. The cost of the physician's defense was estimated to be $25,000. He is now unemployed.

Changing from the civil to the criminal courts saves money for liability insurers. The criminal defendant has to pay for his own lawyer, or rely on the public defender. Also, the insurer will not be liable for paying a damage claim. But is it good for patients? If a lapse in measuring the blood sugar is equivalent to assault and battery, and an excess of blood sugars constitutes Medicare fraud and abuse, just what is a physician caught in this vise to do?

Joining the ranks of the retirees is the only answer that many physicians can see.

The Limits of Criminal Prosecution

Criminal prosecution has its drawbacks for the government or for those who simply want to put a doctor out of business. The criminal defendant is protected by the U.S. Constitution. He is guaranteed a trial by jury; the right to confront and cross-examine his accusers; and protection against double jeopardy. A high standard of proof applies: The prosecutor has the burden of proof and must establish guilt beyond a reasonable doubt. These requirements can be quite burdensome. Furthermore, the government has to compete for scarce U.S. attorney resources in order to prosecute these cases.

A solution has been found: administrative law, administered by bureaucrats. It supplements criminal prosecution, which remains a threat that makes physicians more likely to submit meekly to the bureaucrats.

ADMINISTRATIVE LAW

Administrative remedies against physicians have a historical precedent: The Star Chamber in Westminster Palace, London, once used to curb the power of the British nobility. Because of its own abuse of power, the Star Chamber was abolished in 1641. Its name lives on to signify an arbitrary tribunal, and the concept is coming to life again in our own fourth branch of government and quasi-governmental subsidiaries.

Doctors, of course, are not the only potential targets.

Hospital Peer Review

To see what can happen when doctors become police, judge, and appeals court all in one, we need to look at an example: a real doctor who did lose his license to practice because of action taken by his colleagues, even before the National Practitioner Data Bank was started. He was never able to get a court to even *listen* to the merits of his case.

Dr. Curtis Caine, Jr., was an anesthesiologist who had been in practice for over ten years. He was respected by his colleagues; he lost an election for chairman of his section by only one vote. He was also a man of conviction. He did not believe that it was in the best interest of patients for the hospital to grant an exclusive anesthesia contract for obstetrics to a single group of physicians. He spoke out against the contract, and his view prevailed.

Shortly thereafter, the physicians who had failed to get their exclusive contract contrived to have Dr. Caine summarily dismissed from the staff. The pretext was the death of a patient that Dr. Caine had anesthetized—a patient who was moribund at the time the surgeon decided to operate on him for a complication of a prior surgery. The patient could not have been saved. The surgeon responsible for the complication was never even criticized.

As a result of losing his privileges at this hospital, Dr. Caine's license to practice in Mississippi was revoked. Because Mississippi took this action, other states refused to grant him a license, without considering the facts of the case, on the general principle that "where there's smoke, there's fire." The doctor could not practice medicine for three years. Finally, he found a fellowship in anesthesia, where he was treated like a man who was just out of school. To him, this was like a sentence of penal servitude. He hoped that he would be able to obtain a license from some state upon completion of the program. But several months before the end of his sentence, he was found dead on the floor of his apartment. The autopsy showed heart failure.

At the time of his death, Dr. Caine was awaiting a decision from the Fifth Circuit Court. Because the hospital that dismissed him was a state-owned institution, Dr. Caine had filed a civil rights complaint in federal court. Ultimately, the decision went against him, posthumously, and the U.S. Supreme Court refused to review it.

The Court's opinion, written by Judge Edith Jones, should strike terror into the hearts of all the nation's physicians, since every physician has had patients die: "From the standpoint of a layperson, the situation offers no dilemma: The patient died while under the anesthesiologist's care; therefore, the summary suspension of his hospital privileges was an appropriate remedy."

Hospitals and peer reviewers are presumed to be acting in good faith, even when there is evidence of a personal vendetta against a doctor.

The judge, who never considered any evidence concerning the physician's competence, wrote that "the risk of erroneous decision is . . . tolerable when compared with the state's powerful interest in protecting patient safety." And once an erroneous decision is made, one judge like her can prevent it from being reconsidered.

Ralph Nader could be right. There could be some real bad guys out there. And they might be sitting on the medical executive committee of your hospital or your managed care plan, waiting for an opportunity to ruin your favorite doctor and ensure more business for themselves.

Meanwhile, your favorite doctor may live in fear. Whether or not he realizes it, his decisions may be colored by the need to "Defer, defer, to the Lord High Executioner."

Peer Review Organizations

Another level of medical police action is the Medicare Peer Review Organization (PRO). PROs are agencies that receive multimillion-dollar contracts from the federal government to review Medicare cases.

While would-be rationers ask how many prenatal visits one bone marrow transplant could buy, I'd like to ask how many heart transplants and CT scanners one PRO contract could buy. And here I will answer the question of why your doctor doesn't want to admit you to the hospital.

PROs were initially established to perform "utilization review." Their purpose is to save the government money by denying claims.

Responding to the threat of nonpayment, hospitals established their own utilization review (UR) departments—UR tries to prevent admissions that do not meet Medicare criteria. And if a patient is staying in the hospital too long (that is, longer than Medicare is willing to pay for), a reviewer will pressure the attending physician to discharge the patient. The UR reviewer does this by making telephone calls. He does not write a note in the chart stating that the patient doesn't need to be in the hospital. That would require his signature. He could be held liable for what he says in a written note, and besides, nobody would pay him for actually seeing the patient in consultation!

"It isn't that we don't *want* to write a note," say the utilization reviewers. "It's our lawyers. They tell us not to." To my knowledge, this is the only medical circumstance in which lawyers say something other than "Document! Document!"

The attending physician has several choices: (1) Do what UR "recommends." (2) Fight, knowing that if he loses, Medicare won't pay him either, and the hospital might think twice about renewing his privileges, but if he doesn't fight and the patient does badly, his neck will be on the line in a liability suit. (3) Write ("document") something in the chart that will satisfy UR at both the hospital and the PRO, realizing that if he is caught bending the truth, he can be accused of fraud or abuse.

Having set up one incentive (to skimp on medical care), both hospitals and PROs soon saw the need for an equal and opposite incentive, to keep physicians from responding to the first incentive or at least to punish them for doing so. To "ensure" or at least to document that only unnecessary care was being denied, the PROs undertook "quality assurance," and the hospitals formed quality assurance committees (QACs).

If the PRO reviewer disagrees with a physician's management, he may assign quality points, usually without the physician's knowledge. The points sit quietly in the physician's dossier. If a physician accumulates enough quality points within a certain period of time (this could happen in a single case with a bad outcome), he faces Medicare sanctions. This could mean the loss of his livelihood. Defending himself in an administrative hearing could cost thousands of dollars, even if he ultimately wins.

Thus the shadow of a Medicare bureaucrat looms over every patient encounter. The bureaucrat may have an M.D. degree. He might actually practice medicine, or might have done so in the past. But he has never seen the patient whose care he is evaluating.

Patients may think this is a good thing—if they believe that any randomly chosen agent of the U.S. government is more likely to have their best interests at heart than their doctor, and that doctors function better when terrorized by remote petty bureaucrats.

The PRO Bounty System

Public interest in physician sanctions was aroused briefly by a *Primetime Live* television special in 1991, after HHS Inspector General Richard Kusserow's bounty system was brought to light.[5] In order to gain Level II merit pay, the official who made the initial determination of a physician's fate had to assess 10 percent more sanctions than in the previous year—that is 390 sanctions with monetary penalties amounting to $9 million.

Among the atrocities shown by *Primetime Live* was the case of a respected physician who was hounded with unsubstantiated charges, "by mistake," until he committed suicide.

The former chief of the Medicaid Fraud Unit of Massachusetts from 1978 to 1986, Donald P. Zerendow, reported that

> investigators routinely consider how to maximize the physical, emotional, and financial stress brought to bear on the potential victim. . . . [T]he provider must engage in a risk analysis which weighs payment of the investigator's outrageous dollar demands against public embarrassment and/or the advisability of pleading guilty to a civil count rather than risking criminal prosecution.[6]

Congress Knows: The Gun Is Loaded

Although Medicare penalties are administered through the bureaucracy, the responsibility for them lies squarely on the Congress. Congress created the agencies and deliberately created a draconian set of penalties, which it has intentionally placed outside the jurisdiction of federal courts.

The penalties that can be imposed by administrative law judges need not bear any relationship to the seriousness of the violation; $2,000 per item is the usual amount. If the amounts seem high (they could quickly add up to millions of dollars), the intention of Congress was to set penalties far in excess of the billings as a deterrent to misconduct. Like IRS debts, these penalties may be payable despite bankruptcy.

The Eighth Amendment to the Constitution states: "Excessive bail shall not be required, nor excessive fines imposed, nor cruel and unusual punishments inflicted." However, this amendment applies to criminals, not to persons who "violate [Medicare or Medicaid] program integrity."

Lobbyists for senior citizen groups still say that the penalties for exceeding Medicare charge limits aren't severe enough and enforcement is too lax. They complain to Congress about being "terrorized by high doctor bills."

Someday they may have no doctor bills at all, as more and more physicians avoid Medicare patients.[7] In January 1993, 42 percent of physicians reported restricting the number of new Medicare patients they would accept, and 51 percent restricted the number of appointments available to Medicare patients. Of those decreasing their Medicare practice, 71 percent cited bureaucratic hassles as one reason, and 71 percent cited reduced payment rates as a reason.[8]

The government denies that reduced services are a problem. They note that more doctors are participating in Medicare. It is true that more doctors are signing the contract, but that doesn't necessarily translate into making themselves available to patients.

You don't need to believe the figures. Get out your Yellow Pages and call some doctors yourself.

MEDICAL LICENSURE BOARDS:
POLICING DOCTORS, PATIENTS, OR BOTH

The medical licensure board has the power to sentence a physician to professional death—and the patient to perpetual pain.

THE SENTENCE OF PROFESSIONAL DEATH:
HISTORY, PURPOSE, AND EFFECT

THE POWER of the Board of Medical Examiners is awesome. The threat to use this power is the ultimate tool for forcing physicians to comply with the political agenda of the day; it is increasingly being used for that purpose.

Licensure boards are state agencies. Appointments are through a political process. It is an example of doctors policing themselves. To practice without their approval is a crime.

The medical profession has not always been licensed by the government. Many licensure laws that were a legacy of the Colonial period were repealed between 1830 and 1850. By 1901, most states had reenacted licensing laws, not because of a groundswell of public demand but because of intense pressure from the medical profession, especially the AMA. AMA spokesmen were said to be motivated by "selfless concern for the welfare of a befuddled and helpless public, preyed upon by incompetents and purveyors of poisons."[1] Such is always the rationale for licensure laws. Nonetheless, in most states incompetence is not grounds for delicensure.[2]

Licensure drives up prices. Licensed professionals have a legal monopoly. Everyone knows what happens when one person owns both Boardwalk and Park Place. But the hazard is accepted in the name of protecting the public against poor quality services.

Historically, the main causes for revocation of licensure were dishonorable or unethical conduct, most often a violation of the AMA code on advertising or some activity involving competition on the basis of price. But ethics can cover just about any reason. The Kansas board threatened to revoke the license of a physician who refused to serve in the Persian Gulf war (a politically popular war) while she was a reservist, citing ethical concerns. She served eight months at Leavenworth instead. The board did not question her medical knowledge and competence, just her stand on ethics.[3]

I have no reason to doubt that most members of the Arizona Board of Medical Examiners are reasonable and competent. However, they are political appointees, and there is no guarantee that this situation will continue indefinitely. If licensure boards do abuse their power, the consequences are ruinous for those involved. Boards are under increasing pressure from self-appointed "consumer advocacy" groups and others to ruin more doctors.

Sentencing Patients to Pain

One of the most frequent reasons for board investigations is the alleged overprescription of scheduled drugs such as narcotics. This issue overlaps with policing in the broader sense. The method could serve as a model for the enforcement of practice guidelines. The consequences affect patients more than physicians.

As a medical student in New York City, I had plenty of opportunity to see the results of drug abuse: pulmonary edema in heroin addicts; heart valves destroyed by bacterial infection; life-threatening infections of all kinds; and now of course AIDS. Most of these problems resulted from mainlining street drugs with dirty equipment. But the drug culture itself spawned terrible consequences: lost souls, living only for their next fix, and willing to do almost anything to get it. The addicts were just as destructive of themselves as of others. Some had sclerosed every accessible vein in their body except the one under their tongue, through which they continued to inject drugs.

Public outpatient services see a lot of patients who are "just passing through town" and say they are in dire need of a prescription. They usually complain of migraine or kidney stones. They can't take codeine, so their doctor always gives them that medicine that starts with a *P* ("Percoan?" "Yes, that's it!"). Such patients manipulate the doctor's sympathy, then sell the prescription on the street for an outrageous price. Or they might be addicts themselves, looking for a cheap and relatively safe fix.

If a person is caught peddling his drugs on the street, he might be arrested. Often the police don't even bother. Chances are excellent that a drug pusher will soon be back plying his trade, perhaps within hours.

In contrast, the doctor who prescribed the pills could be out of business for good. So could a doctor who prescribed narcotics for a genuine patient. The doctor is being carefully policed. He is also being used as a policeman against his own patients. Patients with pain, like their physician, labor under a presumption of guilt.

There are no formally stated rules for the use of narcotics to treat pain, except that there is now a Federal Practice Guideline for management of acute pain. Physicians are supposed to use their best judgment. But influential members of the profession are ready, sometimes with evangelical zeal, to pass *their* judgment on the prescribing physician. And medical boards are required by law to review these prescriptions.

When I was a medical student, we were taught to take great care in prescribing narcotics, lest the patient become addicted. There were other ways of managing pain and its consequences. For example, "snake rounds." If patients had a fever after surgery because they were in too much pain to cough, we stuck a tube down their throat. They coughed.

Now the idea that addiction often resulted from the medical use of narcotics has been effectively refuted in the medical literature. In fact, patient-controlled analgesia (PCA) is becoming standard for postoperative patients. Instead of waiting for the patient to develop severe pain, and then making him wait for a nurse to get around to giving the medication, usually in an inadequate dose, PCA allows the patient to determine his own dose of intravenous narcotic, within limits. It turns out that patients actually require less medication if it is given in such a way to keep severe pain from occurring, instead of prn or as needed. And snake rounds are unheard of.

Although attitudes have changed about acute pain and pain in patients with terminal illnesses, chronic pain is said to be different. Narcotics are not considered appropriate in that circumstance. Doctors may relieve pain that is self-limited, either by its nature or the patient's life expectancy. But if there is no natural relief in sight, the patient just has to suffer ("live with the pain"). He can be referred to a multi-disciplinary pain clinic to learn how to cope, using behavioral modification, biofeedback, nonnarcotic pain relievers, antidepressants, anticonvulsants, physical therapy, group psychotherapy, and maybe even hypnosis. Anything but narcotics. An interesting intellectual challenge: how to cope with a problem while forswearing the most effective remedy.

It is sometimes asserted that narcotics don't work in chronic, non-malignant pain. I disagreed with that pronouncement because I believed my patients, but now somebody has confirmed my position in a published article. In a series of 100 patients, only 21 received no benefit from chronic opioid treatment.[4]

Chronic pain patients often engage in "drug-seeking behavior." (It might actually be pain-relief-seeking behavior). Their regular doctor generally refuses to give them narcotics on a regular basis. The only way the patients can get a prescription is to persuade an emergency room doctor to give them a small supply "just this once." These patients may look exactly like drug pushers.

One such patient was a disheveled veteran wearing dark glasses, sitting in a wheelchair due to chronic back pain. He explained to me that Demerol gave him some relief from his pain, and nothing else did.

The next day, I got a stern lecture from the pharmacist. Didn't I know that 100 mg of Demerol by mouth was ineffective for anything except causing addiction! I had to be careful not to be manipulated by these crafty patients!

I didn't prescribe any more Demerol for that patient. A white-haired VA pharmacist can easily intimidate a new physician, especially since she knows a complaint from someone like him can cause all kinds of trouble with the Board of Medical Examiners.

In retrospect, I believe that both the patient and the pharmacist were correct—in a way. At least two thirds of an oral dose of Demerol is destroyed in the liver as soon as it is absorbed. To get the effect of a 100 mg injection, the patient has to take three or four tablets. Indeed, 300 to 400 mg is listed as the oral therapeutic dose in Goodman and Gilman's *Textbook of Pharmacology*, a textbook widely used in medical schools. That is probably what the patient took, knowing that if he admitted it, I would classify him as an addict.

I learned even more about narcotics and chronic pain from another VA patient—Mr. M.—a man who had pain in his stump for years after an above-the-knee amputation. At least every other week, I would see him standing with his crutches, with a mournful expression, waiting for me. I was the only doctor who would write him a prescription for Tylenol with codeine (also known on the street as T-3s). I tried everything else, too. Tegretol, an anticonvulsant. Various antidepressants. Nonsteroidal anti-inflammatory agents. Referrals to neurosurgery, rehabilitation medicine, and orthopedics. Hypnosis. Acupuncture. He applied to enter a study of an experimental pain reliever but was turned down because he took too much codeine. He said that the only thing that helped him was codeine. I did not think he was lying.

Finally, Mr. M. got lucky. He got cancer of the esophagus. With a chest marked for radiation therapy, he got attention in clinics that were unwilling to help him before. The neurosurgeon operated on him for his causalgia. The procedure for interrupting the pain-carrying fibers only works for a short time and is therefore not recommended for patients who are not terminally ill. But during the months that it worked, Mr. M. was able to walk with a prosthesis. After that, he once again needed pain medicines. Because of his cancer, he had trouble swallowing pills, and the liquid cocktails made him vomit. A sympathetic resident started him on morphine injections, then left the service. So there he was again in my clinic, the clinic of last resort. I had the nurse practitioner teach his mother how to give injections. I gave her some Narcan to administer in case she accidentally gave him an overdose. Although she spoke only Spanish, she seemed to understand.

The patient's dose of morphine gradually increased as the expected tolerance developed, but it did not accelerate rapidly as it does for addicts. He reported using three injections of 10 mg each every three hours. He had the needle marks to confirm it.

Everyone was very uncomfortable about this regimen: the pharmacy, the nurses, and the physicians. I had to worry about his prescriptions every time I was planning to be away, because I didn't think anyone else would be willing to write for such large amounts. I had to schedule his clinic visits accordingly. I wasn't always completely sure of myself either. An administrator reported once that he saw Mr. M. on South Sixth Avenue in his wheelchair, "wheeling and dealing." Dealing *what?* I wondered. Soon afterward, there was an opportunity for a test. While he was awaiting his prescription, I had the nurse give him 30 mg of morphine in the emergency room. Near the crash cart. That way, we could intubate him if he stopped breathing. (Patients, especially older women, have stopped breathing on a small fraction of this dose.) Nothing happened. No nodding off, no stupor, no apparent change in mental status. He just said the pain was better. I was convinced that he was taking all of his medicine himself. It apparently gave him enough relief that he could be out and about instead of languishing in his room, waiting to die.

One night, Mr. M. showed up at the hospital late at night. He asked the nurse practitioner to put him in a room and leave him alone. "I'm going to die, and I don't want to die at home," he said. "It would upset my mother."

He died that night, of cancer, not of an overdose.

Sometime later, the administrator summoned me to the clinic. "There's a woman out there who wants to talk to you. She says she's the mother of one of your patients."

Mrs. M., a tiny, elderly Mexican woman, her grief-stained face framed by a black bandana, handed me a brown paper bag and silently went away. The bag contained her son's unused medicines. That much morphine was worth a small fortune on the street.

I thought the pharmacist might have a heart attack when I gave him the bag. "Oh my God," he muttered, as he went to store the medication in the safe.

From this patient, I learned several things: (1) Pain relief is far more valuable than gold. Patients who really have pain do not sell their medicine. (2) Pain patients who are taking narcotics do not behave like addicts, nor do they sit around in a stupor. They seem to become tolerant to the sedative effect of the drug very rapidly. (3) The drug does not stop working, at least not over many months, although some increase in dose may be required, and side effects can occur.

Fortunately, there are not many cancer patients like Mr. M. Most have their pain controlled on relatively small doses of oral medications or with treatments like radiation. But some still do have difficulty finding someone to prescribe what they need. How many is impossible to say. I have heard of one cancer patient who shot himself because physicians were too afraid of the Board of Medical Examiners to prescribe adequate medication.

Knowing what the standard of care is for chronic pain, I knew that Mr. D. was trouble the minute he walked into my office in his back brace, with a handful of prescriptions for Demerol from a physician in another state—probably the only physician who had been willing to prescribe for him. He had been on Social Security disability for years. He had had a number of surgical procedures and was a veteran of pain clinics. He told me he had been moderately successful at achieving a state of relaxation in which his pain was minimized. The problem was, he couldn't do anything while in that state. He had had nerve blocks and all kinds of physical therapy. He had seen neurosurgeons, orthopedic surgeons, specialists in physical medicine and rehabilitation, and psychologists. He was desperate.

I had little confidence in my ability to help a patient like this. But his wife, who was already my patient, had sent him in and pleaded with me to accept him. I had been to a couple of hypnosis seminars and thought it might be interesting to try out some of the techniques I had learned. Also, I believed the patient's assurances that he would not tell me lies. So I took him on. I tried everything I could think of. He thought antidepressants were mind-bending drugs and refused to continue them because they made his thinking fuzzy. Tegretol (an anticonvulsant) didn't help, and I was worried about the potential side effects, including rare but serious things like lethal damage to the bone marrow. Nonsteroidal anti-inflammatory agents (similar to ibuprofen) didn't help him, but they may have contributed to a duodenal ulcer that he developed. We did lengthy, frequent hypnosis sessions. I wasn't able to determine whether they helped his pain. He thinks that they did help in one respect: restoring his self-confidence to the point that he applied for a job.

Mr. D. got the job! Some might think it wasn't a wonderful job. It required a long commute and a lot of overtime. The pay wasn't great. Neither were the surroundings (a state prison). But no physical examination was required. (Patients with any hint of back problems can forget about getting work if a physical examination is required. Employers cannot afford to take the risk of having to pay out the compensation.) And Mr. D. would have the chance to work in his own field. He is a skilled electrician; he enjoys and takes great pride in his work. He thought the job was the best thing that had happened to him for many years.

In order to meet the physical demands of the job, the patient required more narcotics than he had before. I was writing weekly prescriptions for large amounts of Demerol and methadone. I worried about the accumulation of toxic by-products of Demerol; hence the addition of methadone to alternate with it. I was pretty sure that the patient would have withdrawal symptoms if he suddenly stopped taking the medication. In that sense, you could call him an addict. But in many important ways he was unlike the addicts I had treated as a resident. He kept his appointments. He went to work every day, holding the same job for six years. He sat in the waiting room reading the programmer's manual for DBase III. If the Demerol diminished his mental capacity, it probably had less such effect than the pain. And he did not require a rapid increase in dosage to achieve the same effect.

I thought that Mr. D. was a success story. To be working steadily after eleven years of unemployment and unemployability was quite an achievement for him. There was no need to send him to a multidisciplinary pain clinic, because he was doing well. And he was working so hard that he didn't have time to go there. His dosage had increased, but slowly. He was having side effects from his medication but was willing to tolerate them so that he could continue working.

Aside from dread of addiction, narcotics have a remarkably good side-effect profile. Respiratory depression can be fatal, but patients who are on chronic medication are very unlikely to suffer it. In any case, it is readily reversed with Narcan. In contrast, fatal gastrointestinal hemorrhage from nonsteroidal anti-inflammatories like ibuprofen—the preferred, nonaddicting substitute—is not at all rare.

However, the patient and I were not the only judges of the success of the therapy. There is a war on drugs. And there are notorious examples of physicians who prescribe huge quantities of drugs of abuse to Hollywood celebrities, among others. To protect society against the "candy men," prescriptions of scheduled drugs are monitored by computer. Write for too many pills and your number comes up. And Mr. D. was getting a lot of pills. Demerol has a very short duration of action (about three hours), and its potency is low. Three or four 100 mg tablets (the equivalent of 10 mg of morphine by injection) every three hours quickly adds up to thousands of pills.

I got a certified letter from the Board of Medical Examiners, demanding the records of several patients, including Mr. D., and an explanation of my treatment. Then many weeks passed. So many that I thought that my perfectly logical explanation had been convincing. It wasn't. The other shoe dropped. The next certified letter was a demand to appear for an "informal" discussion with the board. By the way, they said, you may bring along an attorney if you like.

This sort of procedure inspires terror in any normal person. Think of it: all those years of study and sleepless thirty-six-hour shifts, resulting in nothing but disgrace and the need to learn some other way of earning a livelihood. All because of prescribing a drug you thought a patient needed, according to your own best judgment, in fulfillment of a sacred oath.

The interview itself is fairly intimidating. It's you and your lawyer in front of a bank of microphones to record every word, along with twenty or thirty people, some physicians and some not, all politically appointed. Somebody acts as prosecutor, reading the charges, then everyone around the table has a chance to grill you. It is informal, which means that there are no rules of evidence. The investigators were concerned about a number of things. For example, the patient once reported that his prescription had gone through the washing machine and asked for another. Didn't I know that story was suspicious? Well, of course it is. However, the record reflected that the prescription that had gone through the wash was never filled. The inquisitor could have determined that fact as easily as I did. But he might not have considered the possibility that the patient was telling the truth. Maybe nobody in his family ever leaves a paycheck or a watch in the pocket of clothes headed for the washer.

I went to that interview with a stack of reprints from the medical literature. I found a few authors who were willing to state for the record that some chronic pain patients really do need narcotics, and that given adequate medication, such patients are able to work. This is by no means a majority opinion. I had no assurance that anyone would have written the same prescriptions for Mr. D. had he been seen in consultation, although I did have a couple of letters from authorities who agreed with me in principle. Thus I did not know whether my treatment would meet the standard of care.

After a lot of questions, some quite hostile, someone made a motion to dismiss the complaint and strike the record. The motion passed.

I did not exactly receive a vindication from the board, just a letter saying they didn't find a reason to revoke my license. At least not at the present time.

For this interview, the legal fee equaled the average net monthly income from my practice. The other costs—time spent in preparation, anxiety, sleepless nights—are incalculable. I could easily understand why physicians are terrified of the Board of Medical Examiners and would not be eager to take over the care of this patient. I have never accepted another like him myself.

As expected, Mr. D.'s drug requirements remained about the same, although his physical impairment gradually worsened. The board kept watching us, and five years later decided that we needed to be investigated again. Another certified letter arrived, demanding copies of the records. This time, an investigator called, a specialist in administrative medicine. His main concern, he said, was that the patient worked at a prison and might be selling his medicine to prisoners.

"You have accused my patient of a serious crime," I said. "Do you have any evidence for it?"

I reminded him that the patient had had an internal investigation at the prison, just because he was bringing scheduled medications to work, and no problem had been found.

The investigator evaded my question.

I think this investigator was a reasonable man. He recognized that this was a difficult case. He didn't want to approve of my management but didn't want to condemn it either. He made a suggestion, which I considered seriously but decided not to follow because it would have provided inferior pain relief at two to three times the cost to the patient, not counting inconvenience and increased side effects.

Many months later, another certified letter arrived—the day after a big newspaper spread about the alleged negligence of licensure boards, as evidenced by the fact that they had revoked fewer licenses this year than last. This time, the board didn't even request to see the records.

The patient came to the hearing, too. He felt that his own good name was under attack because of the undocumented implication that he was a drug pusher. It took him at least half an hour to walk with his cane from his car to the hearing room.

The composition of the board was different this time. They might or might not have the same opinion as the previous group. There is no protection against double jeopardy, this being administrative law.

The procedure was the same as before. The main concern seemed to be that I had not followed the advice of the investigator (who has left the state) and hadn't even bothered to call him back to discuss it with him.

"Did he identify himself as working for the Board of Medical Examiners?" they asked.

At first, that seemed like a strange question to me. Of course he did. Then it occurred to me that the question really was: "How dare you not follow the direction of somebody who works for *us*. Don't you know who we are?"

Generally, I do not call a consultant just to tell him I disagree with him, unless we are both seeing the patient and need to avoid giving contradictory advice. Fortunately, I had taken the precaution of sending the investigator a certified letter, making sure that I understood what the advice was and asking for literature references to support it. I received no answer. So I had assumed that the ball was in his court.

The other main issue was how a general internist, the "LMD," could presume to treat a patient like this, instead of referring him to a multispecialty institution. The fact that he had seen many individual specialists, who all said "I can't cure this case, refer it to LMD," did not suffice.

It was clear that the board is very uncomfortable allowing an individual LMD to stand by her own opinion. Fortunately, the patient had a recent letter from a psychologist. (He had checked into a $10,000 inpatient program of his own volition after finally losing his job due to inability to cope with the physical demands.)

I still have this patient. I do not think of him as a drug addict. He is dependent on narcotics, just as some of my asthma patients are dependent on prednisone and bronchodilators and my heart patients on digoxin. If the drugs are stopped, Mr. D. has more pain, the asthma patients have worse asthma, and the cardiac patients have worse heart failure. Stopping the drugs might actually be fatal in any of these cases; Mrs. D. thinks her husband would have shot himself had he been unable to find a physician who would prescribe narcotics. Of course, continuing the drugs is also dangerous, although in my opinion narcotics are less hazardous than many other drugs that I can prescribe without fear of the Board of Medical Examiners.

What will Mr. D. do if they finally drive me out of medicine? And what will *you* do if your physician is no longer permitted, by guideline and regulation, to ease your pain?

17

....

TO REGULATE AND PROTECT

....

Government is trying to ensure safety through regulation, but the treatment is worse than the disease, whether we measure its cost in dollars or lives.

PHYSICIANS who haven't yet fled the practice of medicine are bracing for an invasion of their offices by swarms of bureaucrats. They are spending thousands of dollars in compliance costs, trying to protect themselves against tens of thousands of dollars in fines for violations of new regulations. The stated purpose of the regulations is, of course, to protect the public health and safety.

These costs will ultimately be paid by patients, although they probably won't get a bill itemized for laboratory regulation or waste disposal. There's no place for dickering about the price. And the costs will be measured in lives as well as dollars.

The fifty-three-volume *Code of Federal Regulations* has grown from 16,502 pages in 1954 to 200,000 pages in 1990, following an exponential growth curve with a doubling time of approximately ten years. This is the type of growth exhibited by bacteria in a culture medium with unlimited nutrients, and by neutrons released in a nuclear chain reaction. To enforce these regulations, there are about 122,000 federal bureaucrats. The combined effect of these regulations is to cost each American household at least $4,000 to $5,000 per year, or about 20 percent of its average after-tax income.[1] (The percentage is higher for the poor; regulation is like a highly regressive tax.) Most of these regulations are concerned with other industries; the practice of medicine was relatively free until recently.

Regulation is far more ambitious than common law. Instead of retroactively punishing evildoers (those who violate rights to be secure in one's life, liberty, and property), the regulators are supposed to ensure a healthful and safe environment, that is, to enforce positive or entitlement rights. The regulators are often proactive in protecting the public.

Laws passed by Congress tend to be very general. The nuts and bolts, the specifics that determine the impact of the legislation in everyday life, are delegated to administrative agencies, the fourth branch of government.

Administrative officials do not bear the title Lord, Baron, or Marquis. They are merely the deputy assistant secretary or administrator or assistant to the administrator, a GS-something. Most of them have no name recognition. They don't need it because their name is never on a ballot. Anonymity, in fact, is an advantage. They are not subject to impeachment. They can be fired, but unless they are political appointees, this doesn't happen very often, not if they keep their heads down and don't draw attention to themselves. They have a ready response to criticism: "We don't make the laws; we just enforce them."

It is dangerous to be misled by a bureaucrat's modest title. Bureaucrats desire respect. And they may be in a position to demand it.

REGULATION VERSUS EDUCATION

Society (or government) can think of two general types of interventions into social problems: regulation or education. For certain problems, education may be held up as the "only answer," laws or regulation being ineffective, unacceptable, or even unconstitutional. For other problems, regulation is necessary or even "urgent."

Currently, we face an epidemic of a deadly disease (AIDS) mostly spread by activities that are or used to be illegal or immoral, such as sodomy, promiscuity, and street drugs. Although the disease itself is supposedly not spread by casual contact, it makes people susceptible to conditions that are—most important, tuberculosis. Sometimes, the tuberculosis is highly resistant to drug treatment. In 1991, one third of all cases surveyed in New York City were resistant to at least one drug. And you can catch tuberculosis on the bus.

What is promoted as the only answer to this epidemic? Education.

There are other problems, however, that *do* give rise to calls for government intervention into almost every aspect of our lives.

CLINICAL LABORATORY "IMPROVEMENT"

At a public meeting in Arizona, a bureaucrat involved in drafting state regulations related to the Clinical Laboratory Improvement Act (CLIA) of 1988 explained how the act came about:

"The program started because the federal government sent out millions of Pap smears to a mail-order place, and women died of cancer of the cervix after getting a falsely negative report. And Congress got mad."

In its wrath, Congress visited CLIA upon every laboratory and physician in the land. The regulations don't just cover Pap smears. They cover *everything* that might be construed as a lab test.

CLIA is supposed to decrease the number of false-negative Pap smears. But because most laboratories are now doing one-slide tests instead of two-slide tests (due to the restrictions on the number of slides a technologist may examine), CLIA is just as likely to *increase* the probability of missing a precancerous change. Even if the tests are better, CLIA will probably *increase* the death rate from cancer of the cervix because fewer Pap smears will be done, especially for poor women at high risk. After regulations similar to CLIA were implemented in New York State, the price of Pap smears tripled. In my office, the price of a Pap smear has already gone from $8 to $55. In some places, it now takes weeks to get a report.

Funds to comply with CLIA have to come from somewhere. Our county health department estimated that it would cost $35,000 to comply so that they could continue to perform simple screening tests for the poor. One of the proposed budget cuts was to close the colposcopy clinic, the only place in town that offered treatment to poor women who had an abnormal Pap smear! Our medical society fought that one, and for once we won.

CLIA will do nothing to *prevent* cancer of the cervix. The cause of most cancers of the cervix is probably human papilloma virus, which is most often a sexually transmitted disease. Disease prevention, as opposed to early detection, is an educational, not a regulatory issue.

So what will CLIA prevent?

It will prevent doctors from doing lab tests in their offices. As many as 70 percent of physicians who previously did some testing will eliminate or curtail that service.[2]

Physicians will stop testing for several reasons. The first is cost. They can't just pass the cost along to patients, either because of government price controls or because the patients simply can't afford to pay.

"Is it within the realm of possibility that a doctor would have to pay $3,000 for the 'privilege' of doing urinalyses for which Medicare pays $5.19?" asked a family doctor at a public meeting with state laboratory regulators.

"It might depend on a lot of things" was the answer.

In other words, it might cost $3,000.

The bureaucrat tried to reassure the doctors who came to the meeting. He won't be coming around to our offices just yet.

"It will take a couple of years for you to get ready for the inspection," he said. "You need to write the procedures. To set up the quality assurance program. To meet the personnel requirements: a clinical director and a technical director. The same person might or might not qualify to hold both positions. It depends on education, training, and years of experience with lab work."

Actually, I could spend the rest of my life getting ready for the inspections. For anything other than the simplest tests, which the patient can buy over the counter and do himself, there would be "proficiency tests" three times a year. Doctors are to prove, repeatedly, that they can tell the difference between red and orange. (Cultures for the fungus causing athlete's foot change the medium from orange to red if positive. This is a "moderately complex" test.)

Another moderately complex test checks for strep throat. Eleven-year-old children can do this test just as accurately as a laboratory technician, with no training beyond reading the package insert.[3] But if I wanted to do it, I would have to be tested several times a year. Being unable to afford either the time or the money, and being a law-abiding citizen, I will decline to do the test.

How many doctors will go back to guessing about the diagnosis of strep throat, despite the current resurgence in rheumatic fever and other complications, in patients who can't afford a fifty-dollar test from the reference lab?

Just listening to the state bureaucrats for an hour at a public meeting convinced me that I had to close my lab. If it hadn't, the 100-page set of draft regulations would have been the clincher.

Lots of people have scoffed or become indignant at my concerns. Why would a doctor not be willing to put up with a little regulation (even a heavy dose of absurdity) in order to serve her patients better? Is that too much to ask? Occasionally, I ask myself that question in a moment of guilt. Then I consider the penalties.

Civil monetary penalties for noncompliance judged to "pose immediate jeopardy" (an undefined term) range from $3,050 to $10,000 per day ($3,050 is the lowest amount judged by HCFA to be effective). Less serious situations call for fines of $50 to $3,000 per day per violation.

The penalties are not proportional to the size of the laboratory; $50 is more than my laboratory ever made in a single day. But a lab that brings in $10,000 per day is on the same scale.

Although these penalties may sound harsh, they are mild in comparison with another clause in the law: a one-year prison term for "any person who intentionally violates any requirement of CLIA '88 or any implementing regulation"—for the first violation. "Second and subsequent violations are subject to not more than three years in prison or fines. . . ."[4]

In other words, the government could send me to prison for a year for saying "that's stupid" and refusing to write down instructions to myself to keep the urine dipsticks in the bottle until ready for use! (That was one issue that concerned the state bureaucrat.)

Now, *would* the government lock me up for a year for something like that? A U.S. court sent a man to jail for six months for dumping two truckloads of dirt on a spot that some bureaucrat thought was a wetland (even though the state's chief soil scientist said it wasn't). If that can happen to a builder of a wildlife refuge, why not to a doctor, especially one who has written a book offensive to bureaucrats?

So what? the public may ask. Maybe it's necessary to ruin a few doctors to save society from the horrors of unregulated lab tests.

There is no evidence that CLIA will improve the lab tests. Even the government admits it, although in convoluted bureaucratic language. And the government hasn't studied whether people will still be able to get lab tests done. The study is required by law, but *that* law disappeared down the memory hole.

CLIA will add more than $4 billion to the cost of medical care. The chief beneficiaries will be the large laboratories, whose competitors will be driven out of business by forcing them to bear 137 times as much as regulatory cost per test performed.

Can you think of a better way to spend $4 billion?

DOCUMENTING GARBAGE

In medical offices, it is no longer enough to dispose of waste properly. There must now be a paper trail left behind as certain regulated garbage goes to a certified hazardous disposal site (as if we didn't already have enough wastepaper). And of course it costs money to transport the garbage, say $33.50 for a two-gallon container of needles.

The rationale is that some medical garbage washed up on a beach in New Jersey. As far as I know, nobody got sick as a result, but a lot of people were disgusted and frightened. There were nationwide repercussions. A television reporter in Tucson came to my office to make a videotape of my garbage. The nightly news showed the camera panning down on my container for disposal of sharp objects. Yes, indeed, there were needles and scalpel blades in there, and they were contaminated, just like the label said.

When I was chairman of the infection control committee at my hospital, we had a report on needlestick injuries every month. Most occurred in the course of treating a patient. Only a few were the result of improper disposal of waste. The regulations wouldn't have prevented most of these. It never was okay to leave a dirty needle in the sheets or to toss it in the regular garbage. The problem was human error, competing pressures like the need to save a patient's life, or just plain sloppiness—not lack of regulations.

My own father was the victim of a needlestick injury. Somebody had left some needles in a paper bag on the ground, and he picked it up to throw it in the Dumpster, to reduce the chance that somebody else might be injured. What to do? Call the police? Call my congressman and tell him we need a new law? This is what I actually did: I told my dad to be more careful. Dumpsters are full of dangerous things.

I also looked at the wound, which was insignificant. I gave him a tetanus shot. He didn't need it for the needlestick, but he is always getting cuts and splinters from his carpentry work, and the needlestick was a timely reminder. I gave him a shot of gamma globulin. The risk of hepatitis was not very high, but why not use the available means to reduce it? We discussed hepatitis B vaccine and decided against it. Then I told him not to worry.

I didn't worry myself either. Although I don't know who was responsible for discarding the needles, the odds were that it had been used to give an allergy shot. I would have worried more about a needle found on the street because it was probably used by an addict. Even then, the risk of a nick from a dried-out old needle was much less than the risk of an injection from a needle that had just been in an infected person's vein. Viral titers decrease with time.

The needlestick in Tucson caused no repercussions in New Jersey.

But what about the syringes on the beach? Syringes aren't a problem anyway unless one uses them to inject something; it's the needle that's the problem for innocent bystanders. Still, people worry about them.

I have heard two stories about the source of the syringes. One is that a navy ship had thrown them overboard without weighting them properly. Another is that they were from the drug trade. The regulations wouldn't have affected either source (especially not the regulations on private doctors in Tucson).

There is also something else on the beach in New Jersey: used condoms, some of them used quite recently. A person with a cut on his foot could step on one and get AIDS from it. The probability is not very high, but it is billions of times higher than the risk of getting AIDS from a syringe or even a needle that has been sloshing around in the ocean for weeks. And what are we doing about it? Exactly nothing, as far as I can tell, not even education. There are all kinds of posters and brochures and comic books exhorting people to use condoms. But I have yet to see a poster that tells people what to do with the condoms afterward.

Doctors don't know what to do with all their garbage either. One pediatrician puts soiled diapers in a plastic bag and sends them home with the parents. The diaper is *not* regulated waste at home, but it *might* be in a doctor's office. After all, the bacterial count of a dirty diaper is about 10 billion per gram of fecal material. An OSHA representative told doctors at one meeting that soiled sanitary napkins were regulated waste if found in an examining room but not if found in the bathroom. Later, in response to a letter, an OSHA functionary stated the first OSHA person was wrong about that. The current OSHA bureaucrat has refused to send written responses to questions.

One OSHA official recommended using common sense and remembering the rationale behind the regulations. (He's not there anymore.)

What *is* the rationale behind the regulations? "Infectious waste" from hospitals contains, on the average, about 1 percent of the concentration of disease-causing microorganisms found in household waste. In other words, household waste has between 10 and 10,000 times as many bacteria per unit volume as hospital waste.[5] At present, there is no evidence that medical waste has caused a health problem, except for sharps, which have caused disease only in occupational settings. Of course, medical waste has not been proved innocent beyond a reasonable doubt, so we will spend $1.3 billion per year complying with the Medical Waste Tracking Act,[6] which will probably *not* keep syringes off the beach in New Jersey.

For that amount of money, we could buy hepatitis B vaccinations for more than 10 million people (hepatitis B is the most common blood-borne disease). Or we could pay for 26,000 coronary-artery bypass operations at $50,000 each.

A WAR ON CHEMICALS

Physicians didn't even have time to get ready for blood-borne hazard regulations before they became aware of the war against chemicals: the chemicals that might conceivably under some circumstances of proper or improper use cause harm to a human being, or the chemicals that might pollute the environment and harm the planet or one of the untold millions of species thereon.

I tried to find out which chemicals were hazardous so that I could be sure my office complied with all regulations. I learned that the enforcers—the Occupational Safety and Health Administration, or OSHA—do not keep a list of hazardous chemicals! I think that is because all chemicals are hazardous, and everything in the world is a chemical. It is impossible to list all the chemicals, and OSHA probably does not want to imply that some chemicals might be outside its jurisdiction. Therefore, they don't keep a list (or didn't at the time I called).

What will OSHA do to enforce these regulations? Will they send inspectors in spacesuits around to rummage through randomly selected doctors' cupboards and garbage cans? So far, it appears they will use other methods, such as anonymous complaints[7]—an excellent way to shut down your competitors.

Physicians' fears of these inspectors are based not on imagination but on news articles. One physician was slapped with a $70,000 fine for violating regulations that were not even final. Among other things, he was cited for failure to have an alphabetically filed MSDS (Manufacturer's Safety Data Sheet) for each of his chemicals, including the acetic acid (vinegar) that he had purchased at Sam's Discount Grocery. (Most doctors, like me, had never even heard of an MSDS before.)

Physicians are not the first to be targeted by the antichemical war. Hospitals had already been fined tens of thousands of dollars, for example, because of minute concentrations of xylene in the wastewater. (Xylene is used to prepare tissue for microscopic examination.) One Tucson hospital has built an $11,500 still to recycle the xylene, in preference to paying $175 per drum to haul the used xylene to a special incinerator. (They used to just pour small quantities down the drain, with no known ill effects.) Xylene is flammable and the distillation could cause a fire, possibly destroying the laboratory and even the hospital and causing deaths and serious injuries. But the hospital can buy insurance against fire. There is no insurance against government fines.

The public has been taught to applaud fines against evil polluters and to worry about things like xylene in the drinking water. In fact, there *is* xylene in the drinking water. After all, it is made from petroleum, and there is petroleum in the ground. In Tucson's artesian wells, the concentration is as high as 4 micrograms per liter, or a scant teaspoonful in a cube of water 100 feet on each side. There may be even more xylene in your town's water. And that's not all. With a sufficiently sensitive analytical method, you could find millions of other chemicals in your water also.

Probably, hospitals with clinical laboratories still exist only because the enforcement of regulations against chemical pollution is not entirely consistent. In other words, hospitals are treated more leniently than gasoline stations, and a large excavation that you might see on a street corner is probably the former site of a leaky gasoline tank rather than a hospital.

A Tucson lumber supplier has a hole in his yard that could swallow a nine-story building. The dirt and crushed rock from that hole are being fed through an incinerator, to remove the minuscule traces of petroleum products that allegedly leaked from a gasoline tank about six years ago. The former owner of the site is bankrupt, and one man is dead. The equipment operator got his clothing caught in the machinery one night and was crushed to death.

Maybe the bureaucrats who forced people to dig that hole will stop before they get to your doctor or hospital. But maybe they won't. In 1992, OSHA officials began to make statements like this:

"Days of freedom from the regulatory community for the medical industry are gone forever."

"OSHA has only civil and criminal penalties, but attorneys who monitor inspections are contacting employees for possible lawsuits."

Physicians will probably have to pay the price of OSHA regulations, unless they fire all of their employees. You don't have to do lab tests in your office, but it is impossible to practice medicine without cleaning solutions, disinfectants, refrigerants, and antiseptics.

How high can the price go? If you have had to buy a prescription drug recently, you are beginning to get an idea (even though drugs are a bargain in comparison with some other things, like a day in the hospital). Drugs are chemicals regulated by still another government agency, the Food and Drug Administration (FDA). It costs about $250 million to bring a drug to market, thanks to the protections of the FDA.

The War Against Inefficacy

The FDA was started to protect consumers against contaminated or unsafe drugs. Then the government started to require proof that a new drug works. (Fortunately, things like aspirin got grandfathered in.) Now the FDA is expanding its role into treatments *not* generally considered to be drugs, such as vitamins and nutritional supplements, and also into medical devices.

Doctors who fear the OSHA inspector, who is armed with a manual for assessing fines, had better be even more certain not to cross the FDA.

The FDA uses guns.

Unproved treatments can kill—so can proved treatments but never mind. Therefore, to protect us against unproved treatments, the government is prepared to kill. I don't mean to risk letting a patient die, as by blocking access to a balloon a surgeon wants to use to treat a defective blood vessel in the brain or to a drug that might benefit a patient with terminal AIDS. I am not speaking of situations such as the FDA's keeping streptokinase off the market for two years, during which it could have saved 22,000 heart-attack victims whose names will never be known. I mean the government is prepared to kill specific, identifiable individuals—"kill," as in the cardinal rule for the use of firearms: *Never point a gun at anyone you are not willing to kill.*

The FDA has conducted a number of armed raids in which firearms were pointed at unarmed, terrified clinic employees. The purpose was to seize vitamins and other unapproved treatments. Arguably, the clinics practiced quackery. Unquestionably, they were unorthodox.

At the present time, the threat of deadly force is being reserved for small fringe groups. The drug industry is controlled by methods that are relatively benign. For example, one company chose to sign a $2 million consent decree (the alternative being a ban of a highly profitable product) when the FDA objected to some wording in the promotional literature. A certified letter had to be sent to every doctor in the country, and all literature that contained the offending statement had to be destroyed. The statement was an unobtrusive one related to an animal experiment—most doctors probably never noticed it.

The FDA is also cracking down on the mention of unapproved ("off-label") uses of approved drugs. Physicians are allowed to prescribe drugs for these purposes, and frequently do so because the drug happens to be the best available treatment for the patient's problem. However, salesmen for the company are not allowed to speak of these uses. The FDA has spies, informants, and hidden tape recorders to be sure that they don't. This is not censorship, because it is *commercial* speech, not *political* speech that is being controlled. In this way, patients are protected from having their doctor hear about the possibility of administering a potassium supplement through a straw. Straws have not been tested in multimillion-dollar studies, only feeding tubes.

"If you can promote the secondary use without approval," said David Kessler (FDA czar under Presidents Bush and Clinton), "where's your incentive to do the testing and the [clinical] trials?"[8]

There *is* no incentive to do $250 million worth of testing on each vitamin supplement because such things cannot be sold for $1 per pill. The same problem exists for mainstream medical therapies for rare diseases: the orphan drug problem. Worse, it exists for diseases that are very common but primarily affect poor people. For example, the world urgently needs new drugs to combat resistant malaria, a leading killer, but pharmaceutical companies are not aggressively pursuing them.

Is There a Better Way?

As I said before, "every drug is a new disease." Sometimes the treatment is worse than the disease the patient already has. But sometimes the disease is worse than the treatment. How do you tell the difference?

That's what you go to medical school to learn.

Then you keep learning all your life.

You learn some things from accredited (or unaccredited) continuing medical education courses and from medical journals and from your colleagues. You learn from patients. You learn from drug detail men; perhaps most important, you learn about the side effects of their competitors' products. And you learn from some extremely unlikely sources. It is even conceivable that you could learn something from somebody who is considered a quack.

The most important thing to learn is that we don't know all the answers yet. There are new drugs and new treatments to be discovered. I would like for them to be discovered, and then I would like the opportunity to find out about them and make them available to my patients.

That's an opportunity I would have had *before* all those huge federal agencies arose to "protect" us from the risks of the unknown.

I would also like the opportunity to prescribe cheaper products so that my patients could afford them and not have to forgo other important things to buy their medicine, or to pay the taxes that buy medicine if we nationalize the whole system.

Where would such products come from?

Imagine this: a company that is not a brontosaurus. A firm that does not have a twenty-story building in downtown Philadelphia, full of high-priced executives, lawyers, and experts on the FDA. A company that has the best scientists, the latest automated equipment, and a lean, mean sales force willing to compete on the basis of price.

Suppose a sales representative of such a company showed up in my office *without* a pile of glossy promotional pieces (that I discard immediately), *without* a fancy notebook computer to store my signature, and *without* a tiny VCR featuring a boring video by some full professor. Suppose he had nothing but some scientific studies and the information that his company's product was one fourth the price of its leading competitor. I'll bet I could remember the name of that product and the dosage regimen, even if the salesman did not leave me a ballpoint pen or pocket calculator. And even if the drug had not undergone $250 million worth of studies to prove efficacy to the FDA, the patient might choose to try it and see whether it helped *him*.

This is not likely to happen. Executives of established brontosauruses can relax. Regulation is there, and it protects *them* above all others.

BACK TO THE FUTURE

Dreams of how things might be if only we had freedom may turn out to be fantasies, perhaps to be realized hundreds of years from now at the end of a long Dark Age.

For the present, it appears that the humble LMD is not the one who will be making use of years of scientific education to prescribe for the individual patient who has come to consult him. The way to the future is the way back to the past, if current trends continue. Specifically, it is the way to nineteenth-century Prussia, not to the Greece of Hippocrates.

In Prussia, medical treatment was determined by the *Geheim Rath* (literally, "secret counsel"), a prestigious professor. In current parlance, he dictated the standard of care. Even if his ideas were as ill-founded as those of Galen, junior professors didn't dare to contradict him. *They* wanted to become the *Geheim Rath* someday!

America is suspicious of dictators, so our new *Geheim Rath* is more likely to be a committee. Our system will be less efficient than the

Prussian system (and inefficiency is a *good* when it is a feature of dictators). It will be called "practice guidelines" instead of a *Geheim Rath*, but it will amount to the same thing. Actually, there is another difference that has become apparent recently. The Prussian *Geheim Rath* was at least a physician. A National Health Board, proposed in the early 1990s to dictate the list of effective medical procedures that qualify for insurance coverage, wouldn't necessarily include physicians.

The LMD of the future won't miss the opportunity to think for himself. He might not know how. But he won't have time for it anyway. He'll be busy filling out OSHA forms, doing CLIA proficiency tests, and filing package inserts and triplicate prescription forms—when he's not attending seminars on how to code an office visit.

Is that the kind of doctor you want?

18

GETTING IT RIGHT

If our goal is to make the sick and the injured well and whole, then the patients, not the managers, have to hold the power.

THE ULTIMATE result of most reform plans would be the destruction of our traditional forms of medical practice—the end of private medicine—except possibly for the elite. No more freedom of choice, no more Oath of Hippocrates, no more heroics to save individuals at all costs. Instead, everyone would have the promised security of a "uniform benefits package," under the management of expert "decision makers" specializing in the calculus of societal costs and benefits.

We have seen some of the results of these concepts.

Some think we can avoid the adverse results by tinkering with the plan by adding an ombudsman here or a multiple-choice option there. But they are mistaken.

In geometry or science we learn that when step after logical step leads to an absurd conclusion, there is only one possibility: The starting assumptions have to be wrong. You can't develop celestial mechanics if you insist on putting the earth at the center of the universe.

And we can't bring healing to our patients if the managers are in the driver's seat.

If we keep the objective—taking care of the sick and the injured—in the front of our minds, we won't confuse medicine with a bureaucratic process. Little boxes and arrows constituting job descriptions and lines of command in a bureaucracy, or sequences of tests and treatments in a practice guideline do not bring comfort and healing to the sick. (We've seen some of the things that they *do* accomplish in this book.)

Medicine is based on the doctor-patient relationship, founded on the Oath of Hippocrates—not on an administrative flowchart.

For all their errors, the reformers are still right about one thing. The system is indeed broken. It is also broke. The only question about its bankruptcy is the date on which it will be declared.

Can it and should it be fixed?

As I said at the outset, I am not going to outline still another plan. I promised I wouldn't. This is not a high school debate case, which has to present a need in the first affirmative and a plan in the second affirmative speech. In fact, I *can't* present the ultimate Utopian one-size-fits-all plan, because *there is no such plan.*

When I started my internship, I thought for quite a while that I was just dumber than the others. But finally my resident blew their cover.

"You sometimes feel that you don't understand what is going on," he said. "Well, I'll tell you a secret. Neither does anybody else."

Finally, I decided that he was right. You can go a long way if you're good at looking intelligent. But there are limits.

William Hsiao, the guru of the Relative Value Scale, may look more intelligent than the rest of us. But he can't fix the system either. It simply can't be done. There is no way that a central agency, however sophisticated its computer, can possibly calculate the worth of millions of medical procedures, much less determine which medical procedures need to be done. In medicine, as well as other areas of the economy, the question "What would you do if you became the czar?" has only one right answer, the one given by Austrian economist Ludwig von Mises: "I would abdicate at once."

There is no right way to do the wrong thing. A central committee cannot make good decisions for individuals, and *you* shouldn't abdicate to *them.* A medical system will, operationally, be a bureaucracy—a labyrinthine, mindless, power-hungry, Kafkaesque monster.

We don't want to replace the present bureaucracy with another that differs only in the details. All bureaucratic systems have the same fundamental problems. The first is that power tends to corrupt. The second is that central planning works about as well for ordering the economy as a central earth works for ordering the motions of the heavenly bodies.

But I am not saying we should give up. Although there is no Utopia, there *is* a better idea.

Why not declare independence from the system and try freedom?

Here's how a free market would bring the best possible medical care to the greatest possible number of people at the lowest possible cost.

Restoring Insurance

Today we have very little true insurance. We have largely replaced it with a prepaid system for consumption of medical care. Our cost problem is not caused by the 4 to 15 percent of the population who are *not* insured, but by the 85 to 96 percent who *are*. About 100 million Americans are *over*insured, according to Senator David Durenberger[1] and large numbers are partly insured by plans that result in cost shifting to both uninsured and overinsured.

As I have explained in the discussion of national health insurance, insurance is for things that you don't want. You don't want your house to burn down, for example. You can't prevent this catastrophe with 100 percent certainty. But you can share the financial risk with others. You can pay an annual premium, which will be used to indemnify others who experience a loss, hoping that you will never have to make a claim yourself. With insurance, it is always better to give than to receive. You would much rather help pay for treating somebody else's heart attack than to have him help pay for yours.

Insurance doesn't pay for preventive maintenance on your house or your car. You pay for that directly.

For true insurance, you have to pay a premium proportional to the risk. (That's one incentive to get the preventive maintenance that lowers your risk.) If you live in a firetrap, the premium on your fire insurance will be very high. If you have a teenage son, the premium on your car insurance will be astronomical. If you are legally blind or have uncontrolled seizures or a history of drunk driving, then you are an uninsurable driver, even if the problem isn't your own fault.

Right, some risks are uninsurable. About 1 percent of our nonelderly population is medically uninsurable, for example.[2] Only *low*-probability events are insurable. Covering *high*-probability events is prepayment for consumption, not insurance.

That does not mean we should do nothing about uninsurable events, only that the method to be used *is not* and *cannot* be insurance, even if we call it that.

I would like to point out two simple things: Car insurance is not the same as transportation. And health insurance is not the same thing as medical care, much less health. To say you can't insure somebody does not mean you can't help to provide what he needs.

You could have lots of health insurance and not be able to get medical care. Maybe the clinic in your town got padlocked by OSHA, and the hospital went bankrupt, and the doctor went fishing, or the rationing board decided that the service you happen to want exceeds the global budget cap or isn't really needed by *society*, even if it means the difference between life and death to *you*.

And believe it or not, you can get medical care even if you don't have insurance. The National Health Interview Survey showed no convincing evidence that the uninsured lacked access to adequate medical care,[3] although they might end up waiting more than seventeen hours in an urban public emergency room.[4] (The problem of long waits or long journeys to see an available provider is probably worse for some insured patients, for example, if the "insurer" is Medicaid or the Canadian government.)

The main problem with being uninsured is the bill you will get after you are treated. For some things, you might have to raise a lot of money ahead of time. If you've been in the hospital or had an operation, that bill could cost you everything you own—if you own anything. *But medical care doesn't have to cost that much.*

I am not talking about cost containment, as most reformers do. They mean we ought to put a lid on *expenditures*, which are not the same as *costs*. I think we should allow people to spend as much (or as little) as they choose for medical care. But they ought to get value for their money. Some medical *costs* are outrageous and they need to be lowered.

If we had real insurance (for catastrophes) instead of prepaid, tax-subsidized plans for the use of medical services, then you might be able to buy medical care for half as much as you'd have to pay now. That means that many more people could afford to pay for treatment even if they had no insurance, and that more people could afford insurance.

Nobody knows for sure how much the price could fall. But there are a number of areas of potential savings: overhead, cost shifting, and wasteful consumption.

Much of the 25 percent administrative overhead goes for claims processing. It costs almost as much to process a small claim as a large one, and there are enormous numbers of small claims. It makes no sense to spend $50 processing a claim for $25 (except to the people who get paid for performing that service). But we process a lot of claims that are worth less than $5 to the beneficiary!

Many reformers recognize that there is a problem here. They propose to solve it by making everybody fill out the *same* form whether the patient received brain surgery or a quick blood-pressure check. Worse, they want to make everybody do it with a computer system that costs more than $7,000. But as everyone who has been to a supermarket knows, it is possible to buy something without filling out any forms at all.

Then there's the cost shifting. Medicare, Medicaid, and managed care plans pay *less* than the full price of the services their beneficiaries consume. This means that other people pay *more* than the full price for services—about 41 percent more, according to a hospital administrator.[5] (That's the other side of a "discount." The people with clout pay less, and the others pay more.)

Then there are the perverse incentives that result from disconnecting the normal market regulator (the price at the time of service). If patients think a service is free or very cheap, they demand more. Doctors are rewarded for supplying more, and threatened with malpractice suits if they don't. How much effect does this have? Nobody knows, but here are two sets of figures worth considering.

The relentless upward spiral in national medical costs and expenditures began just after Medicare was enacted. In 1965, medical expenditures were $205 per capita and 5.9 percent of the GNP. In 1990, they were $2,511 per person and 12.0 percent of the GNP.[6]

Before 1982, the percentage of the Arizona state budget spent on medical services was stable at around 4.5 percent. Indigent care was provided in county hospitals. After the enactment of the state Medicaid substitute (based on an HMO or managed care model), the percentage started increasing and is now between 9 and 10 percent, despite a huge infusion of federal funds.

Direct government spending is not the only problem. Government-created incentives, primarily the tax treatment of employer-purchased medical insurance, have exacerbated the price spiral. Because of government wage-and-price controls during World War II, industry could not increase wages at a time of a severe labor shortage. But it could increase medical insurance benefits, and these were tax-free. This is the historical reason that medical insurance became tied to employment.

If the employer is buying the policy, workers naturally want first-dollar coverage. Out-of-pocket costs have to be paid with their own after-tax dollars, while their insurance premiums are paid with pretax dollars by their employer. And when people cannot use benefits for any purpose other than medical care, they tend to receive more medical care than they otherwise would.

Tax-free medical insurance is only available to *some* workers. Others (including the self-employed and the unemployed) have to pay their own way with after-tax dollars. These others have to produce almost twice as much value in goods and services to be able to pay for the same insurance because of the heavy load of income, Social Security, and state and local taxes.[7] The waitress at a local diner is at a severe disadvantage compared with the corporate executive at Chrysler. She may well be priced out of the insurance market. She also faces much higher costs for medical services because persons with first-dollar, use-it-or-lose-it coverage have bid up the price.

It turns out that workers at the *high* end of the pay scale benefit most from the present structure of the tax code. They are the ones who can gain the most from a tax subsidy simply because they owe the most taxes.

Leaving aside the question of how much the cost of care would diminish if most people had economically sound insurance instead of government-subsidized prepayment, there are actuarial estimates of what it would cost individuals to purchase such insurance. If a family in a city with average medical costs increases its deductible from $250 to $1,000, it would save $1,315 in premiums, almost twice the amount of the increase in the deductible. If the family increases its deductible from $250 to $2,500, it would save $1,749 in reduced premiums, roughly equal to the amount of coverage forgone, considering deductibles and copayments.[8]

Because people have learned to emphasize the *high* deductible rather than the *low* premium, they tend to think that true insurance is "bare bones" or "skimpy." They object that they can't afford to pay the deductible.

It's true—many of them can't. The reason is that the money has been taken away from them, either by the government or the insurance company. Once you have given $1,749 to Blue Cross or Aetna or some other insurance company, it is gone forever, unless you make a claim, in which case the insurance company is not always eager to pay up. The vast majority of people do *not* use that much medical service in any given year. Yet the same people who "can't afford the deductible" are paying about $1 or even more in premiums for every dollar of reduction in the deductible! (Yes, I know, the employer may be writing the check, but it still is coming out of the worker's pocket.)

What if people were allowed to keep the $1,749 that they or their employer don't give to the insurer in a tax-sheltered savings account? And what if they had a use-it-or-keep-it instead of a use-it-or-lose-it option?

Most of them would have money accumulating in that account at the end of the year. *Their own money.*

Think of the possibilities! If the breadwinner became unemployed, the money could be use to pay insurance premiums so that the family did not become uninsured. If the family remained healthy, there would be a substantial nest egg at retirement. For people who are young today, this is extremely important: Social Security and Medicare may be long gone by the time they reach age sixty-five. Or, if we were really radical, we would let people spend their savings any way they wanted. They might start a business or move to a less dangerous neighborhood or send their children to a better school. Or they might waste the money. (When the government does that for them, it is called "stimulating the economy.")

Most people like the idea of keeping their own money.

But there are some people who don't like the idea of medical savings accounts at all. They're the ones who want *your* money for themselves.

Remember that insurance companies skim profits from their gross. The more money that passes through their hands, the more it will stick to their fingers. They want the $1,749 in *their* coffers, not in *your* bank account. In convincing Americans that first-dollar coverage is good insurance, they have done one terrific sales job. And they have had a lot of help from the medical profession as well. Patients would be much more reluctant to agree to expensive procedures of marginal benefit if they were spending their own money. They also might economize by consulting practitioners that the medical establishment disapproves of. Some such practitioners are dangerous, and some of them are ineffectual. The same, of course, could be said for some practitioners who hold all the approved credentials.

Insurers claim that they are all in favor of controlling costs. But who should benefit from the savings? How about insisting that *patients* benefit from any economy measures, not just insurance companies, big business, and the government?

Many insurance companies want to get out of the business of taking risks—never mind that risk taking is what insurance is *for*. They would much rather manage the first $2,500 of your medical spending than take the risk that you will have a heart attack or come down with leukemia. They may very kindly relieve you of the burden of shopping for the best values in routine care. They may provide you with a mammogram, screening blood tests, and a computer printout that tells you the same things that your mother did (exercise, stop smoking, eat your vegetables, etc.). In return, they plan to economize at the high end. If you have chest pain while driving on the highway and end up in the emergency room at Mount St. Elsewhere, the people who should be starting your IV may be on "hold," waiting for precertification from your managed care plan. We spend too much money on people in their last month of life, right? Well, this might just be your last month of life, especially if you don't get high-tech medical care promptly when you need it.

There are some problems with the insurance industry, and these should be reformed.

The most important reform is to sever medical insurance from employment. Insurance should be personal and portable. If you change jobs, you should be able to take your insurance with you, even if your employer paid the premiums. After all, you earned it—insurance benefits are really a substitute for higher wages.

Medical insurance should also be noncancelable, like many life insurance policies are, and there should be built-in protections against unreasonable increases in premiums. In fact, most individuals and family medical insurance policies sold in the 1950s *were* guaranteed renewable.[9] If people found out that such policies were available (and were allowed to buy them), who would ever knowingly buy any other type?

However, there are two very bad ideas now being promoted: community rating and mandatory insurance with defined benefits (many of which you may not need or want).

"Community rating" means that everybody has to be charged the same premium, regardless of the difference in risk. Such policies aren't really insurance because the business of insurance is about pricing risk. If a company is forced to sell insurance on warships headed for the Persian Gulf at the same rate that it offers on a luxury cruise ship, there are several possibilities: The warship would be uninsurable or the cruise ship couldn't afford insurance or the insurer would be out of business.

Community rating is another exercise in involuntary cost-shifting, even though its proponents usually deplore cost-shifting by other means. The principle is "from each according to his ability, to each according to his need."

If we insist on community rating, then we will have to force people to buy insurance. Otherwise, low-risk people will refuse to pay the high price. In fact, a large proportion of the currently uninsured are young, healthy people who have been priced out of the market. And if the insurance company is forced to take all comers at a set price, people will ask why buy insurance when they are healthy if they can buy it at the door of the emergency room? If people bought fire insurance only when their house was burning, the actuarially sound premium would be equal to the value of the house! In other words, it wouldn't be insurance.

How will we enforce a law about buying insurance? Shall we put people in jail if they don't? Shall we seize their house and car? Of course, if they do buy insurance at community rates, they might not be able to afford a house or a car anyway. One way or another, community rating will reduce the living standards of young, healthy workers.

If insurance is so wonderful, why should we have to force people to buy it?

Some think that people are just too dumb and irresponsible to look out for their own self-interest. Surely, there are people like that, but remember that more than 85 percent of the population is insured now and many of the uninsured would buy insurance if the price were reasonable.

What about those who don't? Is it too hard-hearted to *allow* them to bear the consequences of their *own* lack of foresight—say, to go into debt to pay a hospital bill or to face the stigma of being treated like a charity case in a public hospital? Notice I did not suggest putting them in debtor's prison or throwing them out into the street to die on a subway grate.

Is it then compassionate to *force* prudent people to pay the cost of *other* people's poor judgment, by taxing them or driving up the cost of their insurance? (Voluntarily sharing the risk of misfortune is called buying insurance at an actuarially fair price, and voluntarily helping those who are less able is called charity.)

If people are not allowed to enjoy the benefits of self-restraint or bear the consequences of their own overindulgence, they are more likely to take imprudent risks. Turn the rewards and punishments around, and there will be better and more cautious behavior. That's human nature. People have the capacity to choose nobility or depravity, to be sensible or reckless. But on the whole, they tend to respond to incentives.

The guiding principles of insurance reform should be to restore individual responsibility: to put patients back in control of decisions about their insurance coverage and their medical care. And that means putting money back in the patients' pockets instead of taking more of it out.

The role of the government should be to permit (*not require*) medical savings accounts; to revise the tax code that wrecked the insurance market and created the legions of uninsured in the first place; to enact the insurance reforms mentioned above; to repeal expensive state mandates (e.g., hair transplants and in-vitro fertilization) that price perhaps 25 percent of the uninsured out of the market; and to reform its own insurance programs such as Medicare to make them actuarially sound and to prevent cost-shifting (in other words, pay for government subsidies with honest taxes on everyone, not with hidden taxes on the sick). Current Medicare beneficiaries should be allowed to opt out of the program and buy services privately if they wish, without subjecting their physician to intolerable risks of government fines. Future Medicare beneficiaries should be permitted to accumulate money in their medical savings accounts so they will not be forced to rely on the program, which will probably be bankrupt before they become eligible.

If we turn the clock back to more patient choice and less government fiat, will patients make some wrong decisions, some decisions they will regret?

No doubt they will. They sometimes make bad decisions when they elect their senator, choose their marriage partner, buy a house, or join the armed forces. Still, we let them do it.

But when it comes to medical decisions, the medical elite wants to "protect" people. The medical elite thinks that medical decisions are the most complex and important ones in the world. I disagree, but even if they're right and I'm wrong, the question remains: Will the people be better off with bureaucrats in charge of their decisions, even if the bureaucrats have medical degrees? Remember, you can fire your doctor. Can you fire the bureaucrat? It is possible that the medical elite is invariably selfless and well intentioned, caring more about patients' welfare than strengthening its own political power, and that it will stay that way forever. But how much do you wish to stake on that assumption?

If you are committed to one particular reform proposal, why not advocate a demonstration project: free-market medicine and insurance in one community and various reform proposals in others.

You can bet that the elitist reformers would oppose that. Go to a public meeting and ask them. They don't want to try a free market anywhere, and they want their proposal to blanket the country from the outset without any pilot projects or any loopholes, except perhaps for themselves. They don't need to try their ideas on the dogs first.

Could it be that deep down in their hearts, they think the American people *are* the dogs?

REMOVING THE BARRIERS

Once we off-load the unreasonable expectations from the engine of the medical economy (which happens almost automatically when people can benefit personally from economizing), we need to unclog the air intake, plug the leaks in the fuel line, and release the emergency brake.

In other words, start dumping regulations and restrictions into Boston Harbor.

No, I didn't say we should remove the brakes and the steering wheel from the car by repealing the moral law and the criminal laws against the use of force and fraud. And I didn't advocate Shakespeare's prescription ("First, let's kill all the lawyers") so that nobody could collect damages after suffering a tort. I think the tort laws should be expanded so that they apply to bureaucrats, politicians, and lawyers, too.

But all Christopher Columbus rules should be encased in concrete and thrown into the harbor. These are rules that might have saved a life by now had they been made in 1492. After that should come the regulations that do more harm than good: The first principle of Hippocrates—"Do no harm"—should be applied to government regulation. Every new rule should be accompanied by a regulatory impact statement, including all compliance costs, expressed in both dollars and human lives. Lives can be lost through reliance on substitute technology that has hazards different from the technology that is banned, and also indirectly through decreases in our standard of living. On the whole, a wealthier society tends to be healthier.[10]

Someone has suggested the litmus test of keeping only those regulations that applied equally to government officials (who routinely exempt themselves).

But what then? Would we have an epidemic of thalidomide babies?

I think not. I think that *one* thalidomide baby occurring here might have about the same effect as finding cyanide in one bottle of Tylenol or two grapes from Chile. Freedom of information is an important defense. Unfortunately, hysteria all too often drowns out the voice of reason. I think that results from too little freedom, not from too much.

If we hadn't placed our trust so completely in the government, better sources of information might already have developed. For drugs, for example, I wish I had access to a computer database with up-to-date information about the number of patients who have received a drug, the incidence of various side effects, the list of indications for which the drug has been tested, the data from those studies, the manufacturing standards, and the citations for relevant papers in the scientific literature. What about a spreadsheet that would display comparable data for several drugs at a time, the drugs that the *user* wants to see, not the ones selected by the marketing department?

WHAT ABOUT THE POOR?

There are basically two objections to voluntary or free-enterprise solutions that come up virtually every time such a solution is discussed: (1) People are too stupid to make certain decisions for themselves (see above) and (2) the plan will not eliminate all inequity experienced by the poor.

Strangely, objection number two is generally not raised in discussions about involuntary government solutions. But it should be. The question "What about the poor?" really gets to the heart of the issue.

Let's start by asking: What about the poor *now*?

At present, only one out of every eight federal benefit dollars actually reaches an impoverished person.[11] (We're *not* talking about the 28 percent of the federal budget designated for the Department of Defense.) This means that seven out of every eight dollars paid in taxes— *by the working poor* as well as others—is transferred to someone who is *not poor*. That is redistribution *from* the poor *to* the middle class or the rich.

At a public hearing in Tucson about the Arizona Health Care Cost Containment System (which is what we have instead of Medicaid), advocates lined up at the microphone to tell how the people they represented could not get medical services under the AHCCCS (pronounced "access") program. These included: battered children, abused women, pregnant women, disabled elderly, psychiatric patients, AIDS patients, and drug abusers. The first $500 million–plus just didn't stretch far enough for people like this. So where was the money going? You tell me; I don't know. Certainly not to the private family doctors who participated in the program, many of whom soon dropped out because of administrative headaches and nonpayment. (If you can't answer the question either, then don't advocate foisting the "access" solution onto the people of another state.)

The effect on the poor might be one of the best criteria for evaluating government policies with respect to medicine. But we must make sure that competing policies are judged by the same criteria.

When comparing two anticancer drugs, we do not demand that one of the drugs bestow immortality in every single instance, while the other must simply make the patients feel better for a few days. With both drugs, we observe tumor size, length of survival, and side effects.

In evaluating the effects of a national policy, we should not demand that one policy guarantee the end of poverty, or the end of illiteracy, or the end of inequality in medical care, while the other merely needs to assert good intentions. The appropriate measurement is not trillions of dollars spent on government programs (about $2 trillion has been spent on government efforts to eradicate poverty in the past twenty-five years); that's at best an index of good intentions. We need to measure outcome. How many services, and what type of services, are actually received by the poor? Is the average level of service better or worse? Is the number of persons falling below a certain level greater or fewer?

We must be careful not to confuse concern about *poverty* with indignation about perceptions of *inequality*. For example, when I was a medical student at Columbia, there was a lot of indignation about the Harkness Pavilion. When the rich were sick, they came to Harkness in a limousine. They got a nicely appointed private room, often a private-duty nurse, and the most famous doctors in New York. They paid an outrageous sum. They never had to give a thought to the different world located a few feet away—the wards of Columbia-Presbyterian Hospital—even though they were helping to pay for it. Some did think about it, of their own volition, and gave the hospital a generous bequest.

The wards had as many as twelve beds and very few amenities. The patients arrived by ambulance or subway train, never by limousine. Still, they were attended by the same physicians and had their blood drawn by the same medical students as the patients in Harkness. Their surgery was done in the same operating rooms, their x-rays with the same machinery. These patients paid very little if anything. We thought their care was at least as good. And some rich people even said that if they were desperately sick they wanted to be on the ward, where somebody would see them if they suddenly threw up blood and passed out.

Columbia had a two-tiered system. It provoked resentment in many self-appointed advocates for the poor, who are probably pleased that the Harkness is no more. As far as I could tell, it didn't bother my ward patients. Many of them actually seemed grateful to the doctors and students who cared for them.

Did the closing of the Harkness, and the construction of a semi-private room for everybody, diminish inequality? Maybe so. Did it reduce poverty? Clearly not. Reducing inequality does not reduce poverty. It probably makes it worse, judging from the results of radical egalitarian experiments throughout the world.

One thing is clear: Public hospitals (those that still exist) are in much worse financial straits today than they were in the 1960s.

I say that we should let the rich people have their stretch limousines. Let's focus instead on people who (like me) are much more likely to be riding around in a truck—the nonrich. How can we make things better for them, instead of just worse for the rich?

1. Reduce the Cost

In the United States, the principal barrier to medical care is the high cost. The cost is raised, not lowered, by price controls, regulations, additional layers of "management," and other interference with the operation of the free market.

The answer is to eliminate things that artificially prop up prices, as we have already discussed.

Note that most reform proposals focus on *expenditures*, not *cost per service*. They would reduce expenditures primarily by decreasing the number of services delivered. In other words, they would decrease *care*, not decrease *cost*. That means they would hurt the poor.

To reiterate: If we really want to help the poor, we must first decrease cost, as described above. And then for those who still need help, here's the second step:

2. Allow and Encourage Charity

The automatic political response to the existence of a problem is, "There oughta be a law."

Actually, there *is* a law, according to the religious beliefs professed by the majority of Americans. The Hebrew Bible sets some requirements to aid the poor, in addition to according them just treatment under the law. For example, the corners of the field should not be harvested, and some grapes should be left behind in the vineyard. More open-ended requirements are laid down in the New Testament, backed up by potent threats of what will happen on Judgment Day if God says: "I was hungry, and you gave me nothing to eat."

Of course, we would not propose to have the government force people to adhere to a law that they don't believe in or even want to hear about—at least not if it has a religious basis.

Nevertheless, for whatever reason, most physicians do provide many charitable services—$10.2 billion in 1989, according to a survey by the AMA.[12] Physicians in San Francisco estimated that about 39 percent of their average potential gross was not collected because of charity care (not billed), uncompensated care (billed but not paid), and discounts to patients in government programs.[13] Is there any other group in society that gives as much?

Physicians would give more if society did not actually discourage charity by imposing liabilities and punishments. Many physicians have told me they would like to donate their services to a charitable clinic after retiring from active practice. But they can't afford the malpractice insurance.

Physicians who have given large numbers of laboratory services will stop doing so because they cannot afford the cost of complying with federal regulations.

Cost barriers are not the only problem.

There has been a radical change in our perception of the meaning of charity. No longer is it like mercy, that "blesseth him that gives and him that takes."[14] Charity is now considered demeaning.

Patients do not like to ask for services they cannot afford to pay for in full. Increasingly, people prefer to *demand* services as a matter of entitlement or right. They might be ashamed to beg, but they are not ashamed to take, not if they do so with the government as the intermediary. (Actually, they don't have to "beg"—they just have to explain their situation to the doctor.)

Today, we still name hospitals after the Good Samaritan, but the story is being conceptually turned upside down. The hero is now the mugging victim, not the Samaritan who stopped to help him. Did he not have a *right* to be helped, even if the Samaritan had *not* been moved to compassion?

When we identify a class of victims today, we fund a program and establish a bureaucracy. The bureaucracy determines eligibility criteria, based on society's priorities, not Samaritan emotions. The Samaritan's job (he was a businessman, remember) is to pay taxes. The first share of the taxes supports the bureaucrats staffing the program.

The remaining funds buy wine to pour in victims' wounds. (Government programs have to stick with approved treatment methods.) When a mere denarius (a day's wage) proves to be inadequate, the innkeeper is forced to take a pay cut.

Some people fear to rely on spontaneous charity because Samaritans make decisions based on their *own* emotions and values. A Samaritan might be moved to contribute to an open-heart surgery program that operates on blue babies only, discriminating against drug addicts who need replacements for their infected heart valves. Or he might be interested in schools for the mentally retarded (maybe he himself has an afflicted child) and feel completely indifferent to the plight of AIDS patients.

However, public welfare programs discriminate also, based on "public" values, and often against the neediest people. Oregon and Arizona are not unusual. A draft copy of a report prepared for the Saskatchewan Public Health Association stated that

> over and over again the prime client groups hurt by service reductions have been the most disadvantaged groups within our society, the ones with limited public voice. . . . In answering the question of who loses, one concludes that natives, youth, children, the elderly, the disabled, psychiatric patients, the mentally handicapped and victims of abuse are the losers.[15]

Public programs have not eliminated the need for Good Samaritans. They have simply preempted a higher portion of the Samaritans' resources.

However, it seems that some people would actually welcome the demise of the Good Samaritan. A pure, high-minded revulsion against charity or discrimination is not the only possible reason. There are self-interested reasons, too.

If charity supplanted government assistance programs, a lot of bureaucrats and providers would be out of highly paid jobs. Even some physicians have spoken out against too much charity.

In the early 1900s, there were about one hundred dispensaries, concentrated mostly in the industrial East, that dispensed free medicines. They were staffed by volunteer physicians, who used them to teach medical students, gain experience, and advance their careers. But some physicians objected to them:

"Think of it!" wrote one physician. "If a doctor attends a clinic three times a week for 52 weeks, treating daily an average of five patients, every one of whom could pay a moderate fee, say $1.00 (yet this is a small average), what has he done? Simply deprived the profession of $780 in one year."[16]

Hearing physicians' complaints about Medicaid, it seems hard to believe that they would object to a free clinic instead. Yet when Medicare and Medicaid first began, they were a real bonanza for physicians. They got paid for work they had formerly done without charge. Often, the government fee was *higher* than doctors could hope to receive from private patients, especially young parents. But now that many physicians are dependent on the income from the government, fees have been ratcheted down. On the average, a physician can earn about half as much from the treatment of a wealthy Medicare patient as from a young person of modest means who requires a comparable treatment.

Rhetoric about the poor must not distract us from an objective assessment of progress toward the goal of helping them. Let's have a controlled experiment. Why not give doctors a choice? Let them (along with everybody else who can afford it) pay a tax to support a societally defined "basic benefits package," available at their county hospital or clinic, for those who meet government eligibility standards, or allow them to take a tax credit for providing free services to those who meet *their* criteria for neediness. Give the patients a choice, too: the public clinic and the government doctor, or a private doctor who will agree to see them either to receive the tax credit or for a fee that both patient and physician find agreeable.

If too few physicians made themselves available to the poor privately, then the tax could be increased and the public clinic enlarged. If private charity flourished and people preferred it to the public dole, then the tax could be decreased and the public clinic made smaller.

The hypothesis to be tested by this little experiment is that a government middleman works better than private arrangements between individuals—at least if the goal is to maximize the amount and quality of service delivered.

RESULTS VERSUS IDEOLOGY

One way to dismiss an idea that you don't like is to refer to its proponents as "ideologues." It's becoming the American mass-media way: If you can't ignore an idea (the most effective strategy by far), do a rhetorical tar-and-feathers job on it and ride it out of town on a rail.

If you want to be pejorative, you can say that there is an ideology behind an idea. Generally, "ideology" today means "evil ideology."

If you want to be scientific, then you will use a different word: *theory*. Behind every scientific advance there is a theory that generated *hypotheses*, which were then put to the test of experiment.

Let us say there are various theories that explain the existence of certain phenomena. For example, in the Middle Ages, the people were afflicted with unexplained crop failures, mysterious deaths of livestock, vineyards smitten with unseasonable frost, and a rise in human disease and impotence. To protect the people against these clear and present dangers, the Spanish Inquisition came to the rescue. The inquisitors' theory was that all these problems were caused by witches. For a century, they pursued this theory with unflagging zeal (and possibly, in some cases, with all the purest intentions). When problems persisted, the reason was obvious: Some witches were still undiscovered, and the Inquisition needed more resources to track them down.

An alternate theory was that the poor were being victimized by princes, popes, and nature. But this one was politically incorrect.

The witch hunting finally ended when inquisitor Alonso Salazar y Frias made a procedural change. Without ever ruling that witches don't exist, he looked at earthly results rather than heavenly intentions.[17]

From my admittedly idiosyncratic viewpoint, I see two theories locked in mortal combat. One holds that you can't save the health care system while preserving individual liberty and the Oath of Hippocrates. In this view, the poor and the sick are the victims of greedy, selfish, bigoted entrepreneurs. Reform based on this theory is to write a "no-code" order on our allegedly moribund Western tradition, withdraw its life support, and hasten to replace it with something else— something that is based on the good of "society" rather than "rugged individuals."

The alternate theory is that it's the "something else"—the treatment—that is the problem. The people are victimized by bureaucrats and misguided do-gooders, who exploit and worsen naturally occurring miseries, sometimes with all the purest of intentions.

If medicine is to survive as an art and a science, then we must rely on the scientific method. Never mind the cranks, the quacks, the Congress, the deans, the poll takers, the spin doctors, the PR firms, the policy wonks, the AMA, the writers of books, the ideologues, or the lobbyists. Look at the *results* of ongoing experiments: Britain, Canada, Germany, the Veterans Administration, and various U.S. managed care schemes—*all* of the results, not just the Potemkin show-cases that would-be reformers want you to see.

I think that moral relativism is bankrupt, along with the rest of "postmodern" ideology. I think socialism is dead as an intellectually respectable theory. But it may take centuries to bury them, and their derivative plans might bury American medicine in the meantime.

I've told you what I think. You might think I am wrong or even that my ideas are abhorrent. That is okay with me. Let's call a truce in the ideological battle.

But it's past time to do the experiment. Let's put freedom to the test.

APPENDIX: PHYSICIAN OATHS

The Oath of Hippocrates of Kos, Fifth Century b.c.:

I swear by Apollo the physician, by Aesculapius, Hygeia, and Panacea, and I take to witness all the gods, all the goddesses, to keep according to my ability and judgment the following oath:

To consider dear to me as my parents him who taught me this art; to live in common with him and if necessary to share my goods with him; to look upon his children as my own brothers, to teach them this art if they so desire without fee or written promise; to impart to my sons and the sons of the master who taught me and to the disciples who have enrolled themselves and have agreed to the rules of the profession, but to these alone, the precepts and the instruction. I will prescribe regimen for the good of my patients according to my ability and my judgment and never do harm to anyone. To please no one will I prescribe a deadly drug, nor give advice which may cause his death. Nor will I give a woman a pessary to procure abortion. But I will preserve the purity of my life and my art. I will not cut for stone, even for patients in whom the disease is manifest; I will leave this operation to be performed by specialists in this art. In every house where I come I will enter only for the good of my patients, keeping myself far from all intentional ill-doing and all seduction, and especially from the pleasures of love with women or with men, be they free or slaves. All that may come to my knowledge in the exercise of my profession or outside of my profession or in daily commerce with men, which ought not to be spread abroad, I will keep secret and never reveal. If I keep this oath faithfully, may I enjoy my life and practice my art, respected by all men and in all times; but if I swerve from it or violate it, may the reverse be my lot.

DECLARATION OF GENEVA OF THE WORLD MEDICAL ASSOCIATION

(adopted 1948, amended 1966 and 1983):

I solemnly pledge myself to consecrate my life to the service of humanity;

I will give my teachers the respect and gratitude which is their due;

I will practice my profession with conscience and dignity;

The health of my patient will be my first consideration;

I will respect the secrets which are confided in me, even after the patient has died;

I will maintain by all the means in my power, the honor and the noble traditions of the medical profession;

My colleagues will be my brothers;

I will not permit considerations of religion, nationality, race, party politics or social standing to intervene between my duty and my patient;

I will maintain the utmost respect for human life from its beginning even under threat and I will not use my medical knowledge contrary to the laws of humanity;

I make these promises solemnly, freely and upon my honor.

SOVIET OATH (OATH DRAWN UP AND APPROVED BY THE SUPREME SOVIET OF THE USSR IN 1971, WITH ONE ADDITION [ON NUCLEAR WAR] IN 1983):[1]

Upon having conferred on me the high calling of physician and entering medical practice, I do solemnly swear:

To dedicate all my knowledge and strength to the preservation and improvement of the health of mankind and to the treatment and prevention of disease, and to work in good conscience wherever it is required by society;

To be always ready to provide medical care, to relate to the patient attentively and carefully, and to preserve medical confidences;

To constantly perfect my medical knowledge and clinical skills and thereby in my work to aid in the development of medical science and practice;

To refer, if the patient's better interests warrant it, for advice from my fellow physicians, and never myself to refuse to give such advice or help;

To preserve and develop the noble traditions of Soviet medicine, to be guided in all my actions by the principles of Communist morality, and to always bear in mind the high calling of a Soviet physician and my responsibility to the people and to the Soviet state.

Recognizing the danger which nuclear weaponry presents for mankind, to struggle tirelessly for peace, and for the prevention of nuclear war.

I swear to be loyal to this oath as long as I live.

A MODERN HIPPOCRATIC OATH BY DR. LOUIS LASAGNA[2]

I swear to fulfill, to the best of my ability and judgment, this covenant:

I will respect the hard-won scientific gains of those physicians in whose steps I walk, and gladly share such knowledge as is mine with those who are to follow;

I will apply, for the benefit of the sick, all measures which are required, avoiding those twin traps of overtreatment and therapeutic nihilism.

I will remember that there is art to medicine as well as science, and that warmth, sympathy and understanding may outweigh the surgeon's knife or the chemist's drug.

I will not be ashamed to say "I know not," nor will I fail to call in my colleagues when the skills of another are needed for a patient's recovery.

I will respect the privacy of my patients, for their problems are not disclosed to me that the world may know. Most especially must I tread with care in matters of life and death. If it is given me to save a life, all thanks. But it may also be within my power to take a life; this awesome responsibility must be faced with great humbleness and awareness of my own frailty. Above all, I must not play at God.

I will remember that I do not treat a fever chart or a cancerous growth, but a sick human being, whose illness may affect the person's family and economic stability. My responsibility includes these related problems, if I am to care adequately for the sick.

I will prevent disease whenever I can, for prevention is preferable to cure.

I will remember that I remain a member of society, with special obligations to all my fellow human beings, those sound of mind and body, as well as the infirm.

If I do not violate this oath, may I enjoy life and art, respected while I live and remembered with affection hereafter. May I always act so as to preserve the finest traditions of my calling and may I long experience the joy of healing those who seek my help.

The Oath of the Healer, by Dr. Louis Weinstein[3]

In the eyes of God and in the presence of my fellow students and teachers, I at this most solemn time in my life do freely take this Oath, whereby I shall pledge to myself and all others the manner in which I shall live the rest of my days.

I shall be ever grateful to my teachers who have planted the seeds of knowledge, which I shall nurture forever. I thank them for allowing me to see the importance of learning and realize that lifelong study is critically important to becoming a Healer.

I realize that on this day, I become a physician for all eternity. I shall strive to be a person of good will, high moral character, and impeccable conduct. I shall learn to love my fellow man as much as I have learned to love the art of healing.

I shall always act in the best interest of my patient and shall never allow personal reward to impact on my judgment. I shall always have the highest respect for human life and remember that *it is wrong to terminate life in certain circumstances, permissible in some, and an act of supreme love in others* [emphasis added]. I shall never promise a cure, as only death is certain, and I shall understand that preserving health is as important as treating disease. When a patient for whom I have been caring dies, I shall have the strength to allow him or her to die with dignity and in peace.

I shall have as a major focus in my life the promoting of a better world in which to live. I shall strive to take a comprehensive approach to understanding all aspects of life. To become the Healer I wish to be, I must expand my thinking and practice from a system of episodic care to one of a preventive approach to the problems of mankind, including the social ills of malnutrition and poverty that plague the world in which we live.

I am not a God and I cannot perform miracles. I am simply a person who has been given the rights and responsibilities to be a Healer. I pledge to myself and all who can hear me that this is what I shall become.

REFERENCES

1.

1. John Goodman and Gerald Musgrave, *Patient Power*, Washington, D.C., Cato Institute, 1992, p. 356.
2. Robert Axelrod, *The Evolution of Cooperation*, New York, Basic Books, 1984.
3. Frederick Bastiat, *The Law*, first published c. 1850, Irvington-on-Hudson, New York, the Foundation for Economic Education, 1987.

2.

1. Douglas Hofstadter, *Goedel, Escher, Bach: An Eternal Golden Braid*, New York, Basic Books, 1979.
2. Rep. Fortney ("Pete") Stark, speaking at a conference titled "Health Care Reform Under Clinton," Washington Court Hotel, Washington, D.C., January 14, 1993.
3. Correspondence quoted in *Harvey Cushing: A Biography*, originally published 1946, reprinted by The Classics of Surgery Library, New York, 1991, pp. 654–55.
4. Roger J. Bulger, "The 'R' Word: 'Rationing' of Health Care and the Role of Academic Health Centers," *Western Journal of Medicine* 157:186–7, August, 1992.

4.

1. Francis Fukuyama, "The End of History?" *The National Interest*, Summer, 1989, pp. 3–18.

6.

1. James V. Maloney, Jr., "A Critical Analysis of the Relative Value Scale," *JAMA* 266:3453–58, December 25, 1991.

2. C. N. Cofer and M. H. Appley: *Motivation: Theory and Research*, John Wiley and Sons, New York, 1964, p. 454.

7.

1. Christine K. Cassel, Andrew L. Jameton, Victor W. Sidel, and Patrick Storey, "The Physician's Oath and the Prevention of Nuclear War," *JAMA* 254:652–54, August 2, 1985.

2. Nancy S. Jecker, Ph.D., "Striking the Balance Between Fidelity and Justice," *Medical Ethics*, February, 1992.

3. Timothy Ferris, *Coming of Age in the Milky Way*, New York, Anchor Books, 1988.

8.

1. Motion to Affirm Judgment of District Court, *AAPS* vs. *Weinberger*, 1975.

2. Opinion of Judge Nicholas Politan in *Stewart et al.* v. *Louis Sullivan and Medical Services Association of Pennsylvania d/b/a Pennsylvania Blue Shield*, No. 92-417, U.S. District Court, District of New Jersey, Newark Division, Oct. 26,1992.

9.

1. Jack Colwill, "Where Have All the Primary Care Applicants Gone?" *New England Journal of Medicine* 326:387–408, February 6, 1992.

2. George Bernard Shaw, *The Intelligent Woman's Guide to Socialism, Capitalism, Sovietism, and Fascism*, originally published 1928, reprinted by Penguin Books, 1982.

3. William Hsiao, *New England Journal of Medicine* 328:928–33, April 1, 1993.

4. *Medicare News*, February, 1992, published by Aetna, Medicare carrier for Arizona.

10.

1. Mark Thompson, "Plan for Drafting Health Workers Includes Women," *Arizona Daily Star*, June 5, 1993.

2. Presentation at a conference entitled "Health Care Reform Under Clinton," sponsored by *Health Care Reform Week*, Washington, D.C., January 14, 1993.

3. Report from a meeting of the Pacific Dermatologic Association in Vancouver, *The Schoch Letter* vol. 41, p. 46, December, 1991.

4. Studies cited in the *Journal of Legal Medicine,* vol. 10, pp. 433–78, 1989.

5. David E. Rogers, "Medicine and the Social Contract," *The Pharos,* September, 1991, pp. 17–19.

11.

1. John C. Goodman and Gerald L. Musgrave. *Twenty Myths About National Health Insurance,* National Center for Policy Analysis, Policy Report #128, December, 1991, p. 57.

2. Paul Stanaway, "Britain's Sick Joke," *The* (Toronto) *Sunday Times,* June 16, 1991, p. C5.

3. Robert Sade, *Private Practice,* August, 1989, p. 19.

4. Goodman and Musgrave, op. cit., p. 58.

5. John Goodman, *National Health Care in Great Britain: Lessons for the USA,* Fisher Institute, 1980.

6. Anthony Lejeune, "NHS: Confusion and Frustration in Great Britain," *Private Practice,* November, 1990, pp. 9–14.

7. *Daily Mail* (London), June 13, 1991.

8. Lejeune, op. cit.

9. John F. Sheils, Gary J. Young, and Robert J. Rubin, "O Canada: Do We Expect Too Much from Its Health System?" *Health Affairs,* Spring, 1992.

10. Patricia M. Danzon, "Hidden Overhead Costs: Is Canada's System Really Less Expensive?" *Health Affairs,* Spring, 1992.

11. "Recession Forcing Canada to Reexamine Health Care," *The New York Times,* November 24, 1991, p. A20.

12. Goodman and Musgrave, op. cit.

13. Steven Globerman with Lorna Hoye, *Waiting Your Turn: Hospital Waiting Lists in Canada,* the Fraser Forum, May, 1990.

14. Patricia Danzon, op. cit., p. 31.

15. Goodman and Musgrave, op. cit., p. 13.

16. *Globe and Mail,* November 23, 1991.

17. William Goodman, *Canadian Health Insurance: Cure or Catastrophe?* lecture, Association of American Physicians and Surgeons, Great Falls, Montana, June, 1992.

18. William Goodman, *The Canadian Model: Would It Work Here?* Association of American Physicians and Surgeons, 1990.

19. William Goodman, *Canadian Health Insurance: Cure or Catastrophe?* op. cit.

20. Carol Stevens, "Does Germany Hold the Key to U.S. Health-Care Reform?" *Medical Economics*, January 6, 1992, pp. 148–59.

21. Rashi Fein, "Health Care Reform," *Scientific American*, November,[2] 1992, pp. 46–53.

22. Susan Hershberg Adelman, "Let's Use Our Health Care Like the Asset It Is," *American Medical News*, December 14, 1990, p. 27.

23. Susan Hershberg Adelman, "How National Health System Works in Sweden," *American Medical News*, October 20, 1989, p. 48.

24. Goodman and Musgrave, op. cit., p. 45.

25. Hilary Stout, "Infant Mortality Rate in U.S. Fell to Low in 1991," *Wall Street Journal*, April 22, 1992.

26. Joyce M. Piper, Wayne A. Ray, and Marie R. Griffin, "Effects of Medicaid Eligibility Expansion on Prenatal Care and Pregnancy Outcome in Tennessee," *JAMA*, 264:2219–23, November 7, 1990.

27. Carolyn Lochhead, "Cradle to Grave," *Insight*, May 6, 1991, pp. 12–19.

28. John Goodman, Presentation to American Farm Bureau Federation, Chicago, June 22, 1992.

29. Nicholas Eberstadt, "America's Infant Mortality Problem: Parents," *The Wall Street Journal*, January 20, 1992.

30. Goodman and Musgrave, op. cit., p. 45.

31. William Goodman, *Canadian Health Insurance: Cure or Catastrophe?* op. cit.

32. Goodman and Musgrave, op. cit., p. 45.

12.

1. Press conference on April 7, 1987.

2. John C. Goodman and Gerald L. Musgrave, *Patient Power*, op. cit., p. 216.

3. *The Wall Street Journal*, July 8, 1988.

4. *BNA's Medicare Report*, May 1, 1992.

5. Howard Larkin and Brian McCormick, "The Many Faces of Economic Credentialing," *American Medical News*, July 20, 1992, p. 3.

13.

1. Decision of U.S. Supreme Court in *Cruzan* v. *Harmon* quoted in *Connections* (Carondelet Health Care), November 15, 1991.

2. Ashwini Sehgal et al., "How Strictly Do Dialysis Patients Want Their Advance Directives Followed?" *JAMA* 167:59–63, 1992.

3. Sidney H. Wanzer et al. "The Physician's Responsibility Toward Hopelessly Ill Patients." *New England Journal of Medicine*, 320:844–49, March 30, 1989.

4. Robert Spitzer, *Crisis*, October, 1991, p. 45.

5. Robert Jay Lifton, *The Nazi Doctors*, New York, Basic Books, 1986.

6. Council on Scientific Affairs, American Medical Association, "Induced Termination of Pregnancy Before and After *Roe* v. *Wade:* Trends in the Mortality and Morbidity of Women," *JAMA* 268:3231–39, December 9, 1992.

7. From recommendations from a national symposium sponsored by the National Abortion Federation and the American College of Obstetrics and Gynecology, October 25–26, 1990.

8. John M. Thorp, Jr., M.D., and Watson A. Bowes, Jr., M.D., "Prolife Perinatologist—Paradox or Possibility?" *New England Journal of Medicine* 326:1217–1991, April 30, 1993.

9. Ibid.

10. Herbert S. Gross, "Euthanasia Debate" (letters), *New England Journal of Medicine*, 323:1770, December 20, 1990.

11. Aaron Spital and Max Spital, "Euthanasia Debate" (letters), op. cit., p. 1771.

12. Richard L. Brown, "Euthanasia Debate" (letters), op. cit., p. 1771.

14.

1. Joseph A. DiMasi, Ronald W. Hansen, Henry G. Grabowski, and Louis Lasagna, "Cost of Innovation in the Pharmaceutical Industry," *Journal of Health Economics* 10:107–42, 1991.

2. Laurie P. Cohen, "Some Biotech Firms Excel at State-of-the-Art Hype," *The Wall Street Journal*, March 13, 1992, p. C1.

3. Jane M. Orient, Louis J. Kettel, Harold C. Sox, Jr., *et al.*, "The Effect of Algorithms on the Cost and Quality of Patient Care," *Medical Care* 21:157–67, 1983.

4. Jane M. Orient, "Evaluation of Abdominal Pain: Clinicians' Performance Compared with Three Protocols," *Southern Medical Journal* 79:793–99, 1986.

5. Jane M. Orient, "When Do Patients with Chronic Obstructive Lung Disease Need Hospital Admission? Reflections Based on a VA Experience," *Southern Medical Journal* 76:593–602, 1983.

6. *Internal Medicine News & Cardiology News*, April 15, 1992, p. 61.

15.

1. James S. Todd, "Professionalism at Its Worst," *JAMA*, 266:3338, December 18, 1991.

2. Paul Jesilow, Gilbert Geis, and Henry Pontelli, "Fraud by Physicians Against Medicaid," *JAMA*, 266:3318–22, December 18, 1991.

3. See *The Art and Science of Bedside Diagnosis*, by Joseph D. Sapira, edited by Jane M. Orient, Baltimore, Urban and Schwarzenberg, 1990.

4. Cary Copeland, director, Executive Office for Asset Forfeiture, *Asset Forfeiture News*, March/April 1992.

5. *Melashenko* vs. *Sullivan and Kusserow*.

6. Howard Fishman and D. Zerendow, *Psychiatric Times*, September, 1990.

7. *New York Times*, April 12, 1992.

8. Survey by the Association of American Physicians and Surgeons, May, 1993.

16.

1. John Goodman, *The Regulation of Medical Care: Is the Price Too High?* Cato. Public Policy Research Monograph No. 3, 1980.

2. Ibid.

3. Barry Siegel, "At War Over Her Call to Heal," *Los Angeles Times*, September 5, 1992, p. A1, A20.

4. Michael Zenz, Michael Strumpf, and Michael Tryba, "Long-Term Oral Opioid Therapy in Patients with Chronic Nonmalignant Pain," *Journal of Pain and Symptom Management* 7:69–77, 1992.

17.

1. Ronald Utt, "The Growing Regulatory Burden: At What Cost to America?" Institute for Policy Innovation Policy Report No. 114, November, 1991, Lewisville, Texas.

2. Survey by the Association of American Physicians and Surgeons, September, 1992.

3. Daron G. Ferris and Paul M. Fischer, "Elementary School Students' Performance with Two ELISA Test Systems," *JAMA* 268:766–70, August 12, 1992.

4. *Federal Register*, vol. 55, p. 20899, May 21, 1990.

5. Willaim A. Rutala, Robert L. Odetts, and Gregory P. Samesa, "Management of Infectious Waste by U.S. Hospitals," *JAMA*, 262:1635–40, September 22–29, 1989.

6. W. A. Rutala and D. J. Weber, "Infectious Waste-Mismatch Between Science and Policy," *New England Journal of Medicine*, 325:578–82, 1991.

7. Glen C. Griffin, "Who Was the Phantom Accuser of 15 Doctors?" *Postgraduate Medicine*, vol. 92, No. 3, September 1, 1992, pp. 29–40.

8. Christopher Anderson, "FDA Vs. Free Speech Over Drug Promotions," *Nature* 354:421, December 12, 1991.

18.

1. David Durenberger, talk given at United Communications conference, "Health Care Reform Under Clinton," Washington, D.C., January 14, 1993.

2. John Goodman, "A Layperson's Guide to Health Insurance Reform," Policy Backgrounder #121, National Center for Policy Analysis, September 28, 1992.

3. Terree P. Wasley, *What Has Government Done to Our Health Care?* Washington, D.C., Cato Institute, 1992, p. 112.

4. John C. Goodman and Gerald L. Musgrave, *Patient Power*, Cato Institute, 1992.

5. Personal communication to members of Medical Executive Committee.

6. *Nation's Business*, September, 1989.

7. John Goodman, "A Layperson's Guide to Health Insurance Reform," op. cit.

8. Ibid.

9. Goodman and Musgrave, op. cit.

10. Aaron Wildavsky, *Searching for Safety*, New Brunswick, Transaction Publishers, 1988.

11. Neil Howe and Phillip Longman, "The Next New Deal," *The Atlantic*, April, 1992, pp. 88–99.

12. Terree P. Wasley, *What Has Government Done to Our Health Care?* op. cit.

13. Susan Hogeland, "Uncompensated and Undercompensated Care Provided by San Francisco Medical Society Physicians," *West J Med* 149:359–61, 1988.

14. Shakespeare, *The Merchant of Venice*,

15. *Leader-Post Regina*, September 21, 1988.

16. Paul Starr, *The Social Transformation of American Medicine*, New York, Basic Books, 1982, p. 182.

17. William C. Clark, "Witches, Floods, and Wonder Drugs: Historical Perspectives on Risk Management," in *Societal Risk Assessment: How Safe*

Is Safe Enough? edited by Richard C. Schwing and Walter A. Albers, Jr., New York, Plenum Publishing Company.

Appendix

1. Cassell et al., "The Physician's Oath and the Prevention of Nuclear War," *JAMA* 254:652–54, 1985.

2. Louis Lasagna, personal communication: oath as used in commencement ceremonies at Tufts in the late 1980s.

3. Presented in an address to the Arizona chapter of Alpha Omega Alpha and printed in *JAMA*, 265:2484, May 15, 1991.

INDEX